Tempestuous Petticoat

CLARE LEIGHTON

Tempestuous Petticoat

The Story of an Invincible Edwardian

Academy
Chicago
Publishers

© Copyright 1947 by Clare Leighton
Published in 1984 by

Academy Chicago, Publishers
425 N. Michigan Avenue
Chicago, Illinois 60611

Printed and bound in the U.S.A.

Library of Congress Cataloging in Publication Data

Leighton, Clare, 1899–
    Tempestuous Petticoat.

    Reprint. Originally published: New York, Toronto:
Rinehart, 1947.
    1. Leighton, Marie Connor, d. 1941—Biography.
2. Authors, English—20th century—Biography.   I. Title.
PR6023.E46Z7   1984   823'.8 [B]   84-2798
ISBN 0-89733-099-4 (pbk.)

For Charlotte and Hugh
who made me write this book

Contents

1	The Study Table	3
2	St. John's Wood	23
3	Mother's Old Men	38
4	From the Nursery Window	53
5	The Annual Exodus	75
6	Life at the Seaside	91
7	Flowers and Feathers	112
8	The Leightons	126
9	Uncle Jack	146
10	As the Dear Canon Said—	158
11	Education for the Leighton Children	181
12	A New Center of the Universe	202
13	War Years	223
14	The Last Edwardian	251

Delight in Disorder

A sweet disorder in the dress
Kindles in clothes a wantonness:
A lawn about the shoulders thrown
Into a fine distraction:
An erring lace, which here and there
Enthrals the crimson stomacher:
A cuff neglected, and thereby
Ribbands to flow confusedly:
A winning wave, deserving note,
In the tempestuous petticoat:
A careless shoe-string, in whose tie
I see a wild civility:
Do more bewitch me than when art
Is too precise in every part.

—*Robert Herrick*

1. *The Study Table*

I remember peeping through the banisters of the nursery stairs. Up from the kitchen came the smell of food. I was hungry.

"Come here, Miss Clare," my nanny whispered, as she carried me back to the nursery. "And don't you dare to make no noise. You just sit quiet, or you won't 'ave no dinner at all today."

"Shall I poison him?" My mother's voice came up from the study below. "I shall have to get rid of him soon. Or do you think it would be better if I set fire to the house and let him get burnt to death? I can't make up my mind."

Nanny went on with her sewing as though nothing unusual were happening.

"Listen to me, Robert," the voice continued. "You really *must* help me. I'm stuck. I've got to get him out of the way in a hurry, before Ellaline is forced to marry him."

All I could hear in answer was a low mumble. My father never paid much attention to my mother when she asked him questions like this. He was thinking about his own work. While she was planning murders and arson, he roamed the prairies of Canada, among the Indians.

My mother and father were both writers. My mother wrote the melodramatic serials that appeared in the English newspapers owned by Lord Northcliffe, and my father wrote boys' adventure stories. The entire household revolved around my mother's writing, for it was the large sums of money she earned that supported us. My father's work was not supposed to matter nearly as much, because he earned far less.

The melodrama of my mother's stories seeped into our daily life, and even upstairs in the seclusion of the nursery we three children were made aware of the urgency of her work.

Down in the hall sat the messenger boy from the *Daily Mail*. He had been sitting there patiently on the oak settle when we went for our walk that morning. He was waiting for the overdue manuscript as we returned home. Now, with the hour of the midday meal long overdue, he sat there still.

Mother could not seem to find an exciting enough ending.

The household routine was suspended, and a hush lay over us all. A desperate cook downstairs in the darkness of our basement kitchen looked with despair upon the spoiling meal. Upstairs in the nursery the old nanny stopped our noisy games and whispered to us to keep quiet.

"It's very near three o'clock already," she told us. "And you know perfectly well the messenger boy is still down there in the 'all waiting, and they do say the *Daily Mail* can't appear till your mother's sent in 'er instalment. And just now, as I crept past the study door to try to find out 'ow long we'd 'ave to wait for our dinner, I 'eard your mother tell your father that it was no good, she just couldn't seem to think of a way to save the 'eroine. Now if you don't keep quiet and let your mother do 'er work without any of your noise you won't 'ave your dinner till teatime, and you know that perfectly well. What a life, as I always says. What a life."

But we were growing very hungry. Never have noses been flattened against a windowpane with more impatience than were ours as we waited for the figure of the messenger boy to bear the bright green envelope, lavishly decorated with red sealing wax, down the garden path to the gate. That figure meant food. Immediately he had left, the dinner gong would sound.

This was no unusual occurrence. Our mother worked hard three hundred and sixty-four days in the year. Christmas was the one exception, and only on that day was she approachable as a human woman.

"But I get so bored with people pitying me because they think I work too much," she would say as she sat opposite her secretary, dictating an instalment at seven o'clock in the evening, dressed still in her nightgown beneath a pink satin peignoir. "Sometimes it seems to me that the world is getting soft and self-indulgent. Now, look at me. Just because I'm a married woman people expect me to feel faint and tired at times. I remember how worried the editors were whenever I was in a certain condition. But Lord Northcliffe put them in their place. 'Nonsense,' he told them. 'Mrs. Leighton could go on just the same even if she were about to give birth to triplets the very next day.' And he was perfectly right."

My mother was proud of the fact that during the months of her pregnancies she was writing instalments each week of three separate serial stories.

"I shall never forget how I had to rush to get my heroine married to my hero just as the first labor pains were beginning," she laughed. "It's all nonsense—this morning sickness and such. Leave that to the women with no work to do."

Hearing this, I remembered how Grandmamma had once told me that I was almost born into the inkwell, and that it was only because the nurse practically carried my mother upstairs that I first saw the light of day as a self-respecting human being should, from the comfort of a double bed.

Because Mother and Father were always working, the most important room in the house was the study. It was filled with the material for her stories and for my father's boys' books. The enormous table in the middle of the room was cleared one day a year, so that on Christmas Day it might be used for a family party, as the dining room would be too small. Only then was it possible to brush and shake the twelve months' dust from the crimson tablecloth. No servant was ever allowed to touch that table over the rest of the year, and even when we went to the seaside for the summer my mother and her secretary draped a dust sheet over what was left behind upon it.

On Christmas Eve everything was carried into the dining room, covering all the chairs and the floor. This always took the entire day, and dinner had to be eaten up in the nursery. My mother insisted on moving her precious bundles herself, for she would trust them to no one.

These bundles were the most important things in the house. They contained the outlines of the serials she was writing, and if anything were to happen to them she would be unable to remember what she had planned for her villains.

She was never long separated from her bundles. They seemed to be an extension of her own person, and I think I would have considered there was something indecently naked about her if she had walked around without holding one of them in her arms before her. She held it as most women hold a baby, and with the same sense of devotion. So precious were the bundles that, because of her terror of fire, she carried the most recent one with her even when she went to her bedroom to tidy her hair, or took it down to the basement kitchen when she paid her daily visit to the cook, "to keep her in a good humor."

"It's all very well to call me fussy," she would say. "But who, I ask you, can be perfectly sure that a spark won't leap the fireguard in the study during the few minutes in which I am away from the room? People are so unimaginative always. They can never see a thing until it has happened. And then, of course, it's too late."

I often wonder how she ever brought herself to go from the house and leave the bundles behind her. She did, I remember, surround them with dampened cloths, and during the winter she would pour water on the study fire before she went out.

Her bundles were fascinating things. Like the layers of refuse left in France by the people of the Cro-Magnon culture, they were an index to my mother's mind and interests. The base of a bundle was always a spread-open *Daily Mail*. Upon this were scattered numberless unpaid bills. One or two receipted bills were sprinkled among these as a token of her fundamental good faith; but they were usually very old and torn.

"You'll always find that it's the lower classes who rush to pay their bills the moment they arrive," she remarked as she tossed the latest plumber's account into her bundle. "This excessive desire to pay promptly is a sign of lack of breeding. The sensible, aristocratic thing is to wait, and only to pay them when they are accompanied by County Court threats."

The main bulk of the bundle was composed of the outlines of her stories. They were written in longhand with a coarse quill pen, in letters about one inch in height; nobody had ever been able to persuade my mother to write with a steel tip. The outlines were decorated with great blots of ink from the over-charged goose quill, and written on the cut-open paper of brown shopping bags, for Mother had her pet economies. Willingly she might pay twelve guineas for a Paris hat, but she would balance this by saving on paper. And then, because after all she was a woman, among the cumbersome outlines of her stories lay designs for dresses torn from the *Daily Mail*. These she encircled with a thick blue pencil.

During my childhood there was a fashion artist called Bessie Ascough. Each day one of her sketches appeared on the woman's page of the *Daily Mail*. My mother loved these dress designs, and saved practically every one.

"They have," she said, "both style and romance. And that combination is unusual. One day, when I have the time, I shall have all of them made for me by Madame Louise Freeman."

But the designs lay there in her bundles, month after month. They were not being wasted, though, for at odd moments, as she paused in dictating her stories, my mother might be seen gazing through a chipped magnifying glass at any one of the sketches that had happened to work its way to the surface of the bundle. In imagination she clothed herself in these wonderful dresses, and even went to the trouble of pasting together the pieces of newspaper upon which the designs were printed, as they grew torn with age.

One day the bundle would become too unwieldy. And then it was placed in a corner of the study, upon a pile already high on the floor, and old outlines, old bills, old dress designs, faded hair ribbons, love letters from her many admirers, and even forgotten undergarments that awaited mending, gathered the dust over the years. The bundle did not reach this stage, though, until, like a double-decker club sandwich, it had the reinforcement of layers of opened *Daily Mails*, each one of them covered with its collection of treasures.

But it was not only these bundles that cluttered the study table. In the very middle was the enormous glass inkwell. This needed to be big, for my mother used so much ink with her thick quill pens. The great wooden saucer surrounding the inkwell was heaped with the remains of sticks of red sealing wax, because every envelope of raucous green that the *Daily Mail* provided for her manuscripts had to be sealed with dabs of wax along the back flap. And indeed, most of the personal letters she wrote were also secured by a quantity of scarlet wax. Accustomed to the ingenious wiles of her own villains, my mother was melodramatically careful as to the fastening of her correspondence.

"People are so casual about their letters," she said. "They seem to think it's enough merely to lick the gummed surface of the flap. Now a letter to me is a thing of vital importance and so the envelope must be pasted as well. Nobody shall ever be able to say they have received a letter from me which is not properly fastened."

Not content with the paste, my mother always placed the letter within the pages of a book. This book would then be slid between her body and the chair on which she sat, and she would rock upon it for fully five minutes before she considered the envelope safely sealed. But even then, if it were an especially precious and intimate letter, she would look at it with a worried expression and, asking my father for his box of matches, she would cover the entire back flap of the envelope with sealing wax. It was a serious event for her to send anyone a letter.

She used this same paste for her outlines and her manuscripts. The cut-open brown paper of the shopping bags was stuck end to end, as additional ideas came to her, till the length of some pages of her outline would be fully two yards. These pages were folded over and over again till they could lie within the boundary of their bundle. They smelt always of this paste called Stickphast. My mother and the rest of the family loved the smell, which was like the cloves in an apple pie.

"I suppose some people would laugh at me, if they knew about it," my mother used to say. "But the fact remains that I can't seem to work properly unless I sniff at the Stickphast pot from time to time. No amount of expensive perfume could ever take its place."

She could be seen with her nose deep into a pot, as she dictated to her secretary. Perhaps it was this affection for the paste that made her keep the empty pots. They lay around on the study table in all positions and at all angles, with the little picture on the label of one man trying to pull another man off a chair to which apparently he had been stuck in error by this extremely adequate paste.

With her characteristic abundance my mother always used far more Stickphast than was necessary, and we would find odd ribbons and scraps of paper sticking by mistake to her envelopes, and even to her outlines, where the paste had spread beyond its prescribed limit. Sometimes part of a printed page adhered to the back of a letter as she removed it from the book in which she had pressed it, and the envelope would reach its destination with sentences from one of my father's Wild West reference books plastered across it.

One day an especially warm letter from an admirer, that was lying within her bundle, happened to touch a lavishly pasted dress design from the *Daily Mail* that she had backed for strength with a piece of manuscript paper. The love letter stuck to the dress design, and it was only when she was leaving the design with her dressmaker that she discovered what had happened. It was a predicament, but she solved it like a lady and forewent the dress.

My mother hoarded quill pens. She never threw away the discarded ones when their tips broke, and the center of the table, around the great inkwell, looked as though the geese in a farmyard had been having a fight. The main reason she kept these quills was that she grew attached to certain ones, for they served a dual purpose. Not only did she write with them, but she had a passion for being tickled down her back with the feather ends. We were made to sit for half an hour at a time stroking the skin of her back, inside her dress, and around her neck and ears. She closed her eyes in a dreamy manner while this was going on, and, supposing she had fallen asleep, sometimes we would stop; but she always noticed this and made us continue. She said the stroking helped her to get the plots of her stories.

By the side of her main bundle, among the newspapers which were never disposed of, nestled reference books about prison life and a *Manual of Medical Jurisprudence*. Being a writer of melodramas, my mother needed to know about all possible forms of crime and poisoning. What she never did know was that my elder brother Roland and I gathered our first knowledge of the facts of life from the *Manual of Medical Jurisprudence*. When Mother and Father were safely out of the house, we sneaked into the study and withdrew the book carefully from its hiding place. And then we read about the wildest sex outrages and abnormalities, supposing them to be customary. But Mother never knew what conception we had of the facts of life.

Our mother was not the only one to use this study table. To her left, past a barricade of books, sat our father. His was no world of heroes and villains. He lived among Wild West Indians and Northwest Mounted Police, boys' schools and dogs. Walled in, ever since I could remember, by deafness, he was able to write his adventure stories within touch of my mother; for he could not hear her as she dictated her melodramas across the study table to Miss Walmisley, the secretary. This suited him well, as he worshipped my mother so much that he was never happy when she was out of sight. With his minute, copperplate handwriting, so different from my mother's enormous quill-pen scrawl, he covered sheet after sheet with blood-curdling tales about Sergeant Silk of the Northwest Mounted Police, and Kiddie of the Camp of Australia, and sea battles of the days of Nelson.

My father's part of the table was piled high with the history books and accounts of Indians and cowboys he needed for his stories. Innumerable pencil scribbles of canoes and Indian chiefs and dogs also lay around. For deep within my father was the yearning to be an artist. Finding that my mother expected him to go on with his writing, to help in earning the family income, he had tried to satisfy this urge by encouraging me in my earliest enthusiasms.

"You've got to be an artist when you grow up," he would tell me. "It's what I've always wanted to be myself—more than anything else. I shan't feel so bad about it, though, if I see you painting pictures."

And while I was still a very small child he bought me my first oil paints. I was never given much chance to use them, for he was so often up in the nursery with them himself, painting from memory the little brown-sailed fishing smacks we watched in the summer on the North Sea, or heads of dogs, or even, when he felt particularly ambitious, scenes from his own Wild West stories.

Then the seat at the study table beside Mother was vacant for hours at a time, and when Father returned to work Mother would look at him with a cold stare, as though he were a malingerer. He always supposed Mother had not noticed his absence. But he was not really able to slip away unobserved, for this study table was so crowded that any empty space showed up conspicuously.

Each morning my younger brother Evelyn and I were allowed in the study for half an hour after breakfast, while the nursery windows were flung open to air the room. Evelyn was placed on the oak settle near the window and told not to move, while Walmy—as we called the secretary—heaped up books and manuscript notes, to clear a small space by her side where I might sit. But the one stipulation was that we should make absolutely no noise. For, though Mother had not yet started her actual work, she must attend to the daily housekeeping affairs.

As I sat at the table, before the piece of manuscript paper Walmy had given me, silently drawing birds and houses and dogs with a large stub of the blue pencil my mother used to cross out the part of her outline she had finished with, I would hear Mother dictating the day's menu.

The menu was written in an enormous ledger, which contained an account of the meals over many years. If this ledger were to be read now it would give a typical picture of English foods in the early part of the twentieth century. Potatoes and Yorkshire pudding, milk puddings and suet roly-polys; the amount of starch we must have consumed was prodigious.

"I believe in children being properly nourished," our mother always declared. "And you may say what you please about all these new diet fads that are trying to undermine family life, but nothing takes the place of a good mutton chop and a thick slab of currant suet pudding. I don't mean, of course, that you've always got to eat just exactly this. It's every bit as good if you vary it with steak and kidney pie and another kind of boiled pudding—or even, if you like, with roast leg of mutton and blancmange. The important thing is the nourishment."

And so that ledger would record our daily servings of potatoes and meat. But it would also proclaim our extravagance in the matter of puddings. There were always at least four puddings to choose from. On Sundays the number rose to seven, or even eight, with tempting visions of delight such as tipsy cake covered with blanched almonds, looking like an albino hedgehog, or castle baskets filled with whipped cream and cherries and decorated with handles made of angelica stalks. But until we had grown older these were not for us. Up to the nursery went the unvarying portions of milk pudding or suet roll.

I had a special loathing for two things: batter pudding and the skin on the top of tapioca. I refused to eat them. My mother was told of this and on the days when either of these appeared on the menu she sent my father upstairs with his work to sit in the nursery and wait for me to eat the detested pudding.

"I shall stay here until your plate is empty," he always said. "And if you haven't eaten it by five o'clock you will have nothing else for your tea."

We sat on opposite sides of the nursery table throughout long afternoons, Father writing his Wild West stories while I sulked in front of a cold slab of batter pudding drenched in golden syrup.

Sometimes, if Nanny was a bit late in bringing us down to the study, the housekeeping had already started, and timidly we crept to our accustomed places, scarcely daring to breathe. When this happened, I found it hard to behave as I should, for the creative urge within me was stronger even than fear of my mother. With little kicks and pokes at Walmy under the table I tried to bring her attention round to the fact that I lacked my piece of paper and my stub of blue pencil. If this failed, I even risked Mother's anger by whispering to Walmy: "Paper—pencil—paper—pencil." Then my mother stared at me harshly, and Walmy went on writing down: "Cold roast mutton. Mashed turnips. Potatoes baked in their jackets. Currant suet pudding. Stewed rhubarb."

If the household affairs had started, and I missed this chance to get my paper and pencil, I was out of luck, as, before returning to the aired nursery, I had to perform my daily ritual of washing the leaves of the aspidistra. This plant stood on a square black table by the window, in a Benares brass pot. Each morning I went along the passage to the lavatory where, in the damp cold that on winter days made my teeth chatter, I found the blue enameled jug to hold the water, and the old rag with which to sponge the aspidistra. It was an unpleasant job in the winter, for the cold water chapped my hands. The old nurse was upset about this and warned my mother that I would get chilblains; but Mother would not listen to her.

"Nonsense," she said. "No lady ever gets a chilblain. It's only common people who have them. Miss Clare is going to wash the aspidistra every day, weather or no weather."

There was an idea that the plant would thrive more if the London smoke were removed from its leaves.

But this solicitude for the aspidistra was strangely out of keeping with my mother's character, as she never really cared for things around her. Bunches of violets shriveled and died as she forgot to renew their water, and the washstand in her bedroom was littered with discarded lemons which she had used to rub into her skin, and which had turned all conceivable shades of blue and green mold. This lack of care applied also to her attitude towards her own clothes, for the flannel vest she wore beneath her expensive evening dresses was often torn, and she held it together with safety pins, which as likely as not fell below the edge of her short sleeve, to dangle against her arm.

Sometimes these torn flannel vests lay around on her bundles, waiting to be mended. But no one considered this unusual, for there was always a scattering of undergarments over the study. Should the front door bell ring, my mother or Walmy would make a desperate rush for the fireguard, upon which were hanging a few chemises and several pairs of my mother's flimsy, lace-edged drawers.

"The surest way to catch pneumonia is to wear underclothes that have not been properly aired," my mother said as she turned some of her lingerie the other way round, to get it evenly heated. "No flannel petticoat should ever be worn until it has been in front of a fire for at least twenty-four hours. And when it comes to things like chemises and drawers, which go next to the skin, it's always on the safe side to let them go on airing for the better part of a week."

And so the same garments draped the fireguard for days on end, gathering dust and smuts, before they were considered aired enough to be worn with safety. At the advent of an unexpected guest, these chemises and drawers that were snatched up were generally placed hurriedly under a pile of newspapers on my mother's chair. A lacy edge often hung below, for all eyes to see. But sometimes, in her rush, she inserted the undergarments into one of her bundles, where they might be lost forever.

There was another place where my mother's chemises and drawers could always be found. On the top of a sideboard at one end of the study stood a gramophone; the polished oak trumpet looked like the enormous flower of a brown morning glory. This trumpet jutted out into the room, and it was not easy to avoid banging into it.

"Mind the gramophone," warned our mother whenever she heard anyone opening the study door. This grew to be her form of welcome, as other people might say "Come in" or "Good morning." We were never allowed to touch the machine, lest we break it, but though our mother treasured it so, she only played it on the most rare occasions.

"Music," she said, "is nothing to be treated casually. It should be used to enrich a situation."

And so, hearing the sounds of an especially passionate vocal record some afternoon as we returned from our walk, we knew that our mother was in the study, entertaining one of her adoring men friends.

"It does George good to hear a love song from time to time," she remarked. "It counteracts the baleful influence of that depressing wife of his. But then, there's hardly a man in this world who isn't benefited by being warmed and stirred a little."

In the same spirit, though with more mischief, my mother would recite a disturbing love poem during a game of whist, in order to distract a susceptible opponent, while my father, who in his deafness did not hear what was going on, would wonder suddenly why his partner was playing the wrong cards.

But we were always afraid this great wooden gramophone trumpet might harbor dust, which would damage the instrument. The only way to prevent this, we decided, was to stuff something down it.

"Ordinary rags and dusters are far too rough," our mother said. "They might conceivably scratch the polish. The safest thing I can think of is my drawers. There's nothing so soft as silk or mercerised lawn."

Into the gramophone trumpet went the aired drawers, and should my mother be so busy that she did not play any records for some time, there they stayed. But she was inclined to forget she had put them there.

One afternoon a friend seemed dull and depressed.

"What you need, Humphrey, is Caruso's 'Celeste Aida,'" my mother told him. "That will put fire back into your blood. Nothing changes a mood like playing exactly the right music."

She selected the record and wound the machine. But only a

thin little sound emerged from the trumpet. She looked at it in a state of bewilderment.

"That's funny," she said. "I can't think what has happened. This record is generally so loud that even Robert hears it. Something must be wrong."

Suddenly she burst out laughing.

"Of course," she gurgled. "How stupid of me."

Completely unabashed, she plunged her hand down the trumpet and pulled out one pair of pink drawers, one pair of black, and a cream silk chemise.

Lest I should give the impression that my mother completely dominated the study, I must not forget to mention the dogs.

My father was an authority on dogs. Not only did he write books about them, but he also judged them at shows. Consequently, he was always being given presents of dogs by people who hoped thereby to gain his favor. Out in the compound in the back garden were the kennels, where countless litters of puppies would be born. But some of the dogs lived with us in the house. Tita, the favorite Skye terrier, followed my mother from room to room, and Selina, the Scottish deerhound, lay on an oak bench in the study with her long legs sticking straight out before her, catching against everyone who passed that side of the room. Kelpie and Roy, two male Skyes, lived under the study table, where sometimes they started fights in the very middle of my mother's work hours. And then Walmy grew frightened and wanted to leave the room.

"Now look here, Miss Walmisley," our mother would say, interrupting her work for a moment to chide her terrified secretary, "it's perfectly absurd for you to go and get disturbed and frightened. Kelpie and Roy are far too much interested in fighting each other to want to waste time and energy over snapping at your legs. . . . Where were we in the dictating? . . . Oh, yes: 'As he lay in the prison cell, sick with despair, John found himself remembering with

longing the days before the shadows closed in upon him.' Next
paragraph . . . Kelpie, lie down . . . It's all right, Miss Walmisley, don't *think* about the dogs."

But the fight was getting worse. Even my mother grew concerned.

"Robert," she shouted to my father, who was blissfully writing
at her side, in the shelter of his deafness, "I think you'd better see
to the dogs. They're fighting."

My father jerked himself back from his Indians in Canada and
dived under the study table.

When the females came into heat and the sexes had to be separated, Peggy and Pixie went under the study table and Kelpie and
Roy were dispatched to the garden kennels. Our dogs were chiefly
Skye terriers because that breed was supposed to have been the
favorite of Queen Victoria, for whom my mother had had a great
respect.

"Skye terriers are aristocrats," she said. "You can always tell the
class of a person by the breed of his dog. Most people are only suited
by such commonplace dogs as fox terriers or Irish terriers. You have
to be a gentleman to carry off a deerhound or a Skye."

This indoor kennel was fairly easy to manage until a cat passed
the window. The Leighton dogs were allowed to chase cats. When
we went on our walks with the dogs, these cat hunts were one of our
most exciting diversions.

"Catch 'em, Tita! Catch 'em, Selina!" we would call; and the
Skyes and the deerhound tore up the road in wild pursuit of a poor
little tabby.

The glass of the window, though, was a tantalizing obstacle
when the dogs were back in the study. They could not then reach
their prey. Suddenly, into the midst of my mother's love scene
between her hero and heroine, the most terrific barking and baying
started up. Up to her hind legs leapt Selina, as she clawed the window, her hefty tail slashing the aspidistra, and against the lower
part of the window clambered three Skye terriers. But my mother

was completely undisturbed, and the love scene continued, with the passionate avowals shouted loud enough to be heard by Walmy above the din of the dogs, till my deaf father turned to my mother and asked: "What was that you said, Chummie?"

My mother wasn't even much put out when Selina was discovered sometimes stretched over the study table, with her front paws scrabbling among the precious bundles. The keen-nosed deerhound had smelt cold bacon and buttered toast, and was desperately trying to reach it. My parents had a habit of bringing away from the breakfast table slices of bacon, fitted on to neat triangles of toast. My father delighted in shaping the little triangles, as an act of devotion to my mother.

"This is for you, Chummie," he said each morning of his life. "This is to give my Chummie strength for her writing."

The snacks were generally placed on the back of some envelope that had arrived in the morning's mail, and stood around on the study table in readiness for any sudden hunger that either might feel in the middle of the morning's work. Apparently they rarely remembered to eat them, for the toast and bacon slipped under layers of the bundles, or into odd corners beneath the goose quills, where they remained over many weeks, to be joined by halves of Osborne biscuits, or lumps of sugar that my mother intended to put into her handbag, lest, when she was out somewhere, she should suddenly get a severe fit of coughing.

I never understood why our study table wasn't overrun by mice. Undoubtedly there were mice in the house. We caught them in the nursery in traps baited with cold bacon. They haunted the drawers of the washstand in my mother's bedroom. They abounded in the basement. The many dogs in the study must have kept them away. The mice would, else, have had a wonderful time on that table.

One day the study became still more crowded. My father's desire to be an artist grew so strong that he persuaded my mother to give him as a Christmas present a box of oil paints. It was the most wonderful thing. It had three layers of tubes, and dozens of brushes. I would gaze at it in envious awe. Into one corner of the already filled room went an easel, and the boys' stories were abandoned while my father painted a big picture of a beautiful Indian girl in scarlet attire, her black hair streaming behind her, an arrow whizzing past her, as she escaped in a canoe at the edge of some rapids.

But my mother was not happy over this.

"You know perfectly well, Robert, that I have no objection to being the member of the family to earn most of the money," she told him. "That is as it happens—though sometimes, I must admit, I do wonder what it would feel like to be a kept woman. But if I'm to slave away all my days on these potboilers and never have the time to write the *real* literature and the poems that are inside me, the very least I can ask of you is that you also work, instead of enjoying yourself with these pictures."

My father's passion for painting would not be checked. He moved the easel into the unheated back drawing room where, dressed in a muffler and an overcoat, he hoped to be able to paint unnoticed.

But there was trouble ahead. Out of devotion to his Chummie, Father wished to do a portrait of her with his new oils. Yet she would not pose for him. She was honeycombed with superstitions, as could be expected from her Cornish and Irish ancestry. One of the strongest of these superstitions was a fear of being painted or photographed.

"If you allow yourself to be reproduced you will surely die," she declared. "Even the Bible carries this out when it commands: 'Thou shalt not make to thyself any graven image.' I'd do many things for you, Robert; but in this case I must even save you from yourself. What, I ask you, would you do if I were suddenly to die? You'd be in a bad fix, I can tell you. No; most certainly I will not pose."

But in spite of all this, my father meant to paint the portrait.

Over many months, as he sat beside his Chummie at the study table, he would turn his head cautiously towards her, trying to imprint upon his visual memory the shape of her face. Then he would slip from the study, to put down upon canvas in the back drawing room what he had been able to remember.

The several large portraits of my mother he managed to get painted were pathetically bad. But when I remember the difficulties under which poor Father, with no training whatsoever as an artist, worked, I have to admit that they were amazingly good likenesses. I can see one of them now, with Mother staring fullface out from the picture, a large spray of lilac in her straw-colored hair, a purple velvet tunic low over her deep bosom. It was garish yet it gave some impression of her fair beauty and a hint of her wildness, which made her look like the queen of a Border Ballad. Even in the other portrait that I remember, where she is wearing a pink and white boudoir cap and an intimate, low-necked, frilly morning jacket, and holding a pink carnation in one hand, my father managed to show this proud wildness.

For a long while she never knew these portraits were being painted. She rarely went into the back drawing room, and my father would take them off the easel and place them against the wall, behind the piano. She had supposed he was wasting his time with more pictures of Wild West Indian girls, and never troubled to question him. But one day he was working so fondly at this painting that he forgot to look at the clock, and the dinner bell rang without his hearing it. Looking everywhere for him, Mother finally opened the drawing room door, and found herself face to face with the portrait. For many long weeks she went about in fear of sudden death. I think she never quite got over the way her pet superstition let her down.

Though the portraits did her no bodily harm, my father dared not go on with them.

"I may seem to have been able to avoid death this time," our mother admitted after several months of bouncing health, "but that doesn't mean my luck won't change. You must take this escape, Robert, as a kindly warning from Fate. I shall exact a solemn promise from you that never again will you tempt Providence by doing even a pencil scribble of my face."

My father promised; but sometimes I would see him standing in front of a half-finished canvas in the drawing room obviously wanting to take up a paint brush.

For several weeks his spirit was crushed, and he sat closely to his work at the study table, beside my mother, turning out his boys' adventure stories. But it was not very long before he began to slip upstairs to the nursery, and I discovered that his frustration was a great help to me, for he grew even more insistent that I should one day become an artist.

Unfortunately, the things I wanted to paint didn't coincide with what he wished. About this time, when I was six years old, I had a passion for mythological subjects. My father wanted me to paint landscapes or dogs or pretty faces, whereas I struggled stubbornly with a design of Andromeda chained to a rock. Soon he must have realized there wasn't much satisfaction to be found in vicarious painting, for he returned to his writing in the study. Once again that room in St. John's Wood was normal, with its full congestion of workers and bundles, undergarments, aspidistra, gramophone, easel, and dogs.

2. St. John's Wood

The fields from Islington to Marylebone,
To Primrose Hill and St. John's Wood,
Were builded over with pillars of gold,
And there Jerusalem's pillars stood.
                                        —*William Blake*

We lived in a part of London called St. John's Wood. The actual neighborhood can still be found on the map, just beyond Baker Street and Regent's Park; but its spirit vanished many years ago. For St. John's Wood belonged to the age of Romance.

"You have to be worthy of living here," our mother used always to say. "And that is not a question of money or fame. I can think of many very rich and important people who would be incapable of understanding the spirit of the place. They might have heaps of money, but nothing on earth could ever make them belong."

It was a world of individual seclusion. Houses stood hidden behind high garden walls. Garden walls were dwarfed by massive trees. Whatever might take place within these walls was shielded from the

23

eyes of the public. This privacy satisfied our Auntie Pollie's definition of a perfect garden.

"It should be a place," she said, "where you can wash your feet without being seen."

"I entirely agree with you," answered our mother. "But I would go even further, and say that in a perfect garden you ought to be able to walk about completely naked without being seen. And that, of course, is the charm of St. John's Wood. For actually it wouldn't really matter if someone did happen to see you. Even if you chose to walk along the roads in your nightgown no *real* St. John's Wood inhabitant would comment upon it."

Our house, which had the romantic name of Vallombrosa, was satisfactorily invisible from the road. The solid garden gate and the high brick wall were topped with pieces of broken glass bottles, to prevent burglars from scaling them. Against the entire length of this wall grew a row of linden trees. We were proof against the vulgar gaze of passersby. Nobody could know of our thirty-six lilac bushes, or the apple tree in the back garden that blossomed each spring, or the straggly grapevine that draped the wall at the far end of Vallombrosa.

"But then, nobody has any right to know what goes on inside one's garden gate," our mother said. "I have no patience with people who need to live in public. You can always tell them by a certain flat look in their eyes. They have no magic about them. It's as though their outlines end where they end, instead of being surrounded by an aura of glow."

In the St. John's Wood of my childhood most of our neighbors had this "glow." For we lived in the sacred innermost circle, which housed the writers and painters, the actresses and singers, and a few romantic minded but impecunious retired Army officers.

This circle also housed a generous sprinkling of the most select type of "improper ladies." As we went for walks with our nurse we would see male members of the British aristocracy stepping with caution from hansom cabs, in front of closed garden gates. We used to wonder who they were and what they were doing; for they seemed afraid of being noticed.

"And that was the Duke of So and So," Nanny sighed, as an especially dignified gentleman alighted before a blue door in Elm Tree Road. "And 'im with such a beautiful wife, too—as I've seen from their photos in the papers. Upon my word, when you think of what the world's coming to it's about time for the Lord God to descend in the terror and glory of the Judgment Day."

But we never dared to ask what any of it meant, for our nurse wore a forbidding look upon her face.

According to our mother, the outer circle of St. John's Wood started some few streets away from where we lived.

"And it is not imagination on my part that says it is an entirely different world," she contended. "You've only got to walk about fifteen minutes and you'll get into the circle of the 'would-be's'. The people who live there want to look as though they are bohemian. You'll notice that the houses are much grander and they've got more money than we have; but they don't belong to our world. And have you ever remarked how keenly they watch us? They are trying to learn the secret of our magic. But they'll never manage it. You see, they aren't *real*. They don't work."

Our mother was right in what she said. The true St. John's Wood was no romantic setting for the false bohemian. If the "would-be's" could have known how regular our lives were and how hard we worked, they might have been disappointed. These bosky gardens protected houses where pictures were really painted and books were actually written. Artists' models disappeared each morning into garden gates. Hansom cabs arrived each evening to convey celebrated actresses to West-end theatres. Wafted by the breeze, from some open window, came the sound of a singer practising his part at Covent Garden. From time to time, during the day, these workers emerged to take the air. They walked with their dogs and their simmering ideas, round the blocks of houses, and round and round again; but they hardly noticed where they walked. In their minds they were the heroes of a book, or the figures in an oil painting, Mimi, or Hans Sachs. And then, their bodies perfunctorily exercised, they returned to the seclusion of their homes, behind the garden walls, to continue working.

But there was yet another circle in St. John's Wood. It was the outermost circle of all. Nobody with any possible sensitivity or understanding lived there. Within that circle lay the waste lands of Maida Vale and Kilburn, Camden Town and Haverstock Hill.

"And I won't even let Nurse take you for walks in those districts," our mother told us. "You see, though most people seem to overlook the fact, there is every bit as much risk of contaminating the spirit as there is in exposing the body to infection. People who would be scared to death of going anywhere near a case of measles or scarlet fever never think twice about the possible effect of sordid, commonplace atmospheres upon their minds and spirits. I refuse to let my children catch this disease of mediocrity."

Though we were not allowed into these outer regions, we knew a great deal of what happened in our sacred innermost circle. On the daily walks with Nurse there was not much that slipped our notice. And what we didn't know, we guessed, or imagined. For, from our earliest days, we had heard tales of the romance behind these high garden walls with their closed gates.

But these gates were not only guardians of privacy. They presupposed clandestine inclinations. They were often fitted with tiny grilles that could be slid back, so that the owner of the house could put an eye to the opening and examine his visitor without himself being seen. This was supposed to have been especially useful to my mother's father.

Having sold his commission in the 87th Royal Irish Foot, and thereby sacrificed his pension, Captain James Valentine Nenon Connor and his family lived in a dramatically alternating pattern of poverty and riches. Whenever a wealthy relative died and left them some money, my mother and her parents moved to Maidenhead, a romantic, fashionable little place up the Thames, which was notorious for illicit honeymoons. There Grandpapa indulged his extravagant taste for sailing and horses until the legacy had been used up, and so many debts contracted that it was necessary to flee. And then, in the intervals between deaths, the family retired to a miniature house in St. John's Wood, where my dandified, Thackeray-like grandpapa washed the dishes and avoided contact with his creditors. It was here that the little grille came in useful, for at the ring of the bell Captain Connor would go down to the garden gate and slide the shutter just far enough open to let him see who wanted him.

"Captain Connor?" queried the butcher or the baker.

"Captain Connor is not at home," came the reply.

"But you *are* Captain Connor," insisted the creditor, recognizing the voice.

"Captain Connor is not at home," came the answer. And having satisfied his curiosity, Grandpapa slid back the shutter and returned to the house.

Remembering this tale about our grandpapa, who had died before we were born, we used, on our daily walks with Nanny, to watch for one of these grilles to slide open as we passed. But it never happened. We even planned to ring a door bell in the hopes of seeing a ferocious eye appear at a grille. The strict old nurse, however, gave us no chance to do this.

On these same walks we also expected at any moment to see King Edward the Seventh. Had we not been brought up on the legends of our mother's childhood, when the Prince of Wales, as he then was, might be seen disappearing into a garden gate in St. John's Wood, while visiting one of his lady friends?

Our mother was deeply devoted to King Edward the Seventh. No Prince Charming in a fairy tale could have held more magic.

He combined the awesome divinity of a king with the glamour of a passionate lover.

"I honestly believe you think more of that confounded King Edward, whom you will never have the chance to kiss, than you do of any of us who really love you," one of her admirers told her in a fit of jealousy.

Our mother turned to him with a sanctified smile.

"Oh, but you forget," she answered. "Or perhaps you don't choose to remember that I *have* as good as been kissed by him. Never shall I see such a light in any man's eyes as in his. You know perfectly well, George, that I've told you about it many times. Here you keep on saying that you love me so deeply that you'd even die for me, but when I think back to that evening in May I realize that you haven't even the faintest conception of what passion and love really mean."

"To hell with him," shouted the jealous admirer.

My mother was deeply shocked.

"You've no right to say that about a *king*," she reproached him. "But above all, you've no right to say it about King Edward. You happen not to be a woman, so you can't possibly understand. But I tell you, he had everything a woman could want in a lover. There I was, a young girl of about sixteen, walking along Acacia Road by myself, and quoting Byron and dreaming about love, when this hansom cab passes by. I remember it happened near a garden with the lilac in bloom—I shall always think of him when I smell the fragrance of lilac. Something made me look up as the hansom drew near. And there was the Prince of Wales himself, going to see one of his ladies. He leaned forward in the cab, looked me straight in the face and smiled, and sweeping off his silk hat, he kissed his hand to me."

"Nonsense," snorted the jealous George.

"Oh, you may well say 'nonsense'," sneered my mother. "But you weren't there and so you can't possibly know what took place.

Of course I smiled back to him. And then he made a movement towards the little trap door, in the ceiling of the hansom, to tell the cabby to stop; but it was too late. The cabby whipped up his horse, and the next thing I knew I was standing all alone in Acacia Road, against the lilac bushes, with nothing but my dreams."

"H'm. That cabby was probably preparing for his reward in Heaven," said the wounded admirer.

But many years later we were made to suffer for King Edward's gallantry. When he died, our mother felt her grief to be so personal that she put her little children into full mourning for nearly a year. As I played on the beach that summer in my sunbaked black frock, I decided with resentful defiance that never, in all my life, would I be loyal to a king. It was all right to have had to wear black the year before, when Grandmamma died; I had known and loved Grand-mamma. But I hated to wear it for someone I had never met.

My mother, though, had other views. She was even convinced that I had seen him.

"As you go through life," she told me, "I want you always to remember King Edward and to be proud of having seen him at his funeral. It will give you richness of spirit and glamour."

I did not feel either pride or glamour as I fell asleep during the procession. We had been wakened before dawn, to occupy our seats at the window in Edgware Road, above a pawnbroker's shop, for which our mother had paid an exorbitant price. All I can remember across the years is a flag-draped gun carriage and frightening crowds.

I was wrong, though, in feeling I had never known King Edward. My earliest childhood was saturated with him, for he was my mother's idol. It was as if this romantic figure lurked in the thickening lilac bushes in spring, or hid in the blue dusks of early winter. We might see him coming out of a garden gate. He could be within a passing hansom cab.

"I saw *him* again this afternoon," our mother said with a mysterious little smile, when she came upstairs to remove her furs and unpin the Parma violets from her muff. "It was just as I turned the corner of Melina Place. He was going in at that plum-colored garden gate just near the almond tree. He had a bunch of stephanotis in his hand. His back was turned, else I *know* he'd have smiled at me."

We did not need to ask her who the "him" was. The particular quality of our mother's proud smile told us everything. We grew excited ourselves. At any moment we, too, might meet him on our daily walks.

This world had an atmosphere of misty romance which seemed to belong to London, with its violet twilights and the saffron-colored fogs that almost blanketed from sight the gas lamps in the streets. And as it was a world of blurred edges, so it was perhaps inevitably an age of hints and sighs, of clandestine meetings and lingering sentiment. Our mother was a product of this age.

"Don't forget that emotion is nourished by the imagination rather than by actual surrender," she told me as I grew older. "And let me warn you that the rising generation is losing a great deal these days, for there is more romance and passion to be felt in the imagination of an impossible kiss than in all the weekends you young people indulge in. The more you think about sex the less chance there is for romance to enter your life and color it. And without romance, I ask you, what is life worth?"

Our mother lived upon romance, and wove it into her most prosaic daily duties. It was not something to be put aside for special occasions. As she washed her face, or dressed to go out, she quoted poems from W. E. Henley's *Hawthorn and Lavender.*

There was no kiss that day . . .

She paused to splash cold water on her neck—for never in her whole life did she use warm water or soap, believing them to be injurious to the complexion—and then, as she rubbed the juice of a lemon into her skin, she finished one poem and started another.

A sigh sent wrong,
A kiss that goes astray,
A sorrow the years endlong . . ▪

She was growing so emotional that her voice quavered. Tears ran in rivulets down her cheeks and mixed with the dry oatmeal she applied now to her complexion, till her face became covered with fawn-colored paste. But at this point she looked in her glass and saw that she was crying, and, turning her head from me as I sat on the bed waiting to read to her while she dressed, she suggested that we go on with the French play we were in the middle of, while she brushed her hair.

W. E. Henley and King Edward the Seventh were the symbols of my mother's world, against a background of the clop-clop of hansom cab ponies, and flower women by the pavement's edge, selling tightly bunched violets to be pinned on furs, and the sound of the lamplighter's quick step as he walked down the road at dusk with his long pole. It seemed to be a changeless, secure existence, untroubled by outside events. But we three children were not satisfied with this. We felt cheated at having been born in such a time, and wanted something to happen that would be considered important enough to be written into a history book. Our mother's world of melodrama was having its effect upon our minds.

"You don't understand how very lucky you are to be living in these days," she reproached us. "It's a pity you didn't all happen to have been born before the Old Queen died. And it's a pity, too, that you missed the glory of the Boer War. But all the same, you are tasting the fruits of England's greatness, and you should realize that you are very fortunate little children. Why, you might just as easily have been born French, or Italian, or any other of the Europeans."

Our sheltered, secure world was dominated by class feeling. But because both of our parents were writers, it was a very special, peculiar class feeling. It had none of the rigid standards of the "huntin' and shootin' " aristocracy, even though that had been our Grand-

papa's background. It was a snobbishness that included the celebrated poet or the knighted sculptor. For these were the days when
Art was highly paid and romantic, and so long as the artists were
successful, the doors of Society were flung open wide to receive
them. Sir Lawrence Alma-Tadema, R.A., lived in a mighty mansion
with marble pillars, in Grove End Road, which was every bit as
magnificent as the marble backgrounds to his own extremely popular
paintings; MacWhirter, another Royal Academician, earned enough
with his enormous Scottish landscapes to afford an imposing house
with elaborate wrought-iron gateways, and Sir George Frampton,
the sculptor, worked on his statue of Peter Pan for Kensington Gardens in a studio that was almost like a palace. Not only this, but these
artists were visited by members of the Royal Family.

"I've had the shock of my life," our mother said, as she came
back from a round of visits on Studio Sunday, when all the artists
kept open house before sending their completed pictures to the
annual exhibition of the Royal Academy. "I fully expected to see
Royalty in quite a number of the studios I was in this afternoon, but
never did I suppose that timid little Jimmie Faed would have managed to get the Princess Royal along to see those deadly dull landscapes of his. Yes, I tell you, the Princess Royal. And what do you
think he did? Why, instead of letting her see how much honored he
was, he stood in front of his easel, all homesick for that Scotland of
his, and murmured, over and over again: 'Aye, the moor. Aye, the
moor.' But the strangest thing of all was that the Princess Royal
bought the dull landscape. But then, I suppose Royalty has got to
play safe. They mustn't be seen buying anything that might conceivably look fast or wicked."

Though the family lived among writers and artists, our mother
was determined that we should be brought up most correctly. No
hint of anything risqué must be allowed to reach our eyes or ears.

"I do not intend my children to become bohemians," she told
Grandmamma. "Clare worries me by showing symptoms of wanting

to be an artist; but I shall stop that all right. If she had wanted to be a writer it wouldn't have been so bad, but no woman is a lady by reason of being an artist. Only with difficulty can she be a lady in spite of it. . . . And, by the way, Mamma, let me tell you that I simply *will not* have you exposing my children to the risk of meeting that Maude of yours. I mean this. It's nothing to do with me what you may choose to do yourself, but you have got to promise me, here and now, that never, under any circumstances whatsoever, will you even let them catch sight of her."

Overhearing this, we were, of course, deeply curious about "Maude." She became one of the chief mysteries of our childhood.

I never did catch sight of Maude—that is, not face to face. The nearest I got to seeing her was when a shadowy figure slipped out of the back door of Grandmamma's house, just as we were let in at the front door. Grandmamma kept her promise to our mother, though we were tantalized by continual references to the lady.

"Maude came along yesterday in the most marvelous new furs," our grandmamma said with a wink, as she appeared herself in what looked like a brand new sable coat. "And because she can't raise the money to pay my rent this month she handed me over this coat, instead. It's rather nice, isn't it? And it's worth far more than the rent."

My mother tried to look shocked.

"Of course, Mamma, I know it's nothing to do with me who your tenants are, but I do think you might be just a little less obvious about it all."

"Nonsense, Pattie," answered Grandmamma. "Since when have you gone and got so proper? You're jealous of the jewels Maude gives me, if the truth were only known. You'd like some of them yourself, wouldn't you? The way you go on, you'd think Maude was an ordinary sort of 'improper lady,' whereas she's at the height of her profession, and decidedly particular. She has only a very few gentleman friends, and these are, she assures me, of the aristocracy.

And after all, as you yourself have just said, what difference does it make to you who my tenants are?"

Grandmamma toyed with the pearls around her neck, and the rings that sparkled upon her fingers. Judging by the splendor of these substitutes for rent, Maude must have had great charm.

"And when all's said and done, owning house property in St. John's Wood isn't the surest way of earning a steady income," Grandmamma continued. "If I didn't have someone like Maude as a tenant, I'd most likely have an impecunious artist or poet who would never be able to pay the rent. So what are you to do?"

"The one thing you *can* do is to be a little more discreet in talking about her," our mother said. "I wouldn't be surprised if Clare hasn't overheard quite a great deal of what you've been saying. And remember this: I intend Clare to grow up correct and strait-laced. I do not mean her to know about persons like your Maude."

But some years later Maude's name turned up once again in the family. By that time Grandmamma had died, and Maude was nothing more than a memory.

"It was the queerest coincidence," said my mother with delight. "But it only goes to show that real life is every bit as fantastic as the stories one writes."

It seemed that one Christmas, in an unusual rush of maternal exuberance, Grandmamma had given my mother a beautiful sapphire ring. My mother knew perfectly well it had been Maude's equivalent for rent. Only rarely did she wear it, because it was both conspicuous and valuable. One day an important Anglo-Indian government official visited us. As my mother had an engagement later that afternoon, she asked him if he would not like to come part of the way with her in her cab. Pulling off her glove to rearrange the violets on her muff, she was surprised to hear a stifled: "My God!" beside her. She turned round, to see the strong, silent, military face an ashen white.

"What's the matter?" she asked him. "Are you ill?"

But he shook his head.

"Let me look at that ring," he begged. And taking her hand, he examined it lengthily. "Yes," he said, "there's no doubt about it. Absolutely no doubt. It's been in my family for a very long while. But where did you get it? Tell me where it came from."

"Oh that," said my mother, "that was a Christmas present from Mamma."

"Impossible," he moaned. "Impossible. Many years ago I gave that ring to a woman I loved. I would know it anywhere. She was a beautiful woman, I remember, and I was passionately in love with her. Her name was Maude."

It seemed as though he were going to turn reminiscent, but then he thought better of it, and straightened himself as he whispered:

"I can't for the life of me see how it got into your mother's possession, but for pity's sake don't ever mention this to my wife."

In spite of our mother's intention of bringing her children up with the utmost strictness and moral rectitude, there was one way in which she actually encouraged us to sin. She was an ardent suffragette. To our terror she even consorted with women who were planning to kill Cabinet Ministers. This made us afraid she would one day get sent to prison, and we hurried past every policeman we met on our walks, imagining they might be on their way to arrest her.

"Sometimes I get rather worried over Bessie," she confided to our father about a friend of hers. "It seems she has absolutely sworn to kill the Prime Minister, and there's no persuading her against it. Would you believe it? She's the wildest of the lot, in spite of looking such a mouse. Didn't I always tell you that appearances are deceptive?"

But overhearing this, my little brother and I grew scared, for we often saw this friend in the neighborhood. When it happened, we would use every possible device to get our nurse to cross the road, rather than meet her face to face. We suspected that she always carried a bomb with her, and feared it might accidentally explode while she was talking to us.

"But though I don't exactly hold with killing," our mother told us, "I do believe in Women's Suffrage enough to do quite a few violent things. And this is where I would like you children to help me. You can manage it quite easily when you go for your walks. Just get Nurse to take you along Greville Place, where J. L. Garvin, the editor of the *Observer*, lives. You know his house. I've pointed it out to you. He's been writing against the Cause lately in his paper and it's time somebody did something about it. Now, if you *did* happen to have a spare stone in your pockets, and if you *did* chance to throw that stone into the windows of his house as you passed, I wouldn't punish you. In fact . . ."

And our mother looked at us with a warmth that was unusual.

We developed a sudden fondness for taking walks along Greville Place. When nobody was looking, we stole some stones from a roadmender's pile. Day after day, walking demurely on each side of the old nurse, we fingered these stones in our overcoat pockets. We loitered behind her, each waiting for the other to throw the first missile. But something always seemed to hold us back, and with immense relief we would see Nanny turn her head towards us, or notice someone coming down the road; for now it was impossible. We would have to wait till another day.

The stones were never thrown.

This sympathy with Women's Suffrage was an inconsistent thing in our mother's character, for actually she had a contempt for her own sex.

"No woman is really worth talking to if any man happens to be near," she said. "Women, you see, discuss personalities, whereas men talk either about ideas or the work they are doing. You might conceivably say this is the result of education, but I don't believe it would make a scrap of difference. Education for women is a sheer waste of money and time."

But in spite of these views, our mother continued to support the Cause. It was, she held, a sheer matter of principle. The gardener had no right to the vote which was denied to the lady of the manor.

"Why should I want a vote, though?" she asked on her return home from marching through the London streets in a procession of suffragettes. "As it is, I hold the power to control the votes of six— no, eight—men. All of these men will vote as I want them to, to please me, for they think of me as a woman; but directly I get the franchise my power will be taken from me. I shall have become a rival voter, and I shall control one vote only, and that is my own."

Our mother did not belong to an age of sex equality. Hers was the power behind the throne, in a world where women schemed, and the strength of passion lay in its being illicit. St. John's Wood, in Edwardian days, with its misty twilights and the high garden walls, was her rightful setting.

3. *Mother's Old Men*

"Never give yourself to a man," my mother told me when I was growing up. "And I say this to you without any thought for morals. I say this only out of wisdom. A man wants most what he cannot get. That is why the girl in the convent has a glamour and a glow about her that none of you brazen young moderns will ever manage to achieve. And so, if you really want your man, keep everything veiled and hinted at, but not proclaimed."

My mother's greatest wisdom lay in her dealings with men. All men fell in love with her, and she was able always to hold their love. I never knew a man who forgot her, or forsook her, or who managed to free himself from emotional slavery to her. As I began to wonder what the secret of her power was, I decided that it lay, as she said, in the mist of romantic inaccessibility with which she surrounded herself. She was always unattainable, and consequently always to be desired.

"And there's something else I'd better tell you," she added, feeling it was her duty to instruct me about men. "It's what your grandmamma once told me. 'My child,' she said to me many years ago, 'I have only one small piece of advice to give you, but if you obey it there's nothing you can't achieve with a man. My advice is: Fly and they follow. Follow and they fly.' "

I never noticed that my mother did any of the flying she advocated; but then, I was up in the nursery most of the time and knew little of what went on downstairs. I was aware, though, of the irresistible flutey note that came into her voice when she talked with any of her adorers, and I often wished she would use the same warm tone when she spoke to us children.

During the years of my early childhood there were, apart from my father, three men who persistently loved my mother. "Mother's Old Men" Roland called them. Their devotion continued faithfully through to their death, and they followed her movements so closely that one of them even took to living in a caravan, that he might pitch his tent as near to her as possible. Behind the wall of his deafness my father adored her, and, by reason of being a great deal older than she was, had something of a cherishing, paternal attitude towards her. If he felt even mildly jealous of these three men he never showed it. My brothers and I did not know that there was anything out of the ordinary in this multiple devotion. Had not our mother been in love all her life?

"I had my first love affair when I was ten," she told us. "He was a window cleaner in a green baize apron, with a family of eight children, whom I met on my walks in St. John's Wood, and I spent my days quoting Byron to myself about him. Pretty soon we were writing to each other, and he placed his letters in the box attached to the garden gate, and so that my family might not see them through the glass opening he covered the envelopes with a piece of green baize from one of his aprons. This went on unnoticed for quite a long while, when one day Papa happened to look more closely at the letter box as he went out at the garden gate. And there he found a package enclosed within the disguising green baize."

"What happened then?" we always asked, for we loved hearing this story.

"Oh, well, of course there was a terrible row," our mother smiled. "And I had to confess. The poor window cleaner was threatened by the law, and my parents sent me off to a convent in Northern France. They thought I'd be safe there, but actually I proceeded to fall in love at one and the same time with the Mother Superior and the priest, and ended up by becoming a devout Catholic."

But our mother's luck was against her. Her parents thought there was something strange in the tone of little Pattie's letters, and paid her an unexpected visit to France. They found her dressed in black, from head to foot, looking, as her father said, "like a crow in mourning." She was busy doing penance for her sins, and starving herself as well, because she thought thereby to bring herself more closely to the state of grace of the adored priest. The cross Channel steamer next day carried back to England a brokenhearted little girl who spent the time in one of the ladies' lavatories, on her knees, praying to the Virgin Mary that the ship might go down and drown her, so that she need not return to infidel England.

Brought up on these legends of our mother, it was no wonder that we took her adorers as a matter of course. Indeed, we should have felt that there was something wrong if they had fallen away. Adoration was her due.

Of these "Old Men," the one we were most aware of was the novelist who visited our mother three times a week, all the days of our childhood. At exactly three o'clock there was a ring at the front door bell and we rushed to the nursery window to see Mr. Bowles arrive. So punctual was he that you could have set your clock by him. A dapper little figure in a grey overcoat and a top hat, wearing a bunch of violets or a carnation in his buttonhole, and invariably carrying a neat umbrella on his arm, he came up the garden path to the steps with the walk of a little bird, and waved to us at the nursery window. He never failed to wave, and even on rainy days he would slant his opened umbrella to the side so that he might see us.

He was the one we were fondest of, for we were not afraid of him as we were of the other two. Monday, Wednesday and Friday, year in, year out, he arrived. Thus he had arrived before even my elder brother was born. He sat by the hour, adoring our mother, while they talked together about the literary world of London. My mother had very little respect for his brain, and she considered the books he wrote completely worthless and deplorably thin.

"Why anybody takes the trouble to publish them," she said, "is a mystery to me. Ninety-two novels he has written, and if you were to boil the whole lot down into one book you might manage to make something just worth reading while you were waiting at a station for your train on a rainy day. But then, I am always forgetting that most people in the world can only understand trivial books. And any- how, George doesn't expect me to read anything he writes, so why should I bother my head about it? What matters far more is that he has the most perfect mouth I have ever seen in a man. It's a com- plete Cupid's bow. No wonder so many women fall in love with him."

She insisted that she was not one of these women.

"And that's why he is so faithful to me," she added. "What did I always tell you? No man wants a woman who runs after him. It's when she has no feelings for him that he prostrates himself at her feet. There isn't any romance for me about George. He's just a com- fortable little cock robin with pink cheeks and this perfect mouth, to whom I can confide my upset inside, or a chill on the liver. But he loves me so much that I think I could even let him see me if I had a pimple on my nose. Besides, he's very valuable to me, for there's nothing he doesn't seem to know about literary gossip."

And so they sat together through the afternoons, while my deaf father worked steadily at his boys' stories in his chair at her elbow.

Time passed, and outside in the blue dusk the Italian organ-grinder stopped opposite our garden gate, gave a piece of banana to his monkey, and ground out his unvarying *Il Trovatore* or *Cavalleria Rusticana*. A little later, as the dusk deepened, the lamplighter swung down the road with little hurried steps. If it were winter, we would return from our walk with Nanny just after the magic moment when the gas lamps in the street were lit, and Mr. Bowles' top hat and over-coat hung on the oak stand in the front hall, while from the study as we passed on our way to the nursery there came a muffled sound of intimate, warm voices. We would make a noise, hoping Mr. Bowles might hear and call us to come in and see him. But this did not often happen, as he was afraid it might displease our mother. We reached the nursery with the sense of every-thing being as it should, for it would have seemed strange and wrong if that top hat and overcoat had not been hanging there Mondays, Wednesdays and Fridays.

Or if it were late spring, just before we left London for the house in East Anglia, the lilac was in bloom in the garden and it was day-light as we came home to tea. The seasons might change, but that top hat would still be there in the front hall, three afternoons a week, and from the study would come a comfortable sound of soft voices, and the smell of hot buttered toast.

There was a pleasant warmth about Mr. Bowles. He seemed genuinely fond of us, and even took the trouble to come up to see us in the nursery. When he came we had a wonderful time, for we made him tell us about the habitants of Canada. We even forced him to play at Wild West Indians. He had lived in Canada and had seen real live Indians in full war paint. In our minds I'm afraid we contrasted this with our father who, though he wrote about these Indians, had never seen them and knew only what he had been able to read in books.

We also liked Mr. Bowles because we were proud of the way he trusted us. It made us feel we were being treated like grownups.

For Mr. Bowles was married.

"Don't ever forget," our mother would say to us, "don't ever forget that if Mrs. Bowles asks you if you have seen him lately you must say No. You must never tell her he comes to the house. She's a puny-minded woman, and she wouldn't understand. If she knew about it she'd only make it uncomfortable for Mr. Bowles, and you wouldn't like that, would you?"

But the entire family hated this wife, and so it wasn't difficult to keep the secret. Mr. Bowles' honor was safe.

Although Mr. Bowles was the most frequent of the three adorers, the other two equalled him in fervor. One was a remarkably fat old judge who lived near our seaside house at Lowestoft. We had never seen anyone so enormous, and Evelyn and I delighted in counting his chins. His nose was red and swollen as though it had been stung by a bee. His hands were like a bunch of pink sausages. He seemed to us completely unromantic, and we squirmed when we heard him calling our mother his "Beloved Beauty."

Our mother, though, did not seem to object. She went for tedious walks with him along the Front, while he poured out his heart to her. She sat with him for hours on end in the garden at Lowestoft, listening to his romantic philosophy of life. And always it seemed to us that he must be boring her to death; but always she turned to him with one of her very special smiles. There must, we felt, be something to him that we did not understand.

Whereas the winter was more generous to Mr. Bowles, the summer was kinder to this obese judge. It is true that during the winter he often came to London, to see my mother, but it was not possible for him to visit her so frequently then as during the summer months when we lived near to him. He was a devout Catholic. His tiny, thin little wife was an even more devout one and acquiesced in his straying fancies as only a woman who feels sure of her husband in the next world can.

There was one thing about him that distressed us. He was always making awkward statements in a voice that everyone could hear. I remember one day walking along the Front at Lowestoft with Nanny, and seeing the old judge before us, hobbling beside our mother. For he was lame, as well as enormously fat. Suddenly he stopped and, leaning on his thick stick, shouted out loud:

"One hundred of them, my dear. Exactly one hundred women I've loved in my lifetime. And not one of them is fit to touch the little toe of your right foot."

A respectable old couple that was passing at that moment looked round in surprise, hardly able to believe what they had heard. They stopped and stared at this bulky Don Juan, while we blushed with shame for our mother's sake.

Occasionally the old judge took us to parties, for, he said to our mother: "If I love you, my dear, I love your children for your sake." But, though he was generous and kind, we never really enjoyed these parties because he always made himself so conspicuous that we felt awkward and shy. Sometimes he arrived in the open carriage he hired each day to drive up to see our mother, and, his trembling, podgy old hand taking a cigar from his slobbery mouth, shouted that he had come to take us to an open air Catholic service. We went with him to a convent garden, smelling of incense and lilies, where little girls in white dresses sang hymns to Mary, and the poor old judge, once on his knees, had to be helped up by my brother and me to join in the procession. We felt embarrassed by this, and although we loved the smell of the incense, we would escape from him if we could before he had forced us into the carriage.

Judge Talbot, as he was called, was determined to educate his "Beloved Beauty's" children. Once, while I was still very small, Ellen Terry came to Lowestoft to play in Bernard Shaw's *Captain Brassbound's Conversion*.

"When you are a grown woman I want you to be able to tell people that you have seen Ellen Terry act," the old judge said to me in his loud voice. "There won't be any more actresses as fine as she is, with everything getting so commonplace and unromantic. Goodness alone knows what sort of a world you children will have to live in."

And I was taken to the theatre by him and his frail little wife. But it was long past my bedtime, and I grew more and more sleepy, till I began to confuse Ellen Terry with my Aunt Lexy.

"Look at her subtle majesty," the judge shouted to me, as my head began to nod. "That's a woman for you, that is. Look at the way she walks across the stage. Clare, you must remember this all your life. The Lord knows, if I weren't so much in love with your mother that I can scarcely keep my mind free of her even when I'm at Mass, I'd be following Ellen Terry to the end of my days."

The audience hissed at him to keep quiet. But his shouts must have crossed the footlights to the ears of Ellen Terry herself.

The thing that vexed me most about this old judge was the way he encouraged my mother in bringing me up strictly.

"It doesn't matter what sort of morals the men of a country have, so that only the women are innocent as doves," he would say, as he advised her about my education.

Having himself, as he openly declared, loved one hundred women, he was a great romantic on the subject of the purity of woman. I overheard him one day telling my mother, in that huge voice he seemed unable to subdue, that if she were wise she would never tell me anything about the facts of life.

"A woman should come to her husband as innocent as a wild rosebud, my dear," he said. "It is for the man to tell her what he wishes to. That way there is real romance."

And then he quoted, as if to reinforce his opinions, what he considered the finest definition of a woman. It was a poem written, he said with a strange little laugh which I could not see the reason for, by Oscar Wilde. I remembered it over the years, and held it responsible for many severities that were handed out to me.

Lily-like, white as snow
She hardly knew
She was a woman
So sweetly she grew.

"And if *I* don't know what I'm talking about, I'd like to know
who does," shouted Judge Talbot. "When I come to think back to
the barmaids and chambermaids I've been to bed with—"

"Hush," said my mother. "If you talk so loud Clare will hear
you."

"But I'm not talking loud," bellowed the judge. "As I was saying, if anybody on this earth knows what a pure woman is, it's I.
Not that a pure woman is as interesting to go to bed with as the other
kind. I wouldn't say she is. You take Kate, my wife. I love her deeply.
The dear Lord Jesus and our Blessed Lady know I love her. But if
you think I've ever insulted her by making a hack of her—"

"Why can't you talk more softly," pleaded my mother. "If you
go on like this even Robert will hear you. And then he'll imagine all
sorts of things that aren't true."

But the old judge was fully launched now into his romantic
reminiscences, and my mother knew that nothing could stop him.
She shut the study door, and in a few minutes I heard the loudest
record we possessed being played upon the gramophone. My mother
was going to have her own way. Not even the old Judge could drown
"Vesti la Giubba" sung by Caruso.

I wonder whether children have a keener sense of smell than
grownups, or whether they merely lack social reticence in their
minds. I know that I shall always think of my mother's three faithful adorers by their individual scents. Mr. Bowles had a smell of
moustache wax and Turkish cigarettes. There was even a slight scent
of pomade and shaving soap about him; he seemed always so
polishedly clean, and his face shone pink and smooth. It was little
wonder that he was nicknamed "Cupid," for he truly looked like a

cherub. Judge Talbot smelt of warm flabbiness, expensive cigars and Harris tweed suits.

But it was the third adorer whose scent I chiefly remember. And I remember it with distaste. He seemed to smell of moth balls mingled with a whiff of Scotch whiskey. He always wore Highland kilts. He had two sets—winter weight and summer weight—and because the dark green tartan of the Gordon clan didn't show the dirt, they were rarely cleaned. The set that was not at the moment in use was laid by in dozens of moth balls, which were supposed to have a purifying quality to them. Stuck into one of his woolen socks was a great horn-handled knife which terrified us, for we always imagined he might draw it from its scabbard if we displeased him too severely. In the winter, as a concession to the cold weather, he threw a fringed tartan shawl across his shoulders, and held it in place with an enormous cairngorm pin. Below his kilts his knobby knees were so white that they seemed bloodless.

He wore these kilts in the streets of London, though sometimes, when he was going to a fashionable gathering like the Eton and Harrow cricket match at Lord's, he would compromise with custom by wearing a top hat as well. He never seemed to know how ridiculous he looked.

This Scotch adorer was a wild creature. Evelyn and I were terrified of him because he spoke with such a thick Scotch accent that we could never understand him, and whenever he asked us any question we couldn't know how to answer. He was a retired Naval surgeon and, like my father, he wrote boys' adventure stories. Also like my father, he wrote about dogs; he took his huge St. Bernard, Lassie, with him wherever he went, as though she were an emblem of his trade. I can see him now, coming down our road in St. John's Wood in full Highland dress with his shawl floating out upon the air behind him, a top hat on his head, a bunch of red roses for my mother in one hand, and this enormous dog straining at the leash that he held in the other hand. As he passed us with our nurse, he gave me a bang on the head with the bunch of roses, called me "Bonnie wee lassie," and hurried along to his "Mea," as he had named our mother.

I often used to wonder what my mother saw in him. He was a far more insistent adorer than Judge Talbot or Mr. Bowles, but he had neither graciousness nor tact. It is no wonder my father hated him. Perhaps his violence compensated my mother for the timid caution of Mr. Bowles. He carried around with him the impression of imminent danger.

"But you can never go by outward appearances," my mother said. "Alexander is really the most obedient and amenable of the three. There is nothing, in fact, that he won't do for me, if I ask him."

He was a thorough romantic. Letters and poems came from him each day, in an illegible handwriting and purple ink. My mother would put her broken little bit of magnifying glass up to her eye— for her sight was bad, and yet she refused to wear glasses—as she deciphered with difficulty the latest poem he had written to her.

In order to follow my mother in her movements, Alexander took to living in a caravan. No sooner had our family made its annual move to East Anglia, than the breakfast bell rang violently one morning around seven o'clock. We knew then that he had arrived.

"Mea," his husky voice called up the stairs. "Mea, I have come to greet you. I have come to see you while the morning dew is still upon you."

And the tones of a Scotch love song reverberated through the house. Nothing and nobody could keep him out. He forced himself past the housemaid and the cook. As we turned in our beds, wakened by this noise, we knew that back somewhere in a field in the Corton Road he had pitched his caravan, and that he would pester the family until we returned to London for the winter.

Once or twice a year my brothers and I were invited to tea in the caravan. It was a superior affair of polished brown wood, and looked somewhat like a yacht that had been grounded at low tide. But this was no gypsy existence. The Scotchman saw to it that he had everything to make life comfortable and easy. Were he living now, he would have had a luxurious trailer, but in those days he had to rely for transportation upon a horse. As a child I used to picture this horse drawing the caravan all the way across England from the Thames Valley to the shores of the North Sea. Actually both the caravan and the horse came by train, though the caravan was horse-drawn from the Lowestoft railro..d station to its resting place in the field in Corton Road. It moved slowly up the middle of High Street, and the municipal trolley cars accumulated in an impatient line behind it, clanging their bells for this strange obstruction to move out of their way. But the irate old Scotchman leant from the opened half-door at the back of the caravan, and blasphemed into the face of the nearest trolley car driver.

"What blankety-blank damn business have you to frighten my horse with this hellish noise?" he shouted, looking like an infuriated be-kilted Don Quixote with his long moustaches waving in the wind. Once, when the trolley car driver dared to swear back at him, he withdrew into the caravan and reappeared with the horse whip. He even started to brandish it at the driver, but the wise old horse, aware that her master had seized hold of the whip, imagined it to be for her benefit, and broke suddenly into a quick trot, so that the Scotchman was out of reach of the tolley car driver. If the natives of Lowestoft had any doubt as to whether the Leighton family had arrived yet for the summer, they were made certain of it by the sight of this caravan with its blaspheming owner moving slowly up the middle of the town. It was as much an annual event at Lowestoft as the arrival of the first Scotch fishergirls in the fall for the gutting of the herrings, or the Firework Display on August Bank Holiday at the local Yacht Club.

But the Scotch adorer was not alone. He brought with him always a widowed sister and her pale, pimply daughter Maggie. These two women cooked for him and tended him and lived together within the caravan itself. He slept in a tent at the side of the caravan, with his St. Bernard. The old horse Queen was tethered at night to one end of the caravan, so that she might not be stolen; but during the daytime she cropped quietly on the grass of the field where the camp was pitched.

On the rare occasions when we were invited to tea, we used to take sugar and apples for the old horse. We never really got to know the sister and her daughter. They were very shy and completely repressed. They did not visit our house, but sometimes, on our walks in town, we saw the Scotchman strolling along the street with his pimply niece.

"Maggie is the most unattractive young woman I've ever seen," our mother said. "There's nothing to do but despise her."

But I was scared of her, because she never spoke, and I used to wonder what she did all the day long, within the confines of the caravan.

These rare visits to the caravan were not happy times for me. Knowing I was terrified of insects, Roland always took me to a certain big brick that was placed against one of the wheels to prevent the caravan from rolling away. Taking this brick up, he forced me to gaze at the swarm of wriggling earwigs beneath. I was especially frightened of earwigs.

"Let me tell you, Miss Clare," my nurse's words rang in my head, "you'd better be careful of earwigs. It's not for nothing those horrid insects have got that name, for if they creep into your ears they'll nibble at your brain, and you'll go mad."

I suffered on these occasions. Perhaps my fear of the old Scotchman was unfair. It was most certainly tied up with the thought of earwigs.

Although we did not like this Scotchman, we yet worried about him when the nights were wet. For the little tent in which he slept seemed as though it could not keep out the rain. We were always relieved when, next morning, the breakfast bell rang around seven o'clock and his loud voice sang its Scotch love song, to waken our mother; we knew then that he had not been drowned.

Life wasn't easy for my mother at Lowestoft, for there was always the risk of Alexander meeting the old judge. They detested each other, as all rivals do. Even we children were drawn into the problem of keeping them apart, and very often we were sent out to the carriage in front of the house, to occupy the attention of the waiting judge while our mother got rid of her Scotchman.

"If that damn scoundrel in his kilts is there I'm not coming in," bellowed Judge Talbot towards the windows of the house. "But neither am I going to leave," he went on. "I shall stick here in this victoria until the way is clear. If he thinks he can deprive me of my necessary daily sight of my Beloved Beauty's face, he's mistaken. Damn his scraggy bones and his swishing kilts. Damn them, I say."

If these two did happen to meet, they were capable of the meanest and most childish tricks. I remember once how the old judge came to the house and found the Scotch gentleman's top hat out in the hall—for he wore it occasionally to impress my mother, even though this was not London, but the seaside. With all his excessive weight he sat on it, and bashed it in. We delighted in this, if we were able to keep far enough away. But sometimes life became very difficult. That was when Mr. Bowles came down on a visit. Then there were three adorers to keep disentangled. I often wondered how my mother managed it. It could scarcely have been worth all the trouble, unless she enjoyed the exhilaration of being fought over.

Alexander had one most vexing habit, which may have been what caused his wife to leave him. From time to time he took to drink. He took really to drink, until the room was filled with snakes and all creepy crawly creatures, and he sat up in bed with a pistol in each hand, ready to fire at anyone who approached.

This took place only during the winter, when we were back in London and he did not see my mother so often. When it happened his widowed sister sent my mother a telegram. I can see her face as the message was brought to her in the study. "Alexander is at it again," she told my father with a sigh, handing the slip of paper over to him. And even though she were busy with her work, she would go upstairs and put on her coat and hat and take the first possible train to the country, where he lived. For in these attacks she was the only person who had any power over him, and without flinching she went in to him and took the pistols out of his hands and let him sob upon her bosom.

4. *From the Nursery Window*

Most of what we knew of life was learnt from the nursery window. We looked down upon the world, and nothing could be hidden from our sight. We saw the buds swelling upon the trees and the birds nesting in spring; but we saw, also, the cook slinking out to meet her lover.

We were especially fortunate. Many of the bigger houses in St. John's Wood boasted a separate small entrance for the servants, but Vallombrosa had only one garden gate. This meant that we could see everything that happened, for towards this gate converged the paths from the front door and from the kitchen door. There were two bells on the garden gate: one with Visitors engraved around its rim, and the other with Servants. Luckily for us, both these bells rang loud enough to be heard in the nursery, and we could drop our toys and rush to the window in time to see who was arriving. We could hear, too, the slam of the front door, and watch who was leaving the house. So, with our long hours of childhood leisure, we followed the pattern of life downstairs.

In this way we knew things our mother had neither time nor opportunity to learn. For she spent almost all her waking hours within the four walls of the study. Even when she was not actually working, she stayed there with her adorers. Absorbed always in her own world of romance, she was not aware of the drama around her. It was left to us in the nursery to watch the ritual of the days and the activities of servants, relatives and admirers.

Our day of watching started early. We knew the exact moment after breakfast, while Nanny was making the beds in the night nursery, when Dolly, the crippled kitchen maid, would appear with her pail and her kneeling mat, to wash and whiten the steps and polish the brasses on the front door. Down each step she moved on her knees, till finally she reached the tessellated pavement of the garden path. This pavement that led from the bottom of the front steps to the garden gate was a geometric design in browns and reds and slate-greys. It always seemed beautiful to us, but during the short moment when it was wet the colors glowed with a magic richness that only we, looking down from the nursery, knew. The grownups did not dare to walk across this pavement until it was dry, lest their feet got wet and they caught a chill. And that was why it had to be washed as early as possible in the morning, before anyone needed to go out of doors; for our mother had a special terror of wet feet.

"It's the surest way to catch pneumonia," she declared. "I'd rather do almost anything in the world than get my feet wet. Exactly forty-eight hours later I would most certainly begin to sniff, and feel a roughness in my throat. It never fails. Now if we had a gravel path leading to the gate, instead of this paved one that dries so quickly, I would have to stay indoors most of the winter, because of the puddles. As I told your father at the time, it was the tessellated pavement that decided me in taking Vallombrosa."

Evelyn and I must have been heartless little creatures, for we never reflected how the damp cold must have penetrated Dolly, on biting mornings in winter. Rarely did she cross our paths, for she spent her life in the darkness of the basement, helping the cook, where, for five shillings a week, she slaved throughout her days like a drudge in a fairy tale.

But then, we were not supposed to be aware of the servants as human beings. Their personal life was hidden from us, and if we happened upon it we were careful to keep silent. And so when, one morning, it was Albert the knife boy who appeared in a sacking apron to whiten the steps, we feigned surprise. Mother never knew that Dolly's romance had been discussed at length in the nursery. We had listened to the letter she sent to the matrimonial agency, and looked at the photograph of the nice young farmer in Alberta who had written in reply and asked her to come to Canada and be his wife. And when, a month or two later, Dolly reappeared, we kept it quiet that we had watched her sobbingly tell Nanny how the immigration officials in Canada, seeing she was crippled, had turned her back at the docks.

We were ashamed of feeling tender towards poor Dolly.

But once a year our mother treated the servants as human beings. She considered Christmas Day the occasion on which to break down class barriers. The staff appeared then in a "Peace on earth, goodwill to men" atmosphere, to take turns at extracting one of the small gifts from the bran pie. Our mother would not let us have a Christmas tree, lest the candles should topple over and set the house on fire. The bran pie was our festive substitute. The tub stood in the middle of the back drawing room on a large sheet, to prevent the bran from getting trodden into the pile of the carpet. We dived into it, to draw out a present disguised in shape under many wrappings of brown paper. Walmy had been allowed to spend an afternoon and a great deal of money at Shoolbred's, in Tottenham Court Road, buying these gifts. For it was an understood thing that not even my mother and my father must know what lay hidden among the bran.

The ceremony took place at the end of the day, after we had finished opening the countless presents our mother lavished upon us.

"Some people have called me extravagant, giving you children so many expensive toys for Christmas," she once unexpectedly confided to me. "But, you see, I still retain that uncomfortable thing called a conscience, and I know perfectly well I am inclined to neglect my family emotionally over the rest of the year. I simply can't help that. I've got too much work to do. And so all these presents are a sort of salve to my conscience."

Even the servants were included in this extravagance, and received elaborate dresses and hats.

These servants now trooped in at a given order. They stood in a row, in strict precedence: the old nurse, the cook, the parlormaid, the housemaid, the undernurse, and Dolly the kitchen maid.

"Minnie," my mother commanded. And Minnie, the fat bosomed parlormaid who was engaged to the butcher, stepped forward in her frilly starched cap and apron, to draw a shaving set from the bran pie.

"Emily," my mother called next, a sudden sternness in her voice. She imagined my father felt too much tenderness towards this little red-haired housemaid, and as Emily tripped forward to secure her inappropriate gift, my mother gave her a piercing stare, and turned her head immediately then towards my father, to see if he were watching. But my father was gazing with emphasis at the far end of the drawing room. Recently he had been seen coming from the direction of the linen closet, where Emily was arranging the returned laundry; and her face had been crimson, and her red hair disheveled. Or so Walmy had reported. And Walmy, said, my mother, had the unerring eye of a hawk. Even Evelyn and I knew that if Emily didn't soon fix the date of her wedding to the plumber, and leave of her own accord, she would be dismissed. For Mother was deeply suspicious.

Actually we saw more of the servants than our mother knew, or would have permitted. Often they sneaked up to gossip with Nanny. On occasions they came to look out of the nursery window.

Obliquely opposite our house was a big Jewish synagogue. From time to time grand weddings took place there. Early in the morning the palms and potted plants appeared. Then the undernurse was sent down to the kitchen, to inform the staff. This had to be done immediately, in order that the cook might hurry with the preparations for the dinner.

For on these wedding days the kitchen clock was put forward. I have even known the grandfather clock in the hall to have its hands shifted a little, so that my parents should not realize exactly how much too early the gong sounded for the midday meal. I wasn't supposed to know about it, but one day I saw Minnie closing the glass upon the face of the clock and noticed that the morning was decidedly later than I had thought. I was amazed at her daring to do this, as our father never allowed anyone but himself to touch it. He alone might wind it every Saturday, and a special cloth was placed that day on the study table, so that he could dust the clock. It was his dearest possession, an heirloom from Jacobite ancestors. He boasted that Bonnie Prince Charlie had once been hidden inside it, though how anyone could have been squeezed into that space always puzzled me.

Mother had very little patience with this reverence.

"History is something to be created rather than remembered," she told Father. "If only you had done something in your life that would have made the world proud of hiding *you* in some grandfather clock, instead of swelling with pride because Bonnie Prince Charlie, so long ago, happened to be hidden in this worm-eaten old clock your Campbell ancestors owned, it would have enriched the world."

My mother was always mischievous on Sundays and on the cook's day out. She watched for any excessive punctuality of the midday dinner, and delayed her appearance at the table. But she did not seem to notice the tricks played on these wedding days. And we, more loyal to the domestic staff than to the grownups, never told.

Immediately after the dining room table had been cleared, the servants crept up to the nursery, and grouped themselves around the window. Within their breasts stirred romantic longings.

The Abbey Road Synagogue was supported by the rich Jewish community of South Hampstead. South Hampstead was merely an extension of St. John's Wood, but spiritually it was as remote as if it had been Timbuctoo. We were brought up to hold it in contempt, for its values in life were considered false by the creative inhabitants of our part of London. The people who lived there were supposed to think too much about money.

But this was no disadvantage when it came to watching their weddings. Everything was excitingly luxurious.

Along the road came the carriages, with white ribbon bows upon the whips. The horses' tails were decked with white. Any carriage might contain the bride. We held our breath. We were watching romance.

And then she came in a carriage and pair. The horses were white. Long white streamers floated from the coachman's whip.

The bride looked exactly like the bride in a fairy tale. She also looked like the descriptions of the brides in my mother's serials. There seemed little I did not know of brides and bridegrooms, for I was always hearing about them as I washed the leaves of the aspidistra.

Parlormaid and cook, housemaid and nurse, they leaned forward to the window in their excitement, till Evelyn and I were nearly crushed against the wall. But we kept silent. Chivalry demanded that we did not complain. At this very moment our mother might be in her bedroom opposite the nursery, planning the love story of her heroine.

From these virgins now came hushed "Coos" and "Oohs." Our nurse told them to be quiet and stop their nonsense. She reminded them that she had managed to go through her long life without a man, and that it was all a matter if whether you loved the dear Lord enough to live as He would have wanted you to.

"This marriage and sex," she whispered, thinking we couldn't hear her, "it's all just what you make of it, m'say. And there's not much as I don't know of it, single though I am. I tell you, I've seen so many women carrying unwanted babies that it's very near enough to turn me from men."

The satin-clad bride had disappeared into the synagogue. We must wait until the marriage ceremony was over. And now Nanny had something important to tell the servants. During the spring cleaning of my mother's bedroom some of her books had been placed in the nursery for safety. Among these was a set of affectionately inscribed health books written by her Scottish adorer, for in addition to being a retired Naval surgeon, Alexander contributed popular health and beauty notes to the daily papers. These had been collected and published, and the Leighton family used the general volume on sickness whenever anything went wrong with us.

But it was *The Wife's Book of Health and Happiness* that concerned our Nanny now. Out from the third drawer of the mahogany chest that covered almost the entire width of one of the nursery walls, she extracted this volume.

"I think it'd be a most useful thing if you two was to read it," she whispered to the brides-to-be, Minnie and Emily. "I keeps it 'idden always from that there Miss Clare, for it'd never do for 'er to poke 'er nose into it."

She did not know that I had already discovered it, beneath several layers of flannel petticoats and vests, and knew all the symptoms of pregnancy and parturition, as well as the necessary facts about the nursing of a baby and the care of the breasts. At the age of nine I could have put these women servants wise about their forthcoming morning sicknesses and quickenings, and told them the signs by which they could be certain that they had conceived.

Weddings were not the only things we watched. Lovemaking could be seen from the nursery window.

True St. John's Wood inhabitants had a scorn for blocks of flats. It was worse than a scorn. It was a frightened revolt, for we knew that these edifices of communal living endangered the character of the neighborhood. We were a close society, and would have fought the rest of the world for our right to individual seclusion. The high garden walls were no mere idiosyncrasy. They were the symbols of our philosophy. And so we condemned all flats, and, though they were beginning to appear in our most cherished roads, we refused to acknowledge their existence.

"The chief thing I object to about flats is that they are immoral," Mother said. "Immoral, I insist, and not romantic. And they are immoral because everything you do can be seen and known by your neighbors. I always say that the distinction between immorality and romance lies entirely in this: nothing is immoral which is secret, and consequently hurts no one else. I remember how Papa would say with a little laugh that the most important of the Commandments was the eleventh one: 'Thou shalt not be found out.' But he meant this quite seriously. And there was a great deal of truth in it. And so, you see, with the public staircase or lift, where your lover can be observed by everybody, it would be quite impossible in a block of flats to have any true romance."

Obliquely opposite us, at the other end of the road from the synagogue, was one of the few blocks of flats that had been erected those days in St. John's Wood. Our family had the utmost contempt for the building, and decided that only the most commonplace people would dwell in such a barracks.

"No writer or painter or poet or singer could live there," our mother said. "They'd be stifled to death in their souls."

To our amazement we discovered that Dame Clara Butt, the famous singer, actually lived in one of the flats. But even this did not make my mother change her views. She turned, instead, against Clara Butt.

"After all," she said, "you can't expect anything better from anyone who sings in such dull, heavy, tedious and unromantic things as oratorios."

But despite my mother's opinions, I was about to discover romance existing in a block of flats. If you peered out of the nursery window, well towards the right, you could just see the windows of these flats. When the lights came on at night, you could even see into the rooms. On a level with the nursery window was a room with no blinds or curtains. I never knew why this was, but I took it as a gift to me from the gods, for I should not, else, have learnt all I did at that tender age of the art of making love. What I saw was not described by my mother in the stories she dictated. Her heroes and heroines went no further than a passionate kiss. I never heard her say that they took off their clothes.

I have no idea if the lovers in the room across the road were lawful man and wife, or whether I was watching what Mother would have called "true romance." In either case, I believe it must have been very passionate, though I don't think I understood a quarter of what was happening. Standing between the lowered blind and the window pane, to watch it, I did not hear Nurse call to me that it was time to go to bed. But even the spankings she then gave me seemed worth while.

One night the room was in darkness. I was desolate, for I had identified myself so completely with these lovers that it was as if my own love life had been cut off. I did not see them again. But the block of flats was surrounded for me by a halo of romance. After that I never quite understood why my mother objected so violently to flats.

It was not nearly as exciting to look from the nursery window for my mother's admirers to arrive. Compared with the lovemaking I had watched, this seemed strangely dilute. But sometimes there were embarrassing happenings, for we would see when the visits of these admirers overlapped. One was never sure when this might take place, as, though Mr. Bowles was regular in his arrival as night and day, yet sometimes Judge Talbot or Alexander would suddenly decide that they could not stay away from our mother any longer, and arrive unexpectedly upon the scene. This was before the days of the telephone, and unless they sent a telegram there was no way in which they could inform her of their urgent need to see her.

Then, too, there were occasional "also-rans," as Roland chose to call them, knowing that our mother was not greatly interested in these gentlemen. The front door bell would ring, as the various unwelcome admirers arrived and walked up the garden path. We knew them all.

There was a certain astonishingly handsome retired colonel.

"But his looks are very little use to him," I overheard my mother say to my father, "for he's the biggest fool I've ever met. In fact, I'd give a great deal to stop him coming, for he bores me so intensely. But he seems to feel he belongs to the family, just because he had known Papa since their childhood, and because they were at Sandhurst together."

And so he paid us endless visits. Patting Mother's arms just a little higher up each time, he would repeat:

"Gad, how proud your poor papa would have been of you if he could have seen you now."

Then, while he stroked her arms and fingered them too warmly, and looked at her much too tenderly, he would talk by the hour of his early days with her father in Jamaica. He and Grandpapa had been boys there together, for Grandpapa's father had once been Governor of the island. But, my mother complained, the way he made everything he touched on seem utterly commonplace amounted almost to a form of genius.

"Now if *I* had lived in Jamaica I'd have something really worth while to tell about it," she said. "Upon my word, if the Colonel were describing the entrance to Heaven he'd turn it into the vestibule of a local branch of the Y.M.C.A. I wish, Robert, you'd learn how to help me to get rid of him."

But all my father dared to do was to glare at the monocled dandy.

And the old colonel was so busy fondling my mother's arms that he never seemed to notice.

Then there was an eminent editor who developed an infatuation for my mother. He lived a few streets away, and discovered suddenly that we were on his direct route home from the Marlborough Road Underground station. He looked, as we decided, rather like a monkey, and when, on Sunday afternoons, as a means of assuaging in his wife's breast any suspicion of his true feelings, he insisted that he and she should take us two younger children to the Zoo, we always felt that chivalry demanded we should steer him as far away from the monkeys as possible, so that he might not be made to realize how much he resembled them. Roland was very mischievous, and would tell him our mother was out when she wasn't, and enjoy watching the poor man's impatience as he waited his beloved's return. And then, as they talked in the drawing room—for we children had excellent manners, and always felt that we should entertain a guest properly—Roland would do everything he could do to arouse his jealousy, till, he reported, the poor wretch actually got so beyond himself that, not knowing what he was saying, he asked my brother: "Do you keep chickens here in the back drawing room?"

But the most difficult times were on my mother's birthdays. All the people who loved her wished to appear, bringing their offerings. My mother was never any good at coping with large numbers. She preferred an audience of one, in order that she might direct the full force of her magnetism straight upon that person.

"If several people are with me at the same time," she once said, "I feel exactly like a chameleon on a tartan. Not that I take the trouble to try to change myself, in order to fit in with other people; this I don't hold with doing. Perhaps it might be truer to say I feel like a lighthouse that is trying to throw its beam upon everybody at the same moment. It is most exhausting."

From the nursery window we saw the birthday visitors arrive. Grandmamma and her sister Pollie came first; they were always early, so that they might watch everything that went on. Herself a beauty in her day, Grandmamma kept a jealous eye on her daughter Pattie. She even dared to voice an opinion on the various admirers. But lest she might appear to have passed the age of being attractive to the opposite sex, she had her own faithful adorer.

He was a pompous, elderly man, and his name was Charles, and he belonged to some of the most distinguished London clubs. My family never discovered how he managed to pay the club dues, for Charles was an impecunious aristocrat, who preferred to live in one tiny room in Half-Moon Street rather than in a bigger place with a less fashionable address. He might come to South Hampstead to visit my grandmamma by the plebeian Blue Atlas omnibus, but he would wear lilac suede gloves, and a top hat, and an expensive flower in his buttonhole, and always he brought her gardenias and bunches of hothouse grapes. He was inordinately fond of good food, and on her part she saw to it that he was well fed when he visited her.

"Another piece of this good bird, Charles?" I can hear her saying, as she dangled a slither of pheasant in front of his plate with the same sirenlike smile that she had bequeathed to my mother. But they never got married. Perhaps Grandmamma considered it more romantic to keep him hanging about.

Charles must have resembled my mother's father, Captain Connor. Both these men were impecunious aristocrats, and both of them knew how to keep up appearances on practically no money at all. They ran up enormous debts, and washed the dishes at home, but they never let the outside world see them economize, and though Grandpapa had also taken the Blue Atlas from outside the Eyre Arms public house in St. John's Wood, when he had been going into the "West-end," yet he would leave this omnibus about two blocks before he reached his club and, hailing a hansom, arrive before the doors in grand style, where he could have been observed tipping the cabby.

"A gentleman," he is supposed to have said, "is known by the way he tips." And he had lived up to this himself.

But Grandmamma's Charles was not brought to the birthday teas. My mother, in fact, was hardly ever allowed to meet him. He was known chiefly by hearsay. Grandmamma may have been afraid lest he should forsake her for her daughter, or she may merely have wanted to keep an air of mysterious glamour around her own life. Anyway, he always came into her conversation, and, when we went to see her and our great-aunt Pollie, who lived with her, we generally found him at the house. We felt we had to treat him with distant awe, though we knew, too, that we were expected to tell our mother that we had seen him.

Grandmamma was a Trelawny. She had a dark, Celtic beauty which, though striking, was yet less unusual than her daughter's, with the straw-colored hair that my mother tossed around so wildly, like a lion's mane. We often thought our grandmamma wore a wig; her richly coiled curls never varied. But we could not find out for certain.

There was something exuberant and almost blowsy about her.

"If Mamma hadn't unfortunately happened to be born a gentlewoman," my mother once remarked, "she would have made a most excellent and successful lodginghouse proprietress, or even, better still . . ."

But at this point Mother looked round and saw me in the room. Giving an embarrassed little chuckle, she stopped short. I wanted to know what it was that Grandmamma would have been so good at; but I dared not ask. Instead, I listened while my mother went on saying that Grandmamma had a way with her where men were concerned, and seemed to understand them as few women had been known to do.

I never knew whether she had the same power to attract men as her daughter, though there were whispered tales of an earl she had bewitched, and some of her most expensive jewelry was supposed to have been given her by the man who made a popular brand of beer. But she was getting along in years, and had to maintain a certain dignity. Her romances had taken on the purifying patina of the past.

There was no doubt about it, though, that Charles was faithful over a long time, to the very end, and wept openly and unabashed at her funeral.

She was a fearless creature. Neither God nor the devil floored her, she said, and on her deathbed she grew really irate when the family asked if she would not like to be visited by a priest, to make her repentance.

"Have you no better idea of the sort of person I am?" she asked. "Do you know me as little as all that? If you think I'm so mean as to want to cash in at the last moment, I'm sorry for you. I've done without a priest all my life, and I have a greater sense of pride than to haul down my flag and ask for one now. If God's the kind of Person I suppose Him to be, He'd consider me a pretty poor object to cringe at this late hour of the day. No. I'll die alone, thank you."

Aunt Pollie was the one member of the family who never seemed to have had any romance. This was strange, my grandpapa is said to have remarked, because she had fascinatingly high breasts which somehow she had wasted, for they ought to have brought her a good husband. She was short and podgy, but that could not have told against her. Grandpapa seems also to have said this was even desirable, and that no man would ever lose his head over a rabbit-bottomed woman.

For that matter, most of the women those days were well covered. Considering the amount of food they ate, they could hardly have been otherwise. Grandmamma's house smelt at breakfast time of deviled kidneys and mutton chops, and never a morning passed but what some substantial nourishment was taken at eleven o'clock, washed down with a glass of port. Both she and her sister Aunt Pollie were impassioned and superb cooks, and their enormous larder was filled always to overflowing. When we visited them we used to gaze in awe at the chickens and pheasants, the huge sirloins of beef and the fruit pies on the larder shelves. But only very rarely were we invited to stay for a meal, which was a bitter disappointment to us. Instead, we sneaked into the larder when no one was looking and stole little bits off the cold chicken or the sirloin, or dipped our fingers into the fruit pies.

This passion for food even turned Grandmamma into a petty thief. Despite the luxury of most of what she ate, there was one thing in this world she liked better than anything else. It was a really new-laid egg. Her craving amounted almost to a mania, so that had she been living today well-meaning friends would probably have hinted at traumatic unbalance and suggested that she consult a psychiatrist. Many a time she risked her reputation over it, for never could she bear to hear the cackle of a hen without searching for the egg that had been laid. As a very small child I had been for walks with her in the country and, in passing a farm, we had heard this cackle.

"Listen, Baba," said Grandmamma as she dropped hold of my hand. "You stay here a minute like a good little girl and I'll be back again."

She looked around her and then, lifting her skirts and placing a protecting hand over her hat, she crept with difficulty under a gap in a hedge to reach the farmyard. After a few terrified moments in which I stood alone, a tiny speck of humanity in the country lane, I saw first a hat, then shoulders, and finally the whole of Grandmamma reappear through this gap under the hedge, bearing proudly in one hand a warm brown egg. She was always happiest when she knew that the egg was still warm from the hen as it was placed in the saucepan, and on these occasions we hurried home at a pace that was unkind to my young legs, even as the whole episode was a strain on my nervous system. I dreaded lest she should be found out, for had we not been told that we must not steal? Probably the farmer knew all about it, and merely smiled at the eccentricity, for there must have been something amusing and ludicrous in the picture of this dignified matron on all fours, pilfering an egg.

But Auntie Pollie would never have dared to steal. She was a timid creature. She was also supposed to be a weak character, and our mother used her as an example to us of what not to be. Out of her own excessive force, our mother had a deep contempt for anyone who was weak, and, though her aunt had more or less sacrificed her entire life for her when she was a girl, yet she held her in scorn. Any tale that could be told at Auntie Pollie's expense would surely be remembered and repeated. I recollect a legend of what happened to her one day because she ignored my mother's advice, and took a "growler." There was some strange social distinction between a hansom cab and a fourwheeler, or "growler," as it was called. Members of the family were never supposed to demean themselves by entering a fourwheeler.

"For one thing," said my mother, "you run the risk of catching scarlet fever. You will always notice that the lower classes, if they need to go to a hospital, invariably take a growler. There's no law to stop them from entering a hansom, but in the same way that you never see a common person in Bond Street—though there is no barricade to prevent them walking there—so you will never find the lower classes in a hansom cab. A hansom is surrounded by an aura of romance which would frighten a common person, and make him think he was being wicked."

But poor weak Auntie Pollie forgot herself one day and, in a hurry to get somewhere, hailed a fourwheeler. She had only been in the conveyance a little while when the bottom began to fall out. Try as she might, she could not make the driver hear when she rapped at the front window of the cab. And then the ridiculous thing happened. The floor of the fourwheeler parted from the vehicle, and all Auntie Pollie could do was to patter along the road within the shell of the growler, her dainty feet, of which she was so proud, visible beneath the cab, until she reached her destination. The story has a Baron Munchausen flavor to it, but my mother assured us it was gospel truth, and from the moment we were told the tale we could never clear this picture from our mind, and something of the respect that we should have shown our aunt was lacking.

The two things that interested us most in Auntie Pollie were her grey parrot and her banjo. She was devoted to the parrot, and the creature fitted in with her character, for always it seemed as though she were connected with birds. Practically every hat she wore had stiff birds' wings in it, and her brown sealskin coat was trimmed with grebe feathers. And had not Grandpapa said that her high breasts made her look like a little pouter pigeon?

We had heard once that talking parrots swore great oaths, and we would stand by the cage on its table in the back part of the kitchen for the longest time, hoping to learn some swear words with which to shock our nurse.

But Auntie Pollie's parrot, in addition to being this dull grey rather than an exotic yellow and green we would have preferred, was disappointingly well behaved, and the most daring thing it ever did was to call our dead Grandpapa's pet name, "Non," in Grandmamma's voice. Apparently this wasn't as harmless as we supposed, for there was a continual battle going on between Auntie Pollie and her sister's admirer, Charles.

"Pollie," we would hear Charles say in a petulant voice, "you know perfectly well you're up to your tricks again. It isn't pure chance that makes that parrot call out Captain Connor's name. Every time I begin to feel your sister is about to succumb to my charms that damn bird calls 'Non' and reminds her of her dead husband. One of these days I shall slip some poison into the cage. If you think I'm going to let a mere parrot ruin my chance of a home for my old age, you're mistaken."

But Auntie Pollie had her own views on the matter, and I rather think that from then on she encouraged the parrot even more coaxingly to call "Non." At least, I frequently saw her in front of the cage, scratching the parrot's poll as she called the name softly for the bird to imitate.

The banjo, which was the other thing we associated with Auntie Pollie, was kept in a green baize case, in a corner of the morning room, behind the sewing machine. Every time we visited Auntie Pollie we pestered her into playing it for us. She was supposed to have a good voice, and, as she picked the banjo, she sang coon songs. We sat in front of her, fascinated, while she ran through her limited repertory, which began, always, with "My Uncle Ben and Old Aunt Sal." We begged her to bring the banjo with her when she came to Vallombrosa. But our mother would not allow this.

"I don't want you children to get accustomed to it," she said. "A banjo is the most unromantic of all musical instruments. In itself it has been enough to condemn poor Pollie to the life of an old maid."

But I think there must have been more to our aunt's spinsterhood than this banjo. I rather imagine that in her youth our forceful, handsome grandmamma must have monopolized all the men who came to their home. The Trelawny blood in Grandmamma would have balked at nothing. Auntie Pollie was destined to live her whole life in attendance upon her dynamic elder sister.

Unfortunately Auntie Pollie detested Mr. Bowles.

"It's a pure case of jealousy," our mother said. "Pollie is madly in love with him herself—if she'd only be honest enough to admit it. But instead of being frank she goes and invents all sorts of nasty things about him. I wouldn't be surprised any day to hear her say he is trying to kiss her and make love to her. Women are like that, you know. No woman who *really* has men making love to her ever says anything about it. It's always the women who've never in their lives been kissed who complain that men in railway carriages and men who sit next to them at the dinner table are pressing against their knees, or pinching them."

Mr. Bowles insisted on coming to the birthday teas. Knowing

how complicated the situation was growing, we watched for him in a state of apprehension. But we had also other reasons.

He always brought a huge bouquet on these occasions. We had already given our mother our own presents of flowers, and they had cost us pocket money accumulated over many weeks, so that it is not surprising that we felt annoyed when we saw him arrive with his armful of expensive flowers.

Our mother's birthday came at the beginning of February, and custom demanded that, whatever else we might have for her, each of us should give her a potted plant. And so one child would present her with white hyacinths, bound round with crinkly green paper and ribbon, and another would have a pot of daffodils, or tulips, while Roland, who had always more pocket money than we did, would buy an azalea, elaborately decorated with pink and silver paper. These potted plants were smuggled into the house the day before, without our mother seeing, and they spent the night in the back nursery, hidden under the beds, or behind chairs.

Evelyn and I were allowed downstairs for tea only on family birthdays. Our mother's was the earliest anniversary of the year. On this day we had tea for the first time without artificial light. It added a symbolical meaning to the occasion, as though it ushered in the rebirth of spring. Ritual was observed, down to the smallest detail. We must have a walnut cake with white icing, and "jumbles," or brandy snaps, from the local confectioner. These, with our potted plants and a penny bunch of the year's first snowdrops, a new ribbon for our mother's hair, and a present to her from our father of a salmon-pink silk and lace morning jacket, were the elements of the birthday. We would have liked to draw a circle round the family, excluding everyone else. So, as we waited in the nursery for the tea hour, dressed in our party clothes, we resented the ring of the bell that announced the arrival first of Mr. Bowles, then of Judge Talbot and finally of Alexander in his kilts. To us, on this day of our mother's birthday, these were intruders.

But neither was our mother really happy.

"It's a funny thing, Robert," we heard her say. "My birthday is supposed to be for *my* pleasure. Actually, I don't have much chance to enjoy it, because I'm always having to see that people aren't jealous of each other, and start quarreling. First George gets annoyed because I am smiling at Alexander. Then Pollie sulks because I appease George. And then, just as I think everyone is satisfied, and I can settle down to enjoy the Fuller's walnut cake I am so fond of, Louis Talbot makes a remark that shocks Mamma—or so she pretends. I made a great mistake in ever letting all these people know the date of my birthday. If I get any new friends I shall tell each one of them I was born on a different day."

But from our vantage point of the nursery window we saw much besides the friends and admirers who visited our mother. The tessellated pavement dried each morning in time for the punctual arrival of Walmy, who, whatever the weather might be, paused to wave to the two small heads at the window. At exactly half-past ten the butcher boy came for orders, returning an hour later, in his dark blue and white striped uniform, with meat for the family dinner. Just before this the grocer's young man appeared, and the cook would give him the list that had been compiled in the study by our mother and Walmy, while I had sat quietly at the table, drawing with the blue pencil. This grocer man always stayed a long time for, as I once heard the cook tell Nanny, he had "bedroom eyes" where she was concerned, and there was no getting rid of him.

And then, too, there was the greengrocer boy, the fishmonger's assistant, and the poulterer's boy. The gaslit world belowstairs must have throbbed those mornings with excitement and romance.

But there was something else we watched. It was the life beyond our high garden walls.

In the months of winter, when the linden trees of Vallombrosa were leafless, we saw the lamplighter pass along Abbey Road in the violet dusk. Through the closed window we could not hear his step, but we knew when he passed, for, as he lit the first lamp at the corner of the street, it shone into the nursery and illumined the picture of "Baby's First Outing," from the *Illustrated London News* Christmas Annual, that hung on the wall. The primrose gaslight from the street turned our coal fire to deep orange. Soon, now, Nanny would light the incandescent.

But certain sounds penetrated the closed window. At the clanging of a hand bell, in the late afternoon, we rushed to see the muffin man swing along the road, a tray of muffins, covered with green baize cloth, balanced on his head.

"Oh Mother, can't we have some for our tea?" we one day asked.

"Dear me, no," she replied. "They're indigestible, those soggy muffins and crumpets. They aren't for little children in the nursery."

At other times we heard the cart rumble by with logs for sale. As a raucous voice shouted his wares, we looked at the logs in distrust.

"Mother says they're simply swarming with cockroaches," I reminded my little brother. "It's a good thing we aren't anywhere near them."

Street singers and Punch and Judy shows, knife grinders and barrel organs: the life outside our garden walls was filled with events. All we had to do was to look from the nursery window.

But one year, when our father nearly died of pneumonia and we stayed in St. John's Wood until late summer, we found that we could not see half so much when the linden trees were in full leaf. In vain we stared through the thick foliage to see the man calling, "Strawberries all ripe. Ripe strawberries, a shilling a pannet"; and a lyrical voice singing, "Now is the time to buy my pretty lavender" was all we knew of the lavender hawker.

We had one real friend, though, who was as unfailing in his greeting as Walmy. At the corner of the road, outside the synagogue, sat old Charley, the one-legged crossing sweeper. We saw him touch his cap to each passer-by who handed him a coin, and from time to time when he was resting on his upturned wooden crate and nobody was near, he waved his stick wildly in the air towards our window. We would wave back, though I never knew if he could see us do so.

All this while that we were watching so much happening, our mother sat at work in the study. Her bell-like voice rang through the house, clearer than the hand bell of the muffin man or the Italian opera tunes that were played by the barrel organ. She was dictating the stories that paid for the meat and the vegetables, the fish, the butter and the eggs.

5. *The Annual Exodus*

Winter passed, with its fog and rain. Across the road, now, in the garden of the house opposite, the almond was in sudden bloom. The thrushes and blackbirds sang in the trees of St. John's Wood. Little rivers of gold ran down our garden path, on each side of the paved walk, as the crocuses opened to the sun.

Our mother was feeling sad at the coming of spring.

"It brings so many promises it never keeps," she sighed to our father as she looked out of the study window. "And it makes me feel ill and unhappy. I always need a little time in which to be physically fit to claim relationship with the spring. Besides, it's all nonsense to say the spring is meant for the young. It isn't. It's only bearable when you're really old. But then, it actually manages to make you feel old. That blackbird's song takes away all your contentment, and first thing you know you are wanting something without being able to find out what it is you want. Oh, dear me, how I wish it were still the autumn. That is the season for youth and work. The poets knew this. You remember the poem that begins: 'God in His heart made autumn for the young'?"

And she burst out weeping, even while she was quoting this verse. We grew shy, and turned away in confusion as we saw tears drop from her eyes onto the bundle she carried in her arms, till the ink of her outlines was blotted and smudged.

But we did not feel sad about the coming of spring. We knew that in a few more weeks the trunks would be hauled upstairs for the annual migration to Lowestoft.

Each spring the family moved to a house in East Anglia. This annual migration had an Old Testament flavor to it, as though we moved out of Ur of the Chaldees into Canaan. It ought never to have been negotiated in a modern conveyance like a railway train. There should have been camels as beasts of burden, and rivers and deserts to cross.

The first few years of my life we had rented a furnished house for two or three months each summer on the South Coast. It had been exciting to go to a different resort every season, and later on, when we went always to the same place, we often hankered after this change of scene, as over the years of our childhood we grew to know each bush and stone near Lowestoft. For the time came when the Leighton family decided it should have a permanent seaside home, and we bought a half-built house in East Anglia, on a cliff overlooking the North Sea.

"Of course," my mother said, "if we could have found a suitable house for sale that had been lived in and mellowed, it might have been better—though then we'd have had to spend quite a time getting rid of the mental atmosphere left behind by the people who'd lived there before. But as things are, the fact that The Red Croft was only half-built when we bought it ought to make everything pretty safe."

My mother had a deep superstition against building a house. Nothing on earth could have persuaded her to do so.

"But it isn't merely a whim of my own," she protested. "It's a superstition that goes right back to the days of the Bible. Don't you remember the proverb that comes somewhere: 'Fools build houses and wise men live in them'? They knew perfectly well that the surest way to achieve a premature death is to build a house for yourself. It is flagrantly tempting Providence. If you look around you'll see I am right when I say that no one ever lives to enjoy a house he has built."

The migration started a week or two before we actually took the journey by train, for there was so much to be packed. Countless linen chests and trunks appeared on the landings, and in odd corners of all the rooms. I never knew where these were kept over the rest of the year, because there were depths in that St. John's Wood house which we were not allowed to penetrate. Two staircases in Vallombrosa were forbidden to us: the pitch black stairs to the basement, and the equally dark stairway, shut off by a door, that led to the servants' bedrooms in the attic. Between these two floors lay our world; but the outer darknesses were the unknown. Sounds came to us from these regions. The ring of the alarm clock that wakened the servants before sunrise on winter mornings broke into our sleep in the night nursery. As we walked through the hall on our way out, we could hear Dolly stoking the kitchen range, and could imagine the glow of the great banked fire that cooked our dinner. But it never worried us to realize that the servants lived in perpetual gaslight and saw no sun. Only once in all my childhood did I visit our kitchen. That was when our mother and father were away and tremblingly I crept down the basement stairs, challenged by Roland, but terrified of rats and mice.

Though the trunks stood waiting, there was one unpleasant ritual to perform before the packing could take place. My mother's furs must be put away for the summer. Her ermine stole and muff, her sable stole and her skunk-trimmed velvet coat must be protected in pepper from the ravages of moths.

My mother had a great love for furs, and considered that she looked her best in the winter, when she was justified in wearing them. In fact, one of the main reasons for her dislike of the summer months was that she could not be seen in these furs.

"That," she said, "is essentially a sign of breeding. All the common people of the world, you will notice, look their best in flimsy, cheap, gay-colored little cottons and prints. They are the people who are happiest when they are shouting to each other across a tennis court. But the really worth-while women are those who feel most at home in rich furs. And they are in their element when they are quietly indoors. You will see, my child, if you keep your eyes open, that there is a strong line of demarcation between the people who can't seem to wait for the summer, and those who understand the quality of chrysanthemums, and an early dusk, and the magic of lamplight. And nearly always, as I say, it's a case of breeding."

Furs were not only a romantic delight to my mother. They were a symbol.

It was always an especial sorrow to her that she should think it unhealthy to wear a fur coat. I remember her weeping one day because a rich friend, knowing herself to be dying, had asked if she might present my mother with her chinchilla coat.

"I simply had to tell her No," sobbed my mother. "I treasure my health more than a chinchilla coat, and it wouldn't be worth it if I were to die of pneumonia. You notice that no opera singer ever wears a fur coat. She daren't risk catching pneumonia or bronchitis. And neither can I."

And now the romantic half of the year had ended. Her furs must be packed away. Tears fell upon sable and ermine. They were not only caused by pepper.

My mother had no faith in such moth preventatives as camphor. Nothing advertised on the market was to be trusted. She must use household pepper. This pepper arrived in great five pound paper bags, and my mother sprinkled it among her furs with the same lavish abandon with which she pasted her papers together with Stickphast or sealed her envelopes with scarlet wax.

"I dare not let anyone else do this," she said. "My aim is to keep my furs from the moths, and not merely to be able to say that they have been put away. Nobody but myself would think it worth while to rub the pepper thoroughly into the entire surface of the skins."

And so, over several days, my mother dictated her stories to Walmy while she peppered her furs. My mother sneezed. Walmy sneezed. My father bound his nose with a handkerchief as he wrote his stories, and yet he sneezed. Even the dogs seemed affected. But still my mother went on dictating, while she scattered the pepper around her as though it were a libation to some god.

These peppered furs were wrapped securely in old newspapers, and tied with an elaborate network of string. They were put for safety in the top part of the wardrobe in the night nursery, which was the only place in the house with a key. But the pepper seemed to ooze through the packages, and we always sneezed when we opened the wardrobe door.

This sneezing in the spring, though, was as nothing compared with early autumn, when my mother considered it safe to bring out her furs. Walmy was deputed to shake them free of pepper in the back garden, but in spite of this there was an epidemic of sneezing in the Leighton household for many days.

"Is it absolutely necessary, Chummie, to use quite so much pepper?" my red-eyed father dared timidly one day to ask.

But my mother was scornful.

"If Robert thinks I'm going to slave away all my life writing like this in order to get myself a completely new set of ermine and sable each winter, he's wrong," she declared. "Good furs are like family jewels. They come into the category of heirlooms, and are not to be tossed around as though they do not matter."

Once the furs were safely protected against moths, my mother was free to put her mind to the packing for the annual exodus. Not that she did much, for it was Walmy's business to attend to it. Downstairs in the study Walmy was busy amassing my mother's bundles. Into numberless trunks they went: rubbish and unpaid bills, newspapers and dress designs, old love letters and aired undergarments. Everything that lay about in that study was tossed into these trunks, and nothing was sorted. It is not surprising that our luggage was enormous. Even my father's easel and painting materials had to be strapped together and packed.

The only thing of importance we did not take was the gramophone.

"It makes me quite a little sad to leave it behind," my mother said, "for often, over the summer months at Lowestoft, I find myself needing the emotional stimulation of a love song. But it is unwise to risk breaking such a precious thing by taking it on a train."

And so she removed and hid the sound box of the gramophone, in order that the policeman and his wife, whom we always engaged as caretakers at Vallombrosa while we were away—supposing this to be the safest insurance against burglars—might not use it.

"If it were only the police sergeant himself," my mother added, "I would not even remove the soundbox. You can trust a London policeman with anything on this earth—besides, he is generally asleep all the day, when he might want to play the gramophone, and on his beat at night. But unfortunately he is married—though considering he's out always at night it is beyond my understanding what use he can make of marriage—and you can't really trust a woman even when she is a policeman's wife."

But though the entire household was topsy-turvy, my mother went on dictating her serials in the rapidly emptying study. Nothing might interfere with this, and Walmy would try somehow to get everything ready even while she still sat before the typewriter. Up to the very last moment the sound of my mother's voice could be heard, in passionate love scenes.

" 'Oh, my heart's darling, my own, my joy,' " our mother called across the table to Walmy as she gathered together some of her manuscripts. " 'Give me one chance to prove my love. Give me time to earn your kisses. Let me woo you and you shall know'—Miss Walmisley, did you remember to pack the outline of that next serial we have to do for the *Weekly Dispatch*? Where was I? Yes: 'and you shall know the happiness of living in the shelter of a good man's love.' "

The dictating continued even through the last midday meal, with the typewriter placed on the dust sheet that cloaked the dining room table, as my mother decided the destiny of a heroine between mouthfuls of mutton chop.

One year a terrible thing happened. The last meal was finished. The last cord was tied round the last trunk. The enameled hip bath, filled with nursery belongings, was ready to be placed on the roof of the omnibus. Dust sheets covered the beds, and blankets and towels were packed away. The entire Leighton tribe, with all the dogs, stood in the hall, ready for departure. We waited like this for over half an hour, and the dogs grew restless and began to whine.

"Dear me," worried our mother. "Whatever can have happened? All these years I've never known the Great Eastern Railway omnibus to be late like this. And stranger still, the carriage from Trinder's Livery Stable is late also. If they don't come soon now we shall miss our train."

The grandfather clock in the hall ticked loudly as we waited. It struck the hour. By this time everyone was agitated.

"I don't see the ghost of a chance now of catching the train," my mother complained. "What on earth can have happened?"

A sniffling sound came from the far end of the hall, where Walmy was hiding.

"Are you perfectly sure you ordered the conveyances for today, Miss Walmisley?" our mother asked. "You'd better look at the carbon copies of the letters you sent."

The sniffle became a sob as Walmy with difficulty undid the enormous corded chest that held my mother's papers. She searched through this confusion, with all eyes upon her. On to the floor of the hall tumbled the old bills and the unanswered letters, the torn newspapers and the dress designs. When finally she found the carbon copies, her sobbing grew louder.

In the agitation of packing she had ordered both the omnibus and the carriage for the following day. It was no wonder they had not arrived.

Walmy ran to the lavatory to finish her sobbing. My mother kept an angry silence.

It was a good-sized gathering when it assembled for the migration. First there were the heads of the tribe, my father and mother. My mother wore her best, biggest, newest hat in order that it might not get crushed in the packing. My father's coat was covered with dog hairs, because there were so many dogs to assemble. There seemed always to be a new litter of Skye terrier puppies. These were placed in a big hamper, and I remember that they had to come into the railway carriage with us instead of being put in the guard's van with most of the dogs, in order that we could feed them during the journey with Brand's Beef Essence on a half crown, slipped into the interstices of the wicker hamper. Evelyn and I were encouraged to do this, to occupy our minds, and so keep us from being sick.

Then, of course, there were we three children. Although Roland was only five years older than I, he always associated himself with our parents and referred to us two younger ones as "the children," ignoring the three years' difference between me and my little brother. We never resented this, because we loved him. Everything he chose to do must be right. On the occasion of the migration he went to Liverpool Street Station with our mother and father in the separate hired carriage.

Walmy, too, came to Lowestoft with us, and lived in the house over the summer months. This meant that she had to bring her own Skye terrier along, to swell the canine crowd. Our dogs disapproved of this stranger and always started a fight, which added a last minute complication.

And then came the "staff." The old nurse was tired and irritable, wondering at what exact point I would disgrace myself, as invariably I did, by being sick.

"It seems to me, m'say, there's no way as I can stop that there Miss Clare from vomiting," she grumbled. "Even if I lets 'er go without 'er dinner she'd manage it somehow just the same."

Her pockets were stuffed with two or three table napkins, as a precautionary measure.

The undernurse was strapping the last bundles, and the cook, the parlormaid and the housemaid, dressed in their best clothes, waited discreetly downstairs, in a dark corner of the hall, for the omnibus to arrive.

It was an enormous omnibus, as it needed to be, for there were always about eight dogs, as well as the humans. I find myself remembering every bit of that long drive. Past the walled gardens of St. John's Wood, into the grime of King's Cross, and the awful depression of City Road; this was a world we were shielded from. We were not accustomed to such ugliness. The horses that drew the omnibus trotted in a way that made the whole vehicle vibrate. Outside was a grey collection of sordid public houses and chimney pots, beneath a smoke-dimmed sky. Everything smelt of grime and airlessness, frightened dogs and sweaty horses. The ride took so long that it seemed as though we would never reach the station. Suddenly it was all too much for me. True to ritual, I rushed to the hastily opened back window and made my offering to the City of London, while the driver went his way, unaware of the pollution of his omnibus. Out from one of Nurse's pockets came a table napkin, but, as always, it was too late. I had to cross the frightening expanse of Liverpool Street Station with a disfigured coat.

My mother was not exposed to this shame. She and my father and Roland had already arrived at the station, in the carriage hired from Trinder's Livery Stable. They were joined there by a sad little Mr. Bowles and one or two equally sad lesser adorers. Bound together by a common grief, these men forgot their rivalry. We could see them a long way off, at the far end of the platform. My mother's hat looked strangely gay against the grime of Liverpool Street Station, as though an exotic bird had escaped and landed on her head, and the sweep of her fawn-colored shantung dust coat seemed out of place in this smoky setting. She wore this dust coat open, so that the grandeur of her clothes might not be hidden from sight. It was essential that she should be looking her best.

"Don't evér forget, my child," she said to me from time to time over the years, "don't ever forget that the last impression you give a man is important. Never let a man who loves you remember you as anything but your most seductive. If he has seen you for even one careless moment in curling pins, or with a smut on your nose, it is this that he will remember, rather than the times when you were all prepared for him."

And so, now, as she was leaving London for several months, it was especially necessary that Mr. Bowles and the lesser adorers should think of her as they had seen her last on the platform at Liverpool Street Station. She must remain in their memory as a vivid picture of beauty.

But my father had watched for the omnibus to arrive, and hastened to help us as we struggled with the frightened dogs. It was his job to steer all these dogs safely into the guard's van, while Walmy and the two nurses coped with us. As the moment for our departure grew nearer, we saw him taking the dogs, one after the other, for a last short walk up and down the platform, to do their "business," so that they might behave themselves in the van—for quite a few of them lived in the kennels in the back garden, and were not housebroken. Leaning from the window of our reserved compartment, we grew more and more frightened lest the train should start before our father had been able to get himself and the dogs safely inside.

When the train moved out from the smoky station, we saw a group of gloomy men walk slowly down the platform, their heads sunk low. As usual each summer, our mother had left behind her some broken hearts.

I do not know how sad she herself was feeling in the privacy of the separate reserved compartment where she sat with our father and Roland. Evelyn and I were far too much worried with our own terrors just then to be aware of anything. Wedged into corner seats with our backs to the engine, where we had been placed to prevent further train sickness, we did not even hear the ceaseless chatter of the servants.

"How far are we now from Colchester?" we kept on asking in a frightened voice. "Walmy, Walmy, how far?"

We had once been told that the particular part of the earth's surface near Colchester, through which we had to pass, was susceptible to earthquakes. We expected at any moment to be swallowed up in a great opening of the globe, and never felt at ease until we were well past that region.

As we slowed down in the station at Ipswich, a pile of brown wicker tea baskets awaited us. Three of these were delivered into the compartment where our father and mother and Roland sat in state. Four were handed in to us, and Walmy and the old nurse, Evelyn and I started in on our refreshment of strong tea and bread and butter and stale fruit cake. The three servants and the under-nurse, though, were not supposed to have baskets; they rated only separate cups of tea, poured from an enameled urn that was wheeled along the platform.

The journey seemed endless. It was only one hundred and eighteen miles from London to Lowestoft, but journeys in those days were weighty things. With the strange way in which memory retains insignificant details over the years, I remember that we took the three-eighteen train in the afternoon. Three-eighteen down, and two fifty-seven back to London in the autumn; train journeys will always be associated for me with the face of a clock marking one or other of these times. I shall see the enormous clock in Liverpool Street

Station, dim through the veil of fog and smoke, with the hands moving slowly towards the moment of departure. Three o'clock—for we were installed in the compartment a good half hour before the train left—and then the moment when the hands came together, at three-fifteen, and the exciting moment when the minute hand overtook the hour hand, and there were only one or two minutes still to wait.

But the hours passed. Suddenly we could smell the sea. This happened when we stopped at a little place called Beccles. A very old man hobbled alongside the train, shouting the name of the station, and ritual demanded that we should lean out of the window to sniff the air. I am certain the grownups in their separate compartment didn't do this; it would have been too underbred to show such exuberance.

But even though she was a lady by birth, Walmy was not so well brought up. She could not resist our excitement.

"Marvelous. Marvelous," she always said, drawing a deep breath. "Perfectly marvelous. All the ozone of the whole of the North Sea is in this air. Lo-ar, it's good for us. And after a winter in Bayswater, too." For Walmy lived in a stuffy semi-basement flat in Bayswater, all the time she wasn't with us in East Anglia.

It seemed as if new life had suddenly come to us. The servants began to straighten from their wilted exhaustion and even the puppies within the hamper squealed with unusual vigor.

Those were the days when people had a great belief in "sea air." Our family didn't go to Lowestoft to take a holiday. We never took holidays. We went there so that we children should benefit in our health, and in order that our mother and father might go on working with additional vitality. Nobody in our household ever stopped working. Precisely the same pattern of life was led at the seaside as in St. John's Wood, except for seasonal variations such as tea out of doors on fine days in the summer and slightly different hours of working because Walmy now lived in the house with us. But nobody ever dreamed of taking days off to laze or go gadding. Even Evelyn and I worked hard at our studies during the school holidays, in a desperate effort to improve ourselves.

My mother had profound contempt for people who took holidays. She dismissed them as "having something common in their make-up."

"The only real row I ever have with George," she said, "takes place once a year when I discover that he has sneaked off for a holiday. The poor little man is so timid that he is afraid to tell me; but as he is in the habit of writing me a letter practically each day of the week, it isn't easy for him to hide his movements."

And so my mother's face hardened as, suddenly, after a week without a letter, a picture postcard came from Mr. Bowles from "some lower middle class place like Switzerland."

"I have always been afraid that there was something just a little suburban and ill-bred about poor George," she would tell my father with a sneer.

And then, for a day or two, she showed a sudden tenderness towards Judge Talbot or Alexander; for neither of them was off on such a plebeian thing as a holiday. My brothers and I felt sorry for Mr. Bowles when next he came to visit us. We knew how coldly aloof our mother could be when she wished.

For several weeks before he took the rash step, Mr. Bowles would work up to it by saying that of course he wouldn't be able, this year, to afford a holiday. My mother would console him, and say that it didn't really matter, did it? He would then hint that his work was growing somewhat stale, because he needed some new setting for his next story. At this point my mother grew suspicious, and that evening she might be heard talking to my father about it.

"George will be off somewhere or other soon, on one of these travel bureau tours," she would say. "You see if I am not right. And if he does have to do it—and, of course, it's partly that common wife of his who forces him to, to save the housekeeping money while he's away—why can't he choose somewhere interesting and original? Why does he have to go off in such an organised manner? It'll be Switzerland again, I expect. That's such a safe place. His wife knows he won't possibly meet anyone dangerous there. You couldn't. It's filled with schoolteachers. Now look at me. I never take a holiday. And what's wrong with me? Why, nothing."

She showed the same contempt for my uncle. My father's brother was an artist. He was a very bad artist, but as he had married a woman with some money this didn't really matter, because, when she died and left him fairly well provided for, he could go around with all the outward and visible signs of bohemianism without the anguish of having to justify himself by producing any paintings. This uncle was dearly loved by art societies, as he had all the time of the world upon his hands and adored being needed and considered important. And so he was always organizing artists' trips to picturesque countries. Back to us, on the East Coast, came romantic postcards from Palermo, from Spain, from Florence or from Algiers. My mother tossed them over to my father, with contempt.

"There's Jack at it again," she said. "And can't you see him, with all those third-rate artists, thinking himself God Almighty. Little shabby spinsters, who've never in their lives been further than Hammersmith or West Kensington, supposing themselves suddenly the center of romance, and Jack doxing around with them as though he were a legitimate sort of Don Juan. And all the silly little water colors that will come out of it, to be placed on the walls of suburban villas, and to be shown to visitors with a 'and that was the year I was in Italy' sort of sigh. And even Jack himself will be thinking he's truly living at last. He'll be unbearable when he returns—perfectly unbearable. As if travel ever improved anybody. You've got to have it in you yourself, and if you have, you don't need to travel."

But Uncle Jack was wise enough not to come down and visit us for quite a long time after his return from one of these "lower class" trips.

And so this move to the seaside was merely a change of locale, in order that we might benefit by the strong air of Lowestoft. My mother had tremendous faith in this North Sea air. Nothing would take her to any "soft, backboneless place" like Devonshire. She needed the hard bracing quality of East Anglia, and never tired of telling us what happened when she went once to the Lake District.

"That air is no good," she would say. "It just lets you down. Of course those poets wrote. There wasn't any possibility of any vitality to make them do anything else. All your ambition leaves you, and you want to do nothing but live with someone you love in a little rose-covered cottage, on fifty pounds a year, and write sonnets. Now here, on the East Coast . . ."

And she would turn to Walmy and go on dictating the romantic adventures of her latest heroine.

The old judge was always at Lowestoft station to meet us. As the train slowed down, the lumbering figure could be seen vigorously waving a thick stick in the air, to greet my mother. His enormous voice boomed out:

"As I was saying—" But the noise of the porters drowned the rest of the sentence.

My mother and father and Roland, joined now by Judge Talbot, went their way in an open victoria. The rest of us were bundled into the pale yellow omnibus that had been ordered from the Crown Hotel. It was a tight squeeze, for this was a much smaller omnibus than the Great Eastern Railway one in London.

Somewhere, in the luggage van of that train, were the nursery hip bath, my father's easel and the trunks and chests of the Leighton family. But they would appear next morning, by special truck.

The air was filled with the sharp, tangy smell of fish, for Lowestoft was dedicated to the herring. There seemed to be magic in this air. As the yellow omnibus rumbled through the town, burdened with children and servants and dogs, it passed little streets leading to the fish market and the harbor. In the pale light cf a spring sunset the world seemed bewitched. It was the dry, clear light of the North. Here we saw none of the violet mist of St. John's Wood dusks, or the dirty sky of Bethnal Green. Everything was sharp-edged, and pure of color. Excitedly we pressed our noses to the windows of the omnibus as we watched each shop, each street, each loitering fisherman. At this moment we were completely happy.

The yellow omnibus left behind it the town of Lowestoft. It reached Gunton Cliff, and stopped at last in front of The Red Croft. The grownups' hired carriage had already arrived, and waited to take the old judge back to his home. But he was not yet ready. He had not seen his "Beloved Beauty" for many long months. As we and the servants, Walmy and the dogs swarmed into the house, his fat body blocked the way.

"The sun has come into my life again," he shouted, just as the undernurse was carrying a heavy case around his enormous bulk. He brandished his stick in the air and almost hit the poor girl in the face. But he did not notice this. He did not see that he was preventing us from entering the house. Neither did he hear our nurse grumbling.

"If that old man doesn't get out of my way," she muttered below her breath, as she tried to force herself past him, "if 'e doesn't let me get through with these children they'll be dropping to sleep all over 'im."

But the fat old judge was in such a delirium of joy that he saw and heard nothing except his own "Beloved Beauty."

"As I was saying . . ." his voice boomed loud above the barking dogs, the moving of luggage and the whimpers of tired children.

My mother stood in the front hall, in her best, biggest, newest hat, unable to get rid of him. Life in the Leighton family over the summer months of the year had started its traditional pattern.

6. Life at the Seaside

"I can't think what your father does with himself in the garden all this time," our mother often sighed, as she looked out of the window in the house at Lowestoft. "Personally, I find nothing to interest me in a garden. And it would be much better for the family income if Robert didn't waste all these valuable hours out there with that ridiculous hoe. The only good thing to be said for this craze of his is that it does keep him out of mischief."

Actually my father worked in the garden as a background for thinking. Even as my mother evolved the destiny of her heroine while we stroked her neck with the feathery end of her quill pen, so my father developed the plots of his Wild West stories over the mowing of a lawn. The distant look in his eyes as he hoed made us realize that his mind was occupied with other things than flowers. Cowboys and broncos must have galloped across the grass; Indians surely lay in ambush behind the privet hedges.

But the purpose of his gardening did not make things any easier for his children, as he forced us to spend hours at a time in a crouched position, weeding the edges of the paths. We hated it, and feelings of rebellion rose within us when, each evening during the summer, unless it should happen to rain, he made Evelyn and me drag the hose round to the front garden, to water rows upon rows of geraniums and marguerites.

But our father had, also, a real passion for this garden on the East Coast. Fortunately for us, the passion did not extend to the St. John's Wood garden, which was fenced in at the back exclusively for the dogs, but allowed to run wild even in the front. Though we would have hated working in it ourselves, we used to feel ashamed as we compared our wilderness with the lovingly tended gardens of other houses in the neighborhood. The grass of our lawns blossomed and seeded. Tall weeds flourished in the flowerless beds. It was lucky for us that the main charm of Vallombrosa lay in the thirty-six lilac bushes and the row of linden trees, which needed no care.

But on the occasion when we gave a garden party, suddenly the front garden was attended to. I can remember my distress at what I then saw happen.

My father was standing around one morning when we went for our walk, talking to a strange man wearing a sacking apron. When we came back for the midday dinner, there was a big cart outside the front gate, half filled with gorgeous plants—geraniums and marguerites, calceolarias and pelagonias at the height of their flowering. We opened the gate, and there, in the front garden, were three men. They were digging round holes all over the place, and at one end of the grass, near the holly tree, were dozens of potted plants like the ones still out in the cart, waiting to be placed in these holes. The garden looked lovely when all the holes were filled with these plants. But during the party I walked among them in shame.

"I always supposed I was a good judge of character," I overheard one dressed-up lady remark to another, "but I have to admit that for once I've been wrong. Knowing the Leightons as I do, I would never have believed they took such care of their garden. If I'd been asked, I'd have sworn they were the sort of people to let it run wild, while their minds were on their writing. But look at it. It's perfectly beautiful—and with all these flowers in full bloom at just the right moment for the occasion. I must congratulate them."

As I listened, I felt myself turning as red as the geraniums at my feet.

"Don't you see what's happened?" my sense of honesty made me want to cry out. But I was loyal to the family; and I walked away.

It was a dreary business, filling in those holes next day when the party was over; but I felt much more at home in that drab, flower-less place than I had done when it was falsely filled with strange plants in pots.

The garden on the East Coast had many uses. Not only, as my mother said, did it keep my father out of mischief, but it was an excellent place in which to take your daily exercise. Up and down the middle path my mother walked. Fuly dressed in her outdoor clothes, with an elaborate summer hat and a fringed sunshade, she strode the length of the path to the "crazy beds" at the end where the roses grew, near the fence which divided us from a neighbor who, my mother remarked, was "somewhat common" and so under-bred that he kept chickens and hung his washing on a line each Monday; and then, with the disciplined movements of a drill sergeant, she stopped, paused, turned around and marched straight back down the center of the path to the white painted trellis that, covered with climbing roses, separated the garden from the kitchen entrance. She looked neither to right nor to left, neither up nor down. She never saw the pansies that bordered the path, or noticed the rows of annuals that my father grew. This went on for exactly half an hour. It was the summer variant of the walks she took in St. John's Wood during the months of winter, when she would go round and round the block of houses, and round and round again. Nothing could force her beyond these prescribed limits.

"I think I'll just run upstairs and put on my hat and coat and go round the houses," my mother would call to my father. "I've got a bit stuck with this plot. I can't seem to know what to do next."

If he could possibly help it, my father never let her go alone. In a few moments my parents might be seen striding along Abbey Road with several dogs, looking neither to right nor to left. "Round the houses" was one of the first expressions I ever heard. It was one of the most frequently used.

Down at Lowestoft my mother did not even need to go beyond the garden gate.

"Why should I risk having my mind disturbed from my work by walking along the Front?" she always said. "Exercise is exercise, wherever you may take it. You can never tell what interruption to my thinking might not occur on the public road, where I would meet people. An entire day's mood could easily be destroyed if I were to get involved with outsiders."

One of the lawns my father so assiduously mowed was used for croquet. This was the battleground for more bad tempers than would have been thought possible in a well-brought-up family. I can see my father turning in rage to a middle-aged female visitor with whom he was playing. She had sent his ball right to the end of the lawn, and, not knowing his character, had indulged in a superior little smile. This was more than Father could stand, and with a fury that seemed admirably suited to the red-haired, long-moustached Viking chieftain that he looked, he shouted to her: "If you were a man I'd kill you." My mother's adorers delighted in beating poor Father; even the fat old judge would try his hand with a mallet, as he leaned for support on one of us, who had been brought down from the nursery for that purpose. But Evelyn and I were never allowed to play croquet with our parents. It would have been bad for the family morale if we had beaten our mother in a game. Walmy, though, did not in the least mind if we won, and even people like Mr. Bowles would condescend to play a game or two "with the children." Generally we looked on. It was the most exasperatingly slow game to watch, but it was the only form of sport our mother believed in.

"Tennis makes people look hard-faced and strained," she said, as she put on her gloves before being handed a croquet mallet. "And you have only to watch a woman swinging a golf club to know straight away she has no romance in her life. But croquet takes none of the femininity from a woman. She has enough time during the game to think about other things. In this way she does not lose her men."

My mother moved over that croquet lawn with dignity. Her skirts swept the ground as she walked, and whichever adorer happened just then to be playing with her had difficulty in keeping his attention on the game. This was not made any easier by her habit of reciting passionate love poems to her opponents. The games of croquet were played to the accompaniment of Swinburne or Henley, or fragments from the *Indian Love Lyrics*. My mother won most of her games.

The grownups played their croquet in the afternoons. We were allowed to play only when we were not interfering with our parents. And this did not simply mean when they were playing croquet themselves. It also meant that we must keep away from the garden whenever my mother was sitting out there working. Though she never for one moment exposed herself to direct sunshine, she considered it healthy to sit outdoors and work in the open air.

"This is the reason for coming here in the summer," she said as she protected the entire surface of her person, lest a ray of sun should strike her. "Sun is bad for one, but sea air can work wonders."

A wooden cabin was built at the far end of the garden. It stood high above the ground, so that it might not be damp, and beneath it, sheltered from the sun, slept several dogs. Four steps led up to the door. Within this open door, at a little table, sat Walmy, amply provided with pens, ink and paper; for once my mother started work, the stream of words flowed without interruption over several hours. Below, on the path, facing the cabin door, sat my mother, dictating. She was fully dressed, with a Paris hat and a raised sunshade, and sometimes, when it was windy, a spotted veil. On her hands and arms she wore old elbow length white suede gloves that had seen much service in London when they were new. She always looked somehow as though she were taking the indoors to the garden with her.

She sat there on the garden path in the attitude of Britannia on a coin.

There was yet another time when we had to keep away from the garden. This was at tea during the summer months, on the days when the weather was warm and dry. Then the wicker tea table was set up at the very bottom of the garden, on the gravel path, at the point of intersection where the center path was crossed by the path leading to the tool shed on the one side and the cabin on the other. Exactly here it stood, with geometrical accuracy, and round the table were grouped my mother and my father, Roland and Walmy. Why this tea table was not placed a little nearer to the house, I cannot say, as it must have been unnecessarily irksome for the parlormaid to take tablecloth, cake stand and tea service all the way down the path to the bottom of the garden. It wasn't for the sake of privacy, for there was no privacy in this particular garden. Everybody could see everything that happened in it everywhere. That was one thing my mother had against it.

"It's what comes of buying a new house," she complained. "Now if only we'd been able to get an old one, nobody could have seen what we were doing. There would have been big trees in the garden, and high hedges. It's so underbred to live like this in the public eye."

With my mother's upbringing and need for seclusion, it must have been a trial to her. I remember that there was something almost indecently naked about the sight of the group sitting at tea in the middle of a big open space. For there were no trees whatsoever in this newly made garden, and no possibility of shade. When the sun shone strongly my mother raised her sunshade as she sat at the table. The Surrealist painters did not exist in those days, but if a photograph of this family garden tea were to be shown to anyone today, the first expression to come from his lips would surely be the word "Dali." For there was something oddly out of place about it all, down to the detail of Walmy reading a novel to my mother over the tea table, through an enormous magnifying glass. It looked almost as though the whole scene were taking place indoors, and the walls of the room had withdrawn, leaving the tea table standing derelict against a background of the cosmos.

There was probably a great deal of jealous envy in our feelings about this garden tea party. The sun beat in at the nursery windows, till the room became unbearably hot. If we could have had our own outdoor tea party, somewhere in another part of the garden, unseen by the grownups, we would have been happy; but this did not happen. And so the next best thing was to gaze down upon the distant scene, waiting with impatience for the moment when valiant Walmy, remembering the two children in the house, would slip away from the table with a glass dish, at the bottom of which lay a few remaining gooseberries or strawberries, raspberries or greengages.

For fruit in our family was a rarity and a luxury. It wasn't anything to squander upon a nursery. Occasionally over the year a pound of Newtown pippins would be bought for us, and at Christmas we had a big bag of pale, sour oranges from Spain. But generally it was supposed that the stewed fruit we ate at dinner with our milk puddings was enough for any child.

In the summer, though, the Leightons did indulge themselves in fruit for tea. It was the only time of the day my mother dared to eat raw fruit. She was always afraid it would upset her inside, and decided that the least unpleasant time to be inconvenienced would be between the tea hour and the following morning. But this fruit was untold agony to Walmy, who had a terror of wasps. So, too, had my mother, but she denied it, even while she threw her arms around, to beat the creatures off.

"It's utterly ill-bred not to be able to control yourself before a mere insect," she reproached her secretary. "Now look at Robert. There he is, sitting perfectly quiet and still, with a wasp actually crawling up his cheek. That's the way to treat them. They'll never sting you then."

And her own arms would be flung out like a windmill, tossing more and more wasps towards him.

But it was not only wasps that disturbed the garden teas. Sometimes, as the family sat listening to my father or Walmy reading from a recent novel, a thunderstorm crept up unnoticed by them. At the nursery window we saw it happening, and held our breath in fear. Would Mother reach the house in time? For she must not get her feet wet. If she were to be caught in the rain, even for one minute, she would most certainly come down with a cold exactly forty-eight hours later. I have so often watched her as she waited for the forty-eighth hour to arrive, confident of her doom. Generally she managed to achieve the expected cold.

Those days on the East Coast held their rituals. One of the most important was the visit of the "Corton Boy." Three times a week this market gardener from a neighboring village came with vegetables and fruit and flowers. My father never allowed his own flowers in the garden to be picked, and we had to rely upon the "Corton Boy" for house decoration. The cook brought the great basket of flowers into the front hall, where my mother was working. There was no study at The Red Croft; my mother's bundles lay all over her bedroom floor and strayed even into the dining room. She worked in any room that seemed at the moment most convenient. Without pausing in her dictating, she would lift the flowers out from the basket: daffodils and wallflowers, country bunches of mixed flowers, roses and sweet peas, and, later, asters and gladioli. Eight, nine, even a dozen bunches, in the extravagant abandon that was her nature it did not matter how many we bought, if they were beautiful. They lay on the window seats, and among her bundles, waiting for me to arrange them. For in true British tradition I, the daughter of the house, was allowed always to arrange the flowers. It was one of those things that a growing young lady was supposed to do.

But as the summer wore on, my mother took a different attitude towards these flowers. Spring and early summer do not abound with insect life as does the later part of the season. Dahlias came into bloom, and dahlias are proverbial for housing earwigs. If there was anything of which she was truly scared, it was that harmless, creeping insect called an earwig. I have known her to stay up most of a night because she had been unable to track one down that she had seen crawling under the bed. They reduced her to panic.

So, when the "Corton Boy's" flower basket arrived in the season of dahlias, it was never brought into the house. It had to be placed on the steps by the front door. From the safety of the hall, my mother pointed through the window to the particular bunches she wanted, and the cook would lift them from the basket. A bath towel was then produced—for you can see an earwig upon a white surface—and when each bunch had been separately shaken upon the doorstep, the dahlias were enveloped in this bath towel and conveyed to the downstairs lavatory. Here they were left for a while in the basin, to give a chance for any further earwigs to appear. After this, I cut open each bunch and shook and examined each separate flower, so that we might be perfectly certain no single insect nestled still within those fluted petals.

One day I must have done my job carelessly, for suddenly, at the dinner table, an earwig emerged from a large pink dahlia and crawled in the direction of my mother's soup plate. After that I always had to leave the arranged flowers in the vases for several hours in the downstairs lavatory, to make doubly sure there were no loiterers. I have often wondered why we ever bothered to buy these dahlias, considering the potential peril they harbored—not to mention the work they involved.

My mother made very little use of the fact that we were at the seaside.

"The only thing that interests me on the East Coast is the actual sea air," she always said, "and I can get that just as well in the back garden without the bother and waste of time of the long walk down to the beach. But I would like you children to be taken to the beach each morning when the weather is fine. So long as Nurse keeps you away from the part which teems with trippers and bathers, the stretches of sand and the loneliness are good for your souls. This will develop the best in you far more than sitting around in Bellevue Park, among the crowds."

But there were strict rules as to what we might do. Generally we were made to play quietly beside our nurse. The old woman brought her sewing with her, or her crochet work or her tatting, and, resting her back against a breakwater so that there might not be a draught, she spent the long summer mornings keeping watch over us.

If the weather were really hot, our mother issued an order that we could paddle; but this was not encouraged, for there was no telling what harm might not come to us if our heads were heated from the sun and our legs and feet cold from sea water. The uneven distribution of hot and cold was risky. Sea bathing was forbidden. There was an undertow of the tide on the East Coast, which might drag us out to sea. Obediently we built our sand castles, and made our mud pies, and never questioned why all the other children who bathed returned safely to shore.

Occasionally, though, sounds from the populated part of the beach drifted towards us in our select isolation. And then we would hanker after the seaside life of the ordinary child. Farther down the shore stood the line of donkeys, waiting, with the bright-colored fringes over their eyes to keep away the flies, for their little riders. We knew the smell of the hot bodies, and the way the donkeys slashed their tails against their flanks; but never had we been allowed to do more than pat them in passing. Next stood a row of miniature carriages drawn by nanny goats. Into the shouts and laughter of the bathers were mingled calls of men peddling their wares.

"Lowestoft rock, only threepence a stick," shouted one man as he trudged through the sand with his basket full of the sickly magenta confection.

"Fine William pears, all ripe, tuppence each," shouted another.

But sitting quietly beside our nurse as she sewed a flannel nightgown, we munched our midmorning allowance of two Garibaldi or Osborne biscuits. The men did not come as far along as our deserted part of the beach.

"I want you to grow up to have personality," our mother would tell us. "And that means you must do a considerable amount of quiet thinking, by yourselves. You were probably too small to remember it, but I would remind you that when the Duchess of Teck's children played with you on the beach at Bognor *they* weren't allowed to mix with the rag, tag and bobtail. They were intended, you see, for positions of importance in life. Never feel you are missing things if you do not laugh and shout with the crowds."

But in spite of this injunction our eyes often turned longingly towards the goat carriages and the donkeys.

Our mother considered there was healing power in sea water. For this reason, one summer when she had sprained an ankle we were made to bring pails full of sea water back to the house each day. It was difficult not to spill them as we crossed the long stretch of dunes, and climbed the steep slope to the Front. By the time we had reached home and emptied the pails into the basin standing ready in the corner of the hall, there was not much water left. But each evening our mother dangled her weak ankle in the pool of salt water, while she went on dictating her instalment to Walmy. This sea water was never thrown away until it had been renewed; for how was our mother to be sure that the following morning might not be rainy, and her children unable to fetch a fresh supply from the beach?

One summer Mrs. Bowles paid us a visit with her husband. This in itself was not of any great importance, for we disliked her, but it so happened that she was overheard remarking to Mr. Bowles that "Marie" was stouter than she used to be. Our mother was worried. If there was anything she feared, it was losing her figure. She began to diet, but this did not seem to make any difference.

"Robert," we heard her say one day, "I'm sick and tired of eating nothing but water biscuits in order to reduce. It doesn't seem to do any good at all. Now there's something I want to ask you. I've just been reading in a magazine that sea bathing has a slimming effect upon the body. I'm feeling inclined to try it. But first I'd like to know if that undertow of the tide is *really* dangerous?"

Our father managed to convince her that it was absolutely safe, and a carriage was ordered each morning to take her down to the beach. This made him very happy. He had always wanted to bathe. He loved the sea and everything connected with it. But he had never dared to go into the water by himself. He knew that his Chummie would have thought it a waste of his time, when he should be writing his boys' stories. Now, however, he sat beside our mother in the carriage, as it rolled along to the beach, with a look of joy upon his face.

Unfortunately, the bathing machines were a good way off from the select, isolated part of the beach where we sat. We could see them in the distance, being drawn by horses to the water's edge. Sometimes, when our nurse seemed especially occupied with her sewing, we had been known to stray nearer to these machines and watch the bathers bobbing up and down in the ocean. One of my wildest ambitions was to look inside a bathing machine. Perhaps, now that Mother had started to use one, this longing might be satisfied.

But I was not to be so fortunate.

Our parents did not intend to be seen by their children in dripping bathing costumes.

"If one is to retain authority one must be most careful not to be visible in any undignified attire," our mother declared. "Never shall I forget the sight of your grandmamma in hair curlers and a scarlet flannel petticoat, scolding the cook. I lost considerable respect for her—and so did the cook. And I never regained it. But I learnt a most valuable lesson."

On morning, however, Evelyn and I determined to watch our parents bathing. We ran away from Nanny and hid behind the breakwater nearest to the bathing beach.

The carriage arrived. Our mother walked cautiously up the inclined plank that led into the bathing machine, tenderly assisted by our father. She entered her half of the machine, and closed the door. Father then climbed the plank and went into his half. They were hidden from sight as they emerged in their bathing costumes at the other end of the machine, straight down into the water.

At this point we grew reckless. We emerged from our hiding place and crept along the sand until we reached a place where we could watch.

Our mother would have had no objection to being seen by the whole world while still she was dry. Her costume was a dressmaker's creation. Elaborate patterns of white silk braid wriggled over the navy blue serge. The undulating bands of white braid that edged her full skirt resembled the waves of the sea. Even her rubber sand shoes were faced with white, while on her head, though she had no intention of dipping it below the water, she wore a frilled navy and white cap, like a satin mushroom.

My father did not look nearly so attractive. Beneath a bathing costume of horizontal navy and white stripes his arms and legs were pale and lanky.

"Come in further, Chummie," we heard him call to our mother.

"It's quite safe if you keep hold of the rope. Only, don't let go while I have my little swim."

We watched his head of red hair far out at sea.

Our mother was terrified.

"Robert," she shouted. "You'll drown. You'll drown."

But Father could not hear.

It was when he had returned safely to our mother's side at the edge of the water that we were discovered.

"That's it, Chummie," he was saying. "Let the waves caress you. It'll do you so much good. It. . . . Look. There's Clare and Evelyn watching us."

Instinctively they both bobbed down low beneath the water, to be as little visible as possible.

"Go and send them away, Robert," our mother called in a loud voice. "But no; on second thought don't go. You're such a sight in that dripping costume that you'd have no authority whatsoever. You look like a figure in the comic papers."

The punishment was merely delayed.

Very soon after this my mother abandoned her sea bathing.

"It does you more harm than good," she said. "At the end of the morning you are completely exhausted with all the effort, as well as with the actual bathing itself. There's something thoroughly debilitating about it. Besides, it takes up far too much of my time. If I continue like this I won't be able to get enough work done even to pay the butcher's bill."

But the main thing was that it did not seem to have had the slimming effect she had anticipated.

My punishment took the form of having to sit beside the old nurse on the beach each morning for days on end, crocheting lace. This lace was to go round the legs of my flannel drawers. I can remember the pattern even now; it was a series of little triangles, made of rows of blobs. It was the dirtiest lace that ever existed, for I carried it around with me everywhere, knowing that the sooner I finished it the sooner would my punishment be over. Just at this time Nanny was herself making yards of elaborate crochet, six inches in depth, to go down and around a blue linen dress for my mother. I would look at it in awe, as it rippled like magic from the old woman's hands.

"If you make this lace of yours well enough," our nurse said, trying to comfort me as she looked down at the dirty grey crochet I clasped in my fist, "if you do it really finely and keep it clean, I'll let you crochet some lace to go round your mother's new flannel petticoats I'm just going to make."

We were a great family for flannel. It had to be real Welsh flannel, and none of the delicate, ladylike soft white stuff edged with a pale pink selvedge. The stuff of which all our underclothes were made was thick and coarse, and came from the shop in a shade of pale greenish blue with a dark blue selvedge. It had to be "shrunk" before it was made up, and I can see it now, soaking in the nursery bath, so that our vests and drawers might not be too tight after they had been sent to the laundry. This was not used only for us children. Our mother also wore it. She would have expected to die of pneumonia if she left off her flannel vest and flannel petticoat, even on the hottest days of August.

With all her ideas of beauty, she never considered it unromantic to wear these bulky flannel undergarments.

"What good would it do to go around with delicate, thin underclothes and sniffle and drip with a red nose and a chill in the insides?" she asked. "No man would look your way. And after all, the Queen wears thick flannel underclothes, and what's good enough for her is good enough for me."

But she did, at any rate, let herself go when it came to her drawers. I cannot imagine that the Queen of England would have favored the sort of drawers my mother wore. "Regularly indecent and improper, I calls them," said the old nurse, while she helped me cut out a pair I was making for my mother's birthday. But I did not share her views, and, bundled up in my own thick flannel knickers, I vowed to follow in my mother's footsteps the first moment I was beyond her control. I was overcome with the beauty of these rows of lace and insertion on the pair from Paris I was copying. Baby ribbon ran through the insertion and was bunched at the side in what Nanny, who had not understood what the word "chou" meant, insisted on calling "slippers." One day, yes, one day . . .

But when, one day in my late teens, my mother saw me making myself a quite moderately elaborate undergarment, she looked at me in a strange way as she said:

"When a young girl begins to interest herself in her underclothes I begin to interest myself in her morals."

I had no idea what she meant, but somehow the pleasure seemed to have been taken out of the garment I was making.

There was no glamour about the lace I crocheted in my childhood on the beach.

My eyes would stray from the crochet, to watch the ships go by. This was one of our chief delights, and we knew each vessel that passed along the North Sea, and all about it. For, loving the sea and everything connected with it, our father would explain to us where the ships came from. He spent a large part of his days with a telescope, looking out to sea from the top front room he used as a study. The stairway to that room was steep and twisty, and my mother didn't like going up there, which was fortunate, for she never discovered how little work he really did, and how much of his time was occupied with looking out to sea, or painting pictures of fishing smacks.

And so, as we sat on the beach, we watched warships and submarines, fishing smacks, steam trawlers, and shabby tramp steamers with coal from Wales. Sometimes, when we returned home, our father appeared in the nursery and whispered to us to hurry upstairs to his front room. There, on the horizon, would be a four-masted schooner, in full sail. We looked at her through his telescope.

She was even more beautiful than the yachts dotting the sea during the week of the annual Lowestoft Regatta, when our mother spent the afternoons at the Yacht Club with Judge Talbot, dressed in her grandest and most appropriate clothes. Once each summer a sailing ship from Seattle passed. She seemed to have more sails than any ship we had ever seen. In excitement one day I told my mother about this schooner. But my mother scarcely listened. I discovered then that the only ships she was interested in were yachts.

Mother considered herself an experienced sailor. Many years before I can remember, it seems that she and my father used to go off sailing with G. A. Henty, the boys' story writer.

"And this was a great compliment," she said with pride. "Henty always swore he would never take any landlubber to sea with him. He respected his yacht far too much to expose it to this ignominy."

One of her most prized possessions was a photograph of herself on this yacht, sitting beside Mr. Henty. She was dressed as though she were a member of a chorus in a musical comedy which had the setting of the sea, or a character even from *H.M.S. Pinafore*. Her sense of drama always made her dress the part, whatever she might be doing in life. And so, for this yachting expedition, double rows of brass buttons covered the front of her navy blue serge coat, which was trimmed with coils and twists and twirls of white braid. Her hat was swathed in a thick white veil that tied under her chin.

"If you know how to dress properly," she said, "you are aware of which colors are suited to which occasions. Navy blue and white, for instance, are very definitely the only possible colors to be worn either on or near the sea."

She was prepared for anything that was demanded of her, though how much of the actual labor of sailing the yacht was given over to her care I never knew. I rather suspect that my father and the crew did most of the work while she spent a great deal of the time sitting talking with G. A. Henty; for he was very fond of her.

But she ought to have known everything about sailing a ship, because her own father had been a champion sailor. In his spare moments—which were many, after he sold his commission and had nothing to do—Captain James Valentine Nenon Connor made model yachts. During her childhood my mother helped him sew the sails. After his death these yachts were kept for his grandchildren. They lay over the years in our father's top room, waiting for the time when we should be old enough to enjoy them. They were very perfect, beautiful things, but it was our father who eventually got most pleasure out of them. Sad to say, they bored us, and though our mother tried to interest us in them, she had little success. Except for the afternoons when our father dragged us out with them to the Lowestoft Model Yacht Pond, they lay there on the floor, gathering dust, next to Grandpapa's bows and arrows.

These bows and arrows excited us far more. In addition to being a yachtsman, Grandpapa had been a crack archer. During his years of idleness he had, too, made all these bows and arrows. My mother wanted us to be good archers.

"There are certain sports that only well-bred people indulge in," she said. "One of them is fencing, and another most emphatically is archery. You only have to look at the faces and bearing of the members of the Royal Toxophilite Society in Regent's Park, to see that I am right. Any ordinary person can play tennis, or even golf, or billiards; but no easily acquired fortunes will win you entry into the close society of archery."

And so Roland took lessons in fencing, and even we two younger ones were allowed and encouraged to play in the back garden with Grandpapa's oversize bows and arrows.

"It's nearly as good for showing off a woman's figure as playing the harp," my mother remarked, as I struggled with a bow that was far too large for me. "It develops all those curves to the body that men love. Never, my child, be so stupid as to play any game that makes you look like a man."

My mother did not take to archery herself.

"I don't have time for such things," she said. "It's as much as I can do to get my work done and to keep myself neat and clean and see that the household runs smoothly."

Occasionally, though, she did indulge in the wild expenditure of time of hiring a conveyance to take a drive into the country. This was not done out of any love for the countryside; she admitted without shame that the countryside bored her. It was generally used as a means of entertaining some house guest of the female sex.

"You never need to bother yourself to entertain men," my mother said, as she put on her driving clothes. "Men are happy in just talking to you, wherever you may happen to be. They wouldn't mind if they spent all their time with you in a station waiting room, or even in the housemaid's pantry. . . . But women always want to get the utmost benefit out of the expensive railway journey they have taken. And they seem to think they'll get more air when they are moving along in a conveyance than when they are sensibly sitting still."

And so, when we had lady visitors staying with us, Walmy ordered a queer little man with side whiskers, called Tarbox, and my mother, properly attired in a dust cloak, long gloves, and a veil to protect her hat, set off with the guest in the governess's trap, to see the country. If there was any time left over, on their return—for Tarbox charged by the hour—Evelyn and I were allowed to use up the extra minutes.

It was a good thing my mother did not acquire her superstitious terror of horses until the motor car came into existence, else I cannot think how she would have managed to get about at all. As it was, the first taxicabs had already begun to appear on the streets— strange monsters that we would count as children count white horses, for luck—when she paid her visit to Cheiro, the palmist. He was a most celebrated palmist. King Edward the Seventh had consulted him. So had many of his lady friends. So, I believe, had another of my mother's idols, Lord Kitchener. There were not, in fact, many outstanding personalities of the day who hadn't visited him. My mother went, taking Roland with her. Cheiro told them many strange things. None of them ever came true. But the one disquieting thing was the manner of her death. She would, this palmist said, die a sudden death, too early in life, from "some member of the second order of creation."

"But what is the second order of creation?" she had asked him. And he told her that he wasn't sure, but that it might be a horse or a bull. "Mother's Bull," we called it from that day on, and a shiver of terror ran through our bodies. For we believed absolutely in this awful doom. How not, when our mother herself believed in it so completely?

This terror even frightened us on our own account. During our long daily walks up the country roads near Lowestoft, with the old nurse, we trembled if we should see a bull in a field. Perhaps this was the creature destined to kill our mother. Let us hurry past, or turn back. We must get out of range of the beast.

This threat of doom that hung over our mother was especially cruel because her daily life was so deeply controlled by superstitions. The main trend of these superstitions—though there were variants, such as the ill luck of wearing green, or of bringing hawthorn or ivy into the house—was a belief in the law of compensation.

"But why is my Chummie so depressed today?" we would hear our father ask.

"Oh, Robert," came her answer. "It was so lovely this morning, with the sunlight streaming into the bedroom, and I felt so carefree and happy that without thinking what I was doing I sang to myself while I was dressing. It was a most terrible and challenging thing to do, for something unlucky always happens to me during the day. Oh, I know you think I'm ridiculously superstitious, but let me remind you of the old saying: 'Sing before breakfast, cry before night.' And it's true, I tell you. It's absolutely true."

This fear of compensation stopped her from any outward sign of happiness. She was convinced that it was asking for trouble. Strangely enough, she never anticipated good luck in the wake of anything bad that had happened to her. Despite her incomparable spirit and vitality, she went through life with a sense of gloom. Not for nothing was she a Celt.

7. *Flowers and Feathers*

"Let's hurry so as to be back before Father gets up," we would pant as we rushed home with our hands full of harebells and wild roses.

During the summer we went out early to gather these bouquets. Whatever happened, our mother must have a flower at breakfast. Never must she come down to find her plate empty.

Our father was jealous of us in these floral offerings. "Damn those children," we often heard him mutter as he came into the dining room and found we had been there before him. If a little bunch of flowers lay on our mother's plate, he was in a bad temper for most of the day.

All through the months of summer he cherished his rosebuds in the Lowestoft garden so that he might cut them at the exact moment for our mother to wear. He had planted bushes at the bottom of the garden, behind the tool shed, where she would not see them on her daily walks. In that way he might surprise his "Chummie" with some specially perfect bloom.

One morning our father brought a particularly beautiful rose to our mother. The white petals of this Frau Karl Druschki were flawless. He had gone into the garden early enough, he supposed, to outwit his children. Just as he entered the dining room he saw us in the very act of placing our bouquet of honeysuckle on the bread and butter plate. It was too much for him. He snatched the honeysuckle from the table and crushed it in his hands.

"And who do you suppose you are?" he shouted to us in his rage. "I've stood this long enough. Here I spend hours on end growing these roses for your mother, and if you think you're going to put this over on me you're utterly mistaken."

Our mother came into the room with a smile, and she was very kind to our father all that day.

After this we knew we would be wise occasionally to get up late, so that he might sneak out to the garden and cut his rosebuds ahead of us. Luck was with him, also, when the weather was wet, for we were not allowed to go out in the rain. And then the roses he brought in glistened with raindrops.

I don't think our mother would have considered herself decently clad if she had not been wearing flowers. These ranged from the fabulously expensive flings of stephanotis or gardenia she carried upon her evening dress when she went out to dinner in London, down to the nosegays of wild roses we picked for her in the country. But though she liked the rustic posies, her real taste was for those flowers which symbolized luxury and wealth. And so, during the winter months in London, it was always Parma violets or carnations, lilies of the valley or expensive roses that she demanded. This brought her into conflict with our Uncle Jack. I can see her now, arguing fiercely with him one day in the study.

He stamped up and down the room, haranguing her.

"You," he shouted, "you've no idea what beauty is. You only want flowers because they mean that people enjoy giving them to you. You don't love them for themselves. You could never understand the beauty of a dandelion, for example. It's got to be all those shapeless affairs that stand for extravagance. You—"

"Oh, but you're quite wrong," broke in my mother. "It's not because they stand for extravagance that I love them. It's because they represent love and passion and Paris and Nice and all the different men who have been in love with me, and—"

"What did I tell you?" shrieked my uncle. "You're condemned out of your own mouth. It isn't the form of the flowers that matters to you. It's their human association. You don't know what beauty is. You never did. You never could. You—"

He was so worked up by now that my mother burst out laughing at him.

"If you could only see yourself at this moment," she told him, "you'd realize that *you* are no thing of beauty."

Overhearing all this as I passed the study door, I knew exactly what Uncle Jack meant. I had myself suffered from my mother's attitude towards flowers.

It happened one Saturday morning in May.

I had bought a penny bunch of kingcups with my weekly pocket money. They shone like gold as the flower man handed them to me from his basket on the pavement's edge, and I took them home in great excitement, feeling sure my mother would love them. But in this excitement I had forgotten that kingcups were considered wild. The same morning Roland had decided to buy her flowers. In his greater wisdom he had bought three expensive pink carnations. I entered the study to find my mother already wearing these carnations.

"Aren't these lovely?" I cried, as I thrust my kingcups upon her. "They shine like little suns."

But she had no interest in them.

"Thank you," she said without enthusiasm. "I will put them in a vase on the mantelpiece in the back drawing room."

And there they drooped and died, for lack of water; scarcely anyone ever went into the back drawing room. Uncle Jack had been right in what he said. You could not wear a kingcup.

My mother must have missed all these exotic flowers during the summer months at Lowestoft. Even my father's rosebuds lacked the cachet of the florist's shop. And so when, on his periodic visits to the County Court at Norwich, Judge Talbot sent her a box of sulphur-colored carnations, she did not hide her delight.

"I always think there is more real style about a sulphur carnation than about almost any other flower," she murmured as she pinned a large bunch to her dress, and a smaller bunch in her pale yellow hair. "Even after they have faded they retain their sense of distinction."

But my father did not enjoy these carnations. Neither did the Scotch adorer, as he brought his "Mea" rough sprigs of heather to wear in her hair.

Thinking of my mother's flowers, though, I remember that it was when she was going to what the old nurse called "one of your mother's public dinners" that she was most abundantly garlanded.

These "public dinners" were great events. To this day I have no idea what they were or where they took place. They were probably dinners given by my mother's progressive club called the Pioneer or my father's literary club called the Whitefriars. The preparations began early in the morning. Walmy stayed to midday dinner in order that my mother might work in the afternoon, as she would be unable to do so, in her customary manner, during the evening. Not even a "public dinner" might interfere with the ordained number of words she must produce each day.

By this time a long cardboard box would have arrived, containing my mother's flowers. They usually came from Harrod's, and Walmy ordered them at the same time she ordered the electric brougham in which my mother and father slowly but with dignity made their way to the "public dinner." It was supposed to be very daring to go in one of Harrod's electric broughams. Most people still drove behind a horse. One or two, said my mother, were so underbred that they actually went by omnibus.

"If I were forced to go in that common manner," she added, "I wouldn't go at all. It is better to stay at home than to go to Buckingham Palace in a public conveyance. You've only got to watch Mrs. Bowles to see what I mean. She arrives everywhere in an ordinary street coat, with a scarf over her head to keep her hair neat, and wearing stout walking shoes. And she carries a telltale brown holland bag in which are her evening slippers. She might almost be a dancing mistress at a girls' school. Now a lady is dressed for the occasion from the minute she leaves her own front door."

Throughout the afternoon my mother dictated to Walmy. But the work was carried on in the bedroom, instead of in the study, so that she might combine it with dressing. How cold it was in that bedroom! Walmy wore her outdoor coat, and wrapped her legs around with an eiderdown off the bed. At the far end of the room stood an oil stove; but it gave out scarcely any heat. My mother did not intend that it should, for she was convinced that the only way to keep beautiful was to have a really cold bedroom.

"We can learn an important lesson from American women," she said. "They all have skins like shabby parchment. And considering the time and money they're supposed to devote to their complexions, I can only conclude it is due to the fact that they heat their bedrooms. Cold water on the face and cold air all round the face: these are the things that make for beauty."

And so Walmy shivered as she wrote, while my mother kept her own circulation going by vigorously rubbing her face.

Her toilet was a lengthy affair. It began with an elaborate cleaning of her face with lemons and oatmeal. If the top of her washstand was covered with mouldy, used-up lemons, the drawers of the washstand were filled with loose oatmeal. Unfortunately there were many mice at Vallombrosa; and mice like oatmeal. You had always to open these drawers very slowly, and with great care, in order to give the mice a chance to run away. Otherwise one might jump out at you. And my mother was afraid of mice.

"Dear me," she would gasp as she withdrew in a hurry from a baby mouse in the washstand drawer. "This is terrible. This is really terrible."

Walmy was not always quick to realize what was happening, and sometimes she incorporated these frightened exclamations into my mother's story, supposing them to have been dictated.

But at other times the situation grew much more serious. For occasionally the mouse leapt from the washstand drawer and ran wildly about in the bedroom. And then Tita the Skye terrier began to chase it while my mother and Walmy lifted their skirts high above their knees as they sought safety in standing on their chairs.

But there was, my mother always insisted, nothing you could do about it.

"People have been known to tell me we ought to get a cat," she said. "But much as I loathe these mice, I'd rather have them in the house than keep such a common thing as a cat. A cat is almost as impoverishing to the general atmosphere of an establishment as a baby's napkins hanging in the garden."

When the mouse had escaped, and all was quiet again, she went on rubbing the mousy oatmeal into her face. It seemed never to strike her that the oatmeal might not be completely pure and clean.

The next thing my mother always did was to cream her face. She used something called Crème Simon, and the little empty white jars with the tinfoil tops accumulated on her dressing table over the months and years. She never threw them away.

As she rubbed this cream into her face, she dictated. I knew exactly the way she did this rubbing for often, during the afternoon, I was called in to read a French play to her while she dressed, and out of a corner of one eye I would watch her, fascinated, while I stumbled through the "slightly improper" comedy. I could not say how many of these pale blue paper covered French plays I had read to her. I was too small to know where the improprieties lay, even had I been able to understand all the French, but when my mother burst out laughing I would produce a gurgle of my own, to make her feel that I knew it was risqué. It seemed the polite thing to do. On these afternoons before a "public dinner," however, she could not thus indulge herself. She must work.

But sometimes my mother's conscience must have smitten her about the odd kind of French I was reading.

"I really think you ought to know something about French classics," she said once, as she produced Balzac's *Eugénie Grandet.* At another time we wept together over Pierre Loti's *Pêcheurs d'Islande.* While I was still very young she gave me De Maupassant's *Boule de Suif,* and I waded through it with difficulty, bewildered. But she would never let me read De Maupassant when I had grown old enough to understand what he was writing about. She said he was a danger, and might put wrong ideas in my head. And then we returned to the pale blue paper covered plays. Always, to this day, when I read a book in French, I seem to hear a gentle, regular swishing sound, and I remember that it is the stroke of my mother's brush in her yellow hair.

But on these special days it was after tea that the real excitement started. For then we were allowed to help our parents dress.

"Why on earth do we have to go to these pompous affairs, Chummie?" my father shouted from the bathroom. "You know how I loathe and detest putting on a stiff shirt and a white tie. I'd give up my very soul to you, I love you so much, but I will not tie my own white tie."

"That's enough, Robert," my mother would call back. "You know perfectly well that it's an unforgivable social sin to wear a ready-made white bow tie. Clare will come in and tie it for you. She's good with her fingers. And if I find you getting the children to give you any more of these ready-made things as Christmas

presents I'll take them away from you. Don't you *want* to look a
gentleman?"

And so, when I had put the cuff links and studs in my father's
dress shirt, I had to tie his white bow. It was a nerve-wracking
experience, for I had been known to leave a dirty mark on the bow
and once, when I had pricked my finger on one of the safety pins
that held together my mother's torn flannel vest, which had come
undone, I deposited a large spot of blood upon my father's only
remaining clean tie.

My mother dressed now by lamplight. There was magic in this
warm glow. It shone on her pink satin peignoir with its swansdown
edging, and tossed rich black shadows across the bedroom ceiling,
giving a sense of enclosed intimacy to the scene. She was frizzing her
hair; the room was filled with the smell of the hot curling iron.
Outside in the gaslit street a barrel organ was playing. But the
sounds came faintly through the closed windows, and they were
almost drowned by my mother's voice. For, as she fastened the front
busks of her stays, she quoted Swinburne:

> I remember the way we parted,
>   The day and the way we met;
> You hoped we were both broken-hearted,
>   And knew we should both forget.
>
> And May with her world in flower
>   Seemed still to murmur and smile
> As you murmured and smiled for an hour;
>   I saw you turn at the stile.

Right, left, right, left, up the front of her stays the steel loops
alternately fastened, till my mother was encased at last in the tight
curves of these stays. But tight as these curves appeared, they were
not yet to her satisfaction. At this moment I was called upon to help.

I tugged at the stay laces, while my mother went on quoting
Swinburne:

> And the best and the worst of this is
> That neither is most to blame
> If you've forgotten my kisses—

"Can't you pull them just a little tighter?" My mother interrupted the poem to ask me.

I tugged till it seemed to me that she must be going to burst, but she finished the last line of the poem, undisturbed:.

> And I've forgotten your name.

At last she told me to stop. The laces were tied in a secure knot. My mother was ready now for her dress.

With her full breasts forced high above her stays and her frilled taffeta petticoat swirling out below, she looked like a picture on a cover of *La Vie Parisienne*, which I often disobediently looked at when the family was out. I glowed with pride as I gazed at her.

Now, in a pale blue satin dress trimmed with pearls, she was ready, except for the fling of flowers, and the flowers in her hair. What would they be this night? I knew they lay there in that long white box, wrapped in wax paper. And suddenly as we opened the box, the bedroom was filled with their scent: tuberoses, thick-petaled like white kid. We swathed them across the front of my mother's dress, as though it were a ribbon of honor, and the flowers fell into the dip between her breasts. Over her yellow hair we placed a crescent of tuberoses, like a May Queen's wreath.

As she swept from the room and down the stairs, out to the waiting electric brougham from Harrod's, she left behind her upon the night air the scent of tuberoses.

But it was not only flowers that delighted her. She had a passion for hats. Fortunately, the fashion of the day allowed her to indulge this extravagance, for hats were being influenced by *The Merry Widow*, and buried a woman beneath a spreading expanse of feather and flower. This suited my mother's tastes. She was a product of the *Merry Widow* age, and loved this musical comedy so much that she had seen it at least thirty-five times. For her it was the epitome of passion and romance.

Even while she dictated her stories, she would hum the "Merry Widow Waltz," and on her bedroom mantelpiece, in the place of honor, stood a photograph of the actress Lily Elsie, in the part of the Merry Widow. It went to Lowestoft with her in the summer, packed safely in her dressing case among her cosmetics, and was placed, first thing upon arrival, in the center of her dressing table.

"When my mind gets too much cluttered with thoughts of rice pudding and bills," my mother would say, "then I have only to look at Lily Elsie and my dreams return to me."

Daly's Theatre, where *The Merry Widow* was played, became her unfailing fount of strength.

Long after the fashion for Merry Widow hats had passed, my mother managed somehow to give every hat she wore the characteristics of that era.

"Little hats," she said, "are meant for sex-starved, commonplace women that you can shovel up by the hundred, because they are so exactly alike. But a distinguished woman, with a dream, needs a large hat."

And large her hats always were.

The buying of these hats was an event. My mother did not go to them. They came to her. A mouselike creature called Miss Spence, who kept a fashionable hat shop in a little road off Bond Street, notified my mother the minute she had received an especially tempting consignment from Paris—for my mother would only wear a hat that came from Paris. When this happened, three thin, pale young girls would be sitting in the front hall as we returned from our daily walk. Scattered around on the floor were half a dozen enormous bandboxes. From the drawing room came the sound of voices. Miss Spence had arrived, accompanied by her midinettes, and upon each arm of each girl had been hung one of these gigantic bandboxes. It was like the chorus of a musical comedy. It would not have been surprising if the girls had started to dance and sing.

The choosing of her hats was one of the only things for which my mother would put aside her work. It was a lengthy business, because there were always so many hats she wanted, and her conscience would not allow her to buy more than two at a time, or at most three.

It took place in the front drawing room, which was the only room in the house large enough to enable her to walk away and see herself in a mirror.

"It's so silly of women to buy their hats without thinking of the long distance view," she always said. "For this is the first impression the world gets of the hat you wear. By the time a man is close up to you it's your face and your eyes that fascinate him. It's not your hat. But the way to attract him from far off is by your general silhouette; and it's then that the hat counts."

Grandmamma was called in for these occasions, because she always knew what pleased a man; but although Auntie Pollie insisted on accompanying her sister, my mother would never listen to anything she might have to say.

"Your Auntie Pollie has no taste," my mother declared. "Just look at the hats she wears, with the stiff birds' wings stuck on in front, as though a seagull had been impaled on her head. No man would look at a woman twice with such millinery."

And saying this, she stroked the voluptuous sweep of ostrich feathers curving around her latest confection.

But though most of her hats seemed to have this extravagant spread of plumage, occasionally she decided upon something more austere. And then a black velvet brim would be adorned by a crown of ermine, to balance her ermine stole and muff. Sometimes again an especially expensive hat would be severely simple. When this happened, my mother gave me a lesson in the merits of simplicity.

"Always notice," she said, as she stood there in her own elaborate clothing, "that the best things in this world, and the most expensive, as well as those things which are really good style, are invariably simple."

She never realised that she herself rarely followed her own advice. If the winter hats were a riot of feathers, the summer ones were a tangle of secured blossoms.

The rest of her attire was in keeping with this flamboyant millinery. Buttons that buttoned nothing lay in rows upon her dresses, and fringes and curved braid overlapped each other, and fell upon bows of ribbon and elaborate trimmings.

It was impossible to make her conform. Many years later this became decidedly awkward.

For Evelyn was going to be married.

My future sister-in-law came from an orthodox "huntin' and shootin' " family. She appeared in the pages of the *Tatler*, sitting on a shooting stick and wearing severe tweeds at a point-to-point race. Never in her life had she come across anyone like our mother. I promised Evelyn that I would try to subdue Mother's attire for the occasion of the first meeting with his fiancée.

And so I took her to Debenham and Freebody's. If she could not have a dress made especially for her by her own dressmaker, Madame Louise Freeman, who had been trained in Paris, she condescended to go to this shop, which she considered one of the "most exclusive" in London. I let her loose among the afternoon dresses, though I tried to steer her round to some dignified black gown that would have satisfied her future in-laws and at the same time have showed up the fairness of her beauty. But she resisted me, and her eyes strayed to the pinks and blues of the debutante dance frocks at the far end of the row.

"If you think I'm going to allow myself to be made to look like Annie Besant, just because I have a son who's going to be married, you're quite wrong," she said. "Something must have happened to the world, for I have never seen such a dowdy lot of clothes in this place in my life. There used to be glamour in this shop. If you don't mind, we'll call a taxi and go straight back home. I'd rather meet Cynthia any day in this old dress I've got on now, than be made a present of the whole collection of these middle-aged looking garments hanging over on that rail."

Her future daughter-in-law came to meet her in clothes that were impeccably correct. My mother, in the frayed, fringed pale blue silk dress that she was so deeply attached to, behaved with such graciousness and with so much the air of a grande dame that Cynthia was the one to feel inappropriately dressed.

There was, however, one adornment to which my mother never succumbed. Nothing would make her wear jewelry.

"If you cover yourself with jewelry it's as good as proclaiming to the world that you know you are not beautiful. Whoever wanted to place a necklace round a lily? And a woman who has good looks should treat herself as though she were a flower."

She knew, of course, that her particular type of beauty was not suited by adornment; for it would have been like putting trumpery upon a Grecian statue, to clasp a necklace around her sculptured throat. She would wear rings upon her fingers, if the rings were valuable; but I never saw her with brooches or earrings.

"And as for bracelets," she said, as she dissuaded one of her admirers from giving her an expensive one, "they add years to your age. The only women who can wear them with advantage are scraggy ones who want to draw attention away from their bony arms."

But one day when Mr. Bowles was leaving for a lengthy absence in Canada, he gave my mother an amethyst necklace and begged her to wear it always, for his sake. So pathetic was he in his tearful insistence that at last she promised him she would. No sooner had he left the house than she took it off.

"I'm not going to ruin my beauty for any man," she declared.

"But neither will I actually break my promise to George. I will still wear this wretched necklace, but I will hide it from view."

And so, for a long while, she wore it in a muslin bag, pinned between her breasts. But this was far from comfortable and, whenever she moved, the precious stones jingled against each other. My deaf father never heard this noise; but other people did.

"Whatever has Mrs. Leighton got underneath her dress that makes that queer sound?" one visitor was heard to whisper to another.

It became so embarrassing that finally my mother decided she was justified in breaking her promise to Mr. Bowles. She laid the amethyst necklace safely away at the back of one of her dressing-table drawers.

8. *The Leightons*

"Don't forget, my children," our mother said as she told us that Grandmother Leighton was arriving that morning to pay us a visit, "don't ever forget that my family has always considered I married beneath me. They were so upset at my running away with your father that when finally I gave them our address Mamma refused to send me on even a pocket handkerchief."

We were supposed to share this contempt for our father's relatives, and everything was done to prevent us from coming into contact with them.

When we were small we associated the Leightons with intimidating people like our grandmother. She was aged, and very Scotch. I never saw her in anything except an old lady's attire: black satin dresses fastened at the neck with cameos or gold brooches filled with someone's hair, mauve and white silk ribboned caps, and, when the weather was cold, a lace shawl wrapped around her shoulders. For a Christmas or a birthday present I was always forced to make something for her out of black satin, which I hated. Not only did I object to the color, but I hated it because my nurse made me sew these satin aprons and knitting bags on the beach, during the months of summer. As the sun beat down on the black material till it was almost too hot to hold, and my eyes strayed to Evelyn paddling at the water's edge, I stitched resentment into every hem.

Grandmother Leighton was aware of my mother's feelings about her family, and it made her angry.

"I would remind you, Marie," she told my mother in unavailing self-defense, "that I am a Campbell of Breadalbane. There is nothing in your inheritance to surpass this. Even a Trelawny is a mere upstart."

But she was less forceful a character than my mother, and all she got in return for trying to uphold her own ancestors was a steely coldness.

The visits Grandmother Leighton occasionally paid us in St. John's Wood were uncomfortable affairs. She wanted to get to know her grandchildren, and insisted on taking us for walks. She seemed so very old that we were always afraid she would die suddenly in the road—which, oddly enough, she did some years later when, at the age of ninety-seven, she stole from her house unnoticed, to mail a letter, and fell on the icy pavement. Not only did she take us through some of the "common" streets in St. John's Wood that were forbidden to us lest we catch an infectious disease, but, too, on these walks she gave us advice we didn't understand.

"There is one sin I hope my little grandchildren will never fall into," she often said as we plodded slowly along the pavements, "and that is self-abuse. No child is too young to start sinning in this terrible way. The road to madness and hell can begin in the nursery. I will leave you some booklets on this subject, to read at leisure."

The booklets had frightening titles, such as *Are You Sinning, Brother?* which made us feel sure we had already sinned without knowing it, and were on our way to hell. But we had no idea what this terrible sin was, and we did not dare to ask. All we knew was that our mother always searched the nursery after Grandmother had left, and scooped up any of these pamphlets she could find.

"Trust these really good people to have their minds fixed on the dirt and evil of the world," she stormed, as she burned the offending literature in the nursery fireplace. "As my mamma always told me, it is safer any day to leave your children in the company of a rake than to place them for half an hour in the care of a vicar's wife. The rake does the evil thing and keeps silent, whereas the virtuous woman gets satisfaction out of discussing what she does not do."

When Grandmother Leighton wasn't preaching us sermons we didn't understand, she was giving us dull books like *Ministering Children*. We dreaded lest she should ask us if we had enjoyed them, for they bored us so much that we left them only half read. But the most troubling thing about her was the ear trumpet that looked like a black snake. It had a queer smell to it that reminded us of an empty church.

"Nobody with any sense of style or beauty would be seen with such a trumpet," our mother declared. "And let me tell you, Robert," she added, shouting to our deaf father, "if ever you suggest using this hideous, impoverishing contraption I will pack up and leave you straight away."

We grew even more frightened of the ear trumpet after this, so that, when we had to hold it to speak to our grandmother, we always seemed to forget what we had meant to say. Considering these embarrassments, we were glad when she left.

But perhaps it was my father who suffered most. My mother held him responsible for all the "underbred" habits of our grandmother, and immediately a visit was over a general spiritual disinfecting took place.

"Please remember, Robert," she told my father, "I only married you to get away from my own people and write books. You know perfectly well I never intended having anything to do with your family. It's bad enough having your old mother up here, but whatever happens, I'm going to keep the children out of the way of contamination."

Listening to these tirades against my father's side of the family, I was bewildered as to what she meant. Everything about the Leightons seemed so respectable—more respectable, in fact, than my mother's relatives. That was probably what irked my mother, who considered respectability a sign of lack of breeding. She was distressed, also, because my father's parents had been Unitarian.

"It's a funny thing," she said, "but no ladies or gentlemen can be Unitarian. Neither, for that matter, can they be any kind of Nonconformist. It's as though there are as many social levels in the next world as in this. And, my dear Robert, when it comes to the next world, definitely I do not expect to meet your family there."

And so it was much against the grain that she would have to agree to our paying an occasional visit to the Leighton family in the village in Berkshire called Swallowfield, where Grandmother lived with her three unmarried daughters.

These visits never lasted more than one day. Fortunately for our happiness, while we were actually spending that day at Swallowfield we could forget the shadow of impending punishment which lay before us. For never did we return home but what our mother would tell us we had become "common," and a doll or a toy engine or some other treasure would be sacrificed upon the altar of "good breeding." We did not understand what had happened in us to displease our mother so, but as we grew older we had a suspicion that anything we enjoyed automatically must be wrong.

We were taken to Swallowfield by our father. The journey itself was an event. Trinder's brougham, smelling of old leather and straw, fetched us from the door of the house in St. John's Wood. The day was so enchanted that the smallest detail took on a glow. Even Roland, who rarely associated with "the children," seemed friendly on these occasions.

"Why doesn't Mother come us sometimes?" I asked

Father as we sat in Paddington Station, waiting for the train to start. But he looked worried at this question and, muttering something about her being behindhand with her work, he changed the subject.

When we reached the town of Reading we plunged into a dark livery stable. As a treat we were allowed to choose our horse for the six mile carriage drive out to Swallowfield. So rarely were we given any freedom that this sense of power intoxicated us. We walked from horse to horse, unable to make up our minds.

Generally we brought Selina, the Scottish deerhound, with us. She was an exciting complication, for invariably, on the drive into the country, she caught the scent of some animal—a deer, we were convinced, though we never saw it—and leapt right out from the open carriage. She had to be chased over several fields and coppices. It was as though even Selina felt the unaccustomed freedom. We always arrived at our destination covered with mud.

Our father seemed like a child who had played truant from school. All of us were very happy.

Swallowfield was a paradise of strawberries and roses. The lanes and woods in spring were sulphur with primroses, and sweet with the songs of nightingales. The Meadow, where the Leightons lived, was far up a leafy lane called Spring Piddle, beyond sight of any other house. The most interesting thing about this place was that it had no gate. The lane merged imperceptibly into the garden, which was a feature practically unheard of in England. This was no mere oversight. It was a symbolic gesture, but a gesture that, my mother said, was in itself enough to prove that our grandmother was not well-bred; for well-bred people demanded privacy. Years earlier our grandmother had accompanied her husband to America. There she had been impressed by the lack of hedges and gateways and fences, and had determined to have a gateless garden for herself. The path flowing unobstructed from The Meadow into Spring Piddle was a clarion call tc earth brotherhood.

The garden was gay with flowers, and quivered with bees. We were allowed to pick these flowers. We watched while our Aunt Jean removed the honey from the hives. We ran in the fields and played hide and go seek up the lane. We gathered strawberries in June, and apples in September. For one day we could forget the dull walks with Nanny, who never let us move from her side, lest we got overheated and caught a chill.

Our bliss must have been evident on our return when, next morning, Mother paid her daily visit to the nursery to see us and to ask the nurse if our bowels were working properly.

"You are always completely spoilt by these visits to Swallow-field," she told us, as she carried off our most cherished toys. "The only way I can teach you a lesson is by making you suffer."

If Mother had only known, her rival was not the despised Leighton clan, but the unaccustomed sense of freedom, and a comb of honey and a basket of ripe strawberries.

There was one member of the Leighton family whom my mother disliked more than any of the others. This was Aunt Sarah. My mother said she had outstanding malice. I never myself saw it, but when she felt she needed to influence us more strongly against the Leightons, Mother would insist that Aunt Sarah had once stated: "When I cannot bite with my teeth I bite with my tongue."

Oddly enough, there were certain similarities between my mother and this aunt. For one thing, Aunt Sarah, also, wrote stories. But whereas my mother's serials were filled with bloodcurdling melodrama, my aunt's tales were gentle, sentimental romances. As these sugary stories appeared in several of the weekly papers, Grandmother sent them up to us with pride, anxious to prove that the Leighton women were intellectuals. And then Mother would smile and say:

"Of course, when you read one of Sarah's love stories, it's only too evident that she couldn't possibly understand anything about love, and that no man in his senses could ever have wanted to kiss her—the poor, ugly little creature."

She never knew of my virgin aunt's hopeless passion for a well-known Dante scholar of her day. Aunt Sarah, on her part, had the deepest contempt for my mother's lack of true emotion.

"Your mother," said my aunt, in a sudden burst of incautious confidence, "is all wrong in her values. She is absolutely incapable of feeling love. All she wants is worship and adoration from men. She could never understand the joy of sacrifice and service."

But not only did my mother dislike Aunt Sarah; she considered her the most dangerous of all the Leighton influences. She had not worried over Aunt Jean while she was still alive. Aunt Jean had been the domesticated member of the family, with no interest in ideas. The story went that her lawyer fiancé had jilted her the day before her marriage, deciding at the last moment that she was too ugly to live with; the shock to her pride, my mother said, had humbled her and kept her in her place. It had, the family believed, led to her early death. Even Aunt Lexy, the black sheep of the family, was not supposed to be so much of a danger. This may have been because the Leightons themselves were ashamed of her. The Leightons were strictly upright, and tolerated no deviation from the straight path. For they were Scotch, as well as being Unitarians. But my mother considered Aunt Lexy the only member of the family worth knowing.

Aunt Lexy had gone on the stage.

It wasn't thought quite "nice" to go on the stage, even though Irving had been knighted and a number of King Edward's lady friends were actresses. It had to be admitted, though, that Aunt Lexy was as "legitimate" as she could be, for she acted in Shakespeare, with Ben Greet, and was in the same company for a time as Sir Henry Irving and Ellen Terry. Actually it was because she resembled Ellen Terry and got her "calls" that she was thrown out of that company. And so, when in my earliest childhood, I sleepily watched *Captain Brassbound's Conversion* with my mother's old judge, I was not altogether wrong in being reminded of the derelict old aunt.

Aunt Lexy had started life correctly. She had even been engaged to a clergyman. But some ferment was at work within her. She could not see herself in the quiet life of a country vicarage. And so she jilted her clergyman and ran away. She went on the stage, with her Venetian red hair that fell down to her knees, and the romantic name of Alexes Leighton which nobody ever believed to be really her own.

She was not a beautiful woman. Her eyebrows and lashes were so fair as to be scarcely visible. Her nose was decidedly large. But, even as she resembled Ellen Terry in appearance, so did she share with her that element which can best be called temperament, or magnetism. My mother was slow to praise another woman's looks, but she admired Aunt Lexy.

"If I were a man I'd fall in love with Lexy any day," she said. "She has more charm than most beautiful women put together."

From the first moment I met Aunt Lexy I had been tacitly warned against her; not by my mother, but by family pressure on the Leighton side. I must have been a tiny child, for, I remember, I had been sent to stay with the Leighton grandmother at Arborfield, in Berkshire, to be out of the way while Evelyn was born. Aunt Lexy's stage days were now over, and she was a broken creature. Some time earlier she had gone to America with Olga Nethersole's company, to act in *Sappho*. The play had been considered immoral, and withdrawn. This, with all its implications and difficulties, proved too great a strain for poor Aunt Lexy. She sought solace in drink. Unfortunately the habit grew upon her, and she had to be brought back to England, where she needed to be cared for from that time on.

"But how much more worth while she is, in her wrecked condition, than all the self-consciously upright members of the Leighton family," our mother insisted. "It makes me positively angry to see how ashamed they are of her. They should be proud to show her off, instead of keeping her hidden always, like a skeleton in the cupboard."

Even as a tiny child I must have been aware of Aunt Lexy's magnetism, for whenever I saw her I felt a strange excitement. I did not then know anything about her, but I noticed that she lay around in the house at Arborfield doing nothing while my austere, spinster-ish Aunt Jean did all the housework. And yet, indolent though she seemed to be, Aunt Lexy was the lovable one, rather than Aunt Jean.

I remember her in the morning room of the old house, dressing me up in all kinds of fancy garments. Sometimes a lace curtain transformed me into a bride; at other times she covered me with the family jewels and I became a rich lady; or, again, we ransacked the drawers upstairs in my grandmother's bedroom and, collecting all the artificial flowers we could from my grandmother's discarded bonnets, Aunt Lexy said that I was someone called Ophelia. And then she stood off from me at the far end of the room, pretending she was the audience in a theatre. Clapping her hands, she said: 'Splendid. Splendid." One frightening morning she acted her favorite part of Lady Macbeth and, sending me into the kitchen for the bread knife, towered above me, declaring: "Infirm of purpose, give *me* the dagger."

But just as I was decked out in some exciting costume, Aunt Jean walked in, her hands white with flour.

"Shame upon you, Lexy," scolded Aunt Jean, wiping her hands on her apron. "How dare you go on so! You'd think you'd given us enough trouble without trying to put immoral ideas into little Baba's head. One actress in the family is one too many. Come along, Baba, and help me with the dinner."

She carted me off to the kitchen, beyond the reach of moral contamination, and made me sit in a chair and shell peas.

But Aunt Lexy called to me, as I disappeared:

"Which do you love most, your Aunt Lexy, or your Aunt Jean?"

Suddenly the Leighton blood within me asserted itself, and as the scrawny Scotch arms of my Aunt Jean kneaded the dough for the bread, some sense of justice made me answer: "Aunt Jean." Even to this day I can see the figure of Aunt Lexy wilt as I denied her.

When I returned to London to confront a new baby brother, I found my values in life swimming around me in confusion, and overheard my mother saying to my father:

"Robert, if there's anything extra needed to make me sure never to be careless and have a baby again, it's the way that child Baba gets ruined when I send her down to your mother. In a few weeks they undo all the good of the training I've given her since she was born. She's a common littie thing, now, instead of a little lady."

But in spite of all this, Aunt Sarah was the one whom my mother most distrusted. During my childhood I was kept from her as much as possible. It was only when I had grown up that I began to know her.

Then she became my greatest friend.

Over those many years of friendship I realized why my mother feared her influence upon us. For one thing, Aunt Sarah had a contempt for class distinctions. To her all men were equal. Her father had been a Scottish poet whose philosophy of life was a mixture of Robert Burns and Walt Whitman and who had instilled into his children a feeling of the innate dignity of the human being. He had spent some time in America and, whereas my grandmother had brought back with her a longing for a gateless garden, he had returned fired with excitement over the New World, and the brotherhood of man. I never met this grandfather; he had been killed in an accident long before I was born, while he was still young; but I felt that I had known him well, for Aunt Sarah never tired of telling me about him. Looking from his photographs almost like a twin brother of Lord Tennyson, he seemed to have been a noble character. A great part of Aunt Sarah's idealism stemmed from his example.

And thus it was natural that my aunt should have a special contempt for the pastimes of the aristocracy. The very thought of fox hunting maddened her. Unfortunately she was continually being exposed to this particular sport; for her nearest neighbor was the Duke of Wellington, upon his Stratfieldsaye estate. I can remember the fierce glee with which she told me of her successful thwarting of His Grace's pleasure.

"The unemployed were up the lane here last week," she said to me in a feigned casual voice one day, as she poked the living room fire.

I started in surprise, for her home in Swallowfield was a good six miles from the nearest town of Reading.

"But they didn't come as far into the country as this, did they?" I asked.

My aunt smiled whimsically.

"Yes," she said, "they were up the lane. They were here, as large as life; all their pink coats and their horses and their hounds. And the Duke himself, sitting his horse and leading them all."

"And what happened?" I asked, for I could see that she was bursting to tell me.

"Well," she said, "they came up the lane as far as where this garden begins. They even started to come up the path. It's the first time in my life I've ever wished we had a garden gate."

Listening to her so, I began to realise how absolutely right it was that my mother should have lived behind high walls and a solid garden gate, while this Leighton garden merged into the country lane with no gate whatsoever. It seemed to me that the two cultures were as well shown by this as by anything. . . . And now I could see the Berkshire Hunt bearing down upon my tiny little aunt as she walked to meet it—for I knew that was certainly what she had done.

"Yes," she went on, "there they all were, surging up the garden path, and with the horses trampling upon my flower beds. So I went out to meet them. 'Well?' I said to the Duke as he reined in his horse. 'Well?' But the Duke did not seem to understand. 'The fox has got away in your orchard, ma'am,' he said. 'The hounds want to be after him.' 'The fox is welcome to the safety of my orchard,' I answered him calmly. And at that he grew so angry that his face turned the color of his coat. 'But madam,' he said, 'the fox, I tell you—' 'Good morning, sir,' I bowed to him. 'Good morning. And will you please have the goodness to call your dogs off my garden.' It made him mad to hear me call those hounds 'dogs.' It just isn't done. And that's exactly why I did it. With that I drew myself up and stood there in the middle of the garden path, looking him straight in the face. And he couldn't move, you see, for if he had he'd have knocked me down on my own land. 'But the fox, madam. He's in your orchard.' 'And he couldn't be in a safer place,' I snapped back at him. I was losing my temper, for some of the hard-faced women in the hunt were beginning to grumble. They had no manners, and seemed to consider me a nuisance. 'And I'll be obliged if you will please call your dogs and horses together and leave my garden,' I went on severely. 'Perhaps you are not aware that you are trespassing?' And I stood there, without moving, till the Duke turned his horse and led them all down the path again and out into the lane. I liked to think of that fox, safe among my apple trees. . . . It was a grand morning, I can tell you, a grand morning."

She gave the fire a vicious poke, and the flames glowed upon the look of triumph on her face.

She knew that in obstructing this hunt she had defied the whole fabric of England.

But I was careful never to tell my mother this story. She would have called my aunt a cad for interfering in such a sacred thing as a fox hunt.

What possibility was there that these two women might agree?

The only wisdom was in keeping them completely apart. And so I visited my aunt, but refrained from telling my mother.

My mother said that Aunt Sarah was something dreadful called a Socialist, and that she read terrible books that no well-brought-up woman would have on her shelves. Actually my aunt introduced me to the books of Edward Carpenter and Havelock Ellis, Lowes Dickinson and E. M. Forster. But she also opened up to me the world of American literature. Sometimes, when I felt mischievous, I would tell my mother about these writers I had discovered. And then she would lift an eyebrow and look at me in a superior manner.

"None of them really matters," she declared. "They are eccentric highbrows, and lack the stamp of the professional. Now if Sarah were to give you books by people like Robert Hichens or W. J. Locke, there'd be some sense to it. However, I suppose I ought to be glad she isn't the sort to get you started on Elinor Glyn or Ouida. These stuffy things she's interested in can't actually do you any harm."

My mother had a passion for Ouida. A copy of *Moths* was always hidden among her bundles in the study. It was falling to pieces from over-use, as she would often pause for a minute or two in her dictating to reread some favorite love scene. It helped her, she said, to keep in the mood for what she was herself writing.

I was never allowed to read Ouida. She was supposed to be far too improper for a young girl, though an exception was made in the case of *Two Little Wooden Shoes*, which, had "a minimum of sex" in it. My mother was strict about the books I read. This was part of her promise to Judge Talbot to bring me up as innocent as a wild rosebud. Being forbidden to look at it, naturally I managed to read *Moths*. I used to slip into the study when the family was out and skim through as many pages at a time as I safely could. But the sad thing was that I found myself disappointed. Where were the passionate love scenes that gave my mother such thrills of emotion? Why, even, was I forbidden the book? Many years later I admitted to having read *Moths*, and asked my mother what was so improper about it. She seemed surprised and grieved that I had been unaffected.

"When I was a young girl, I also disobeyed my mother," she confessed to me. "During those times when we were hard up and had no servants, I was made to dust my parents' bedroom, and I found that my mother kept a copy of *Moths* in a drawer of one of her cupboards, hidden underneath some flannel petticoats. Each morning, while I was supposed to be busy dusting, I managed to read a few pages. My whole existence was transformed by the glow of the book, and I went about all those days in a haze of emotion."

There was something to me very enviable about my mother's impressionableness. She would be reminded of a particular line or verse of a poem, and carry it around with her for hours or days, or even weeks. She wrote me once that she had been interrupted that particular morning from her work because of waiting for the chimney sweep.

"He is unromantic but necessary," she added. "But there is a touch of spring in the air and all the while the verses of 'This month the almonds bloom in Kandahar' are running in my mind."

As likely as not, when the chimney sweep arrived she quoted these verses to him from *Indian Love Lyrics*, mixed in with the directions about the chimney to be swept, till he grew confused, and wondered what was happening to him.

All the while that she was living in this world of romantic poetry, she was vituperative against Aunt Sarah who was, in her own way, living an identical life of books. But my mother could never understand the particular intellectual color of my aunt's life. She had never heard of Calderon, and the name of Camoens was probably unknown to her. And so, living alone in the country, my aunt spent her days in the world of writers, even as my mother wove the *Indian Love Lyrics* or Swinburne and Henley into her business with the chimney sweep. Had they ever been able to meet, without knowing who the other was, it is even possible that they might really have liked one another.

Years later, after my father had died and my mother was completely alone, the parallel between her and Aunt Sarah was still more strange. For outwardly they were living such similar lives, while yet the entire range of their values was different. In her house in Hertfordshire my mother was free to shape her day as she chose, so that she could write to me: "And, by the way, I've just discovered that I've forgotten to have my breakfast, and it's just one o'clock, and a lovely day, too," while, down in her house in Berkshire, my aunt was living her own queer diurnal rhythm. This rhythm was thoroughly sensible, and yet, if the people in her village had known of it, she would have been considered even more of an eccentric than she already was. For her entire life revolved around her passionate need for reading.

During the winter months my aunt went to bed when the birds did; but before she could shut her bedroom door there were four trays to prepare. And so she laid out her tea tray, her supper tray, a tray with a saucepan of milk and a tin of Ovaltine for midnight refreshment, and a breakfast tray. These were placed on chairs in her room, as near to the bed as possible in order that she might not have to travel far to reach her next meal. On the round table by her bed stood a methylated spirit stove and a box of tobacco and cigarette papers. Aunt Sarah smoked unceasingly, even in the days before it became the fashion. She made her own cigarettes and her remarks seemed always to be accompanied by the action of rolling a cigarette, while her sentences were broken by a pause for the licking of the paper.

Having placed nearest to her the tea tray, which she would need first, she got into bed and started her reading. She read books in five languages, though, like all the women of our family, she had had practically no schooling whatsoever. She despised translations, and felt strongly that Cervantes should be read in Spanish, Dante in Italian, Balzac in French and Goethe in German. Some little time after the last bird had finished his evensong, she reached out for the matches and started the spirit stove, for her tea. While the water was heating she lit the oil lamp, which was the only form of artificial illumination in this house—the daily cleaning of the wicks was an art of enormous importance, for only if the lamps were well trimmed could my aunt read with comfort over the hours of darkness. At this moment she would decide to draw the curtains, as no longer was there any light from the sky. And then, as she waited for the water to boil in the tiny aluminum pan, she would roll a cigarette, and turn over in her mind what she was reading.

The lamp shone with a warm glow upon the shell-thin Japanese teacup and saucer, and upon the silver milk jug and sugar bowl. Even though she lived alone, she treated herself always to the best china and the best silver; Grandmother Leighton had trained her children that what was not good enough for guests was not good enough for the family. Her tea finished, she pulled the Jaegar shawl closer around her shoulders—for she did not want to bother to keep the coal fire in the grate too high—and settled down to two or three hours of solid reading. As the feeling of hunger overcame the excitement of the story, she would push aside the used tray and draw towards her the supper tray.

Raised on vast quantities of meat, potatoes and suet puddings, I found it difficult to get accustomed to the food she ate.

"You've only got to see what Sarah eats to realize she is an eccentric," my mother said. "Whoever could possibly imagine there was any nourishment for the brain in figs and dates and lettuce and garden vegetables? If you were to place a good beefsteak before her she'd have a fit and tell you we had no right to kill animals."

"But she *does* eat meat," I interrupted. "She's trying a diet which is almost entirely meat."

My mother would not believe it.

"You must be mistaken," she told me. "I am perfectly certain that what you suppose to be meat is really a chopped nut affair that has been cooked in some way or other to look like meat—mock cutlets, I think they call them. You've only got to read a sentence or two from any one of your Aunt Sarah's stories to know that she's a food fad and a vegetarian and an anemic homespun crank. If I ever find you eating salad I shall know you've become a Leighton; and you will be beyond salvation."

Meanwhile, my aunt would be sitting up in bed, devouring minced beef upon her supper tray. She had been experimenting with a diet called the "Salisbury cure," which consisted of nothing whatsoever but meat and hot water. My mother was right in saying that Aunt Sarah was an eccentric in her diet. But now, though, she was beginning to doubt the wisdom of the "Salisbury cure" and had started again on "reformed food," and brews of medicinal herb teas.

This supper finished, she would read past midnight, and sometimes well into the small hours of the morning, until she began to feel sleepy. And there, at the other side of the round table, stood her nightcap of milk and Ovaltine, waiting to be heated. If there had been any neighbors close enough to see it, the light in Miss Sarah Leighton's bedroom window might have been noticed through most of the hours of darkness.

But before this light could be turned out, an important ritual had to be observed. "Bobs" must be remembered. "Bobs" was her pet robin. On the ledge by the opened window she placed the lid of a matchbox, through which was inserted a heavy pair of scissors. Upon the top of the matchbox lid she put a dab of butter. This was her alarm clock; each morning, at exactly twenty-five minutes past eight, "Bobs" flew in at the open window for his breakfast of butter and, pecking at it, he made a noise with the heavy pair of scissors. My aunt then would wake and smile at the little bird, knowing it was time for her own breakfast.

This continued over many years. It might have gone on longer if her brother, my Uncle Jack, had not died. She went to London for several weeks, to attend to his affairs. Before she left Swallowfield she asked the village policeman to come up to The Meadow and, telling him to keep his eye on the place each day while she was away, she tipped him five shillings as she begged him to give the robin his butter. The butter was placed in a closed tin on the porch, but though the English are notoriously sentimental about birds, this particular policeman must have been slightly casual in keeping his promise, for on her return Aunt Sarah found "Bobs" had lost his endearing ways and no longer visited her in her bedroom. Neither did he, as the summer came around, ever again alight on the toe of her foot, or on her book, as she lay in a hammock under the chestnut tree, reading.

My mother did not know any of this, for I kept silent always about the life at The Meadow. But if she had known she would have had little sympathy. Hers was a world of dogs rather than of birds.

"You can always tell whether people are well-bred or not by whether they love dogs," she used to say. "And isn't it so exactly right that not one single member of the Leighton family—except your father, who, of course, isn't really a Leighton any more—not one single member of the family owns a dog? They're the sort that ought to have quantities of common tabby cats. And I rather suspect they know all about birds. It's strange how the people who know the names and habits of birds seem to be the ones who never *do* anything important in life."

Aunt Sarah ran through an enormous quantity of books. When Uncle Jack went for holidays abroad he had difficulty in finding enough literature to occupy his sister while he was out of the country. The length of Proust's novels was an answer to prayer, and enabled him to travel farther afield with a clear conscience; but should he be away unduly long, and the Proust novels be finished, Aunt Sarah was never really at a loss. She fell back upon "running through Balzac once again," or "having a look at Dickens or Trollope."

Mudie's Library was a household word in our family, both with my father and mother in London and with Aunt Sarah at Swallowfield. Every Tuesday and Friday afternoon of my childhood an imposing horse-drawn closed vehicle with a liveried coachman stopped before the gate of Vallombrosa and "Mudie's man" came up the garden path, dressed in a brass buttoned overcoat and a silk hat. By a thick leather strap he carried a pile of books. They were the latest novels for my mother and father to read over tea. Up in the nursery we could hear the steady drone of my father's voice, as he read these books aloud to my mother from the start of the five o'clock tea until half-past six, when Walmy appeared for the evening dictating.

But Aunt Sarah had none of this regular twice a week service. Uncle Jack selected her literature. Living in Bloomsbury, not far from Mudie's headquarters in New Oxford Street, he spent a great part of his days in the Library, discovering books that were worth reading. And then an enormous crate was sent down to Aunt Sarah at The Meadow. It was a wonderful thing to be visiting her when one of these crates arrived. She acted like a drink addict before a sudden vista of endless bottles. A wild light came into her eyes, and her hands trembled as she began to open the crate. When there was a book she wanted to possess, though, she became independent of her brother and ordered it through the village boy who left her daily newspaper. Once, however, she was in a predicament.

"I really don't know what to do," she complained to me. "I own everything any of the Powys brothers has written; but now John Cowper Powys has just brought out a book called *In Defence of Sensuality*. I dare say it's perfectly innocuous, but, I ask you, how do I dare to order a book with such a title? Before I know where I am, I might ruin my reputation for respectability in the neighborhood."

She felt so upset about it that I bought the book for her in London and sent it by mail, securely wrapped.

The books she read, however, were not by any means always innocuous. She chose the unexpurgated editions of the classics, and reveled in their licentiousness. But it was the romantic attitude towards love that really interested her. Over our sewing, on the long dark evenings of my visits to Swallowfield, she told me the plots of the books she had read since I was last there. Her voice grew tender at the remembrance of the love passages.

"And then, one day, when he had waited for her several years, they again met. And still she resisted him—for quite a long time. But he was persistent and, of course, at last she gave way and it was the 'chose ordinaire.'"

After that she gave up any interest for, she said, at this point the story always lost its originality.

"It's not for nothing that I call the sex act the 'chose ordinaire,'" she added. "That's just what it is. It has neither beauty nor variation. The only part of sex that is worth while is romantic love."

There was a great deal in common between Aunt Sarah and my mother.

9. Uncle Jack

"It's strange what a world of difference there is between an artist and a writer," my mother sighed. "An artist *used* to be romantic, but I ask you, where today can you find the painter Ouida wrote about in *Two Little Wooden Shoes*, with his deep-set soulful eyes and his brown velvet coat? As I pass the St. John's Wood Art School and watch those anemic degenerates emerging I feel sure there can be nothing more pitiable than an art student."

My mother's opinion was colored by her contempt for the Leightons. Both Aunt Sarah and Uncle Jack were artists.

Aunt Sarah was a bad artist. She was, if possible, inferior to her brother. Art was her less important form of expression; the romances she wrote mattered to her far more.

They had attended the South Kensington Art Schools together, but whereas Uncle Jack had managed to get accepted into the Royal Academy Schools, Aunt Sarah had failed. She did not seem to have resented this, for she worshiped her brother, and spoke with awe of the four foot high stump drawing of the Venus of Milo which had opened the sacred portals to him and which, framed in gold, hung above his bed in his Bloomsbury flat, looking cold and dismal in the grey light of winter. So greatly did she worship him that she felt bewildered and hurt because I did not appreciate his work.

"You young moderns have lost all subtlety," she told me one day, as I showed her my most recent sketches. "Now when we were art students—Jack and I—we never used such harsh colors or sharp contours. We were taught always to bring a gentle tone of brown into all our pictures, for harmony. And we knew the beauty of dim outlines."

This contempt Aunt Sarah and Uncle Jack felt for my painting almost reconciled my mother to it, even though she had no real use for an artist who wanted to paint anything other than beautiful women or romantic situations.

"If I had seen you draw or paint even one pretty face, I'd think there was some hope for you," she sighed as she looked at a complicated problem picture I had just finished, called 'The Call of the Blood,' in which a handsome young priest prayed before a crucifix, with the wraith of a beautiful woman around his shoulders.

Uncle Jack was visiting us just then, and my mother turned to him for support.

"And what do you think, Jack?" she asked in her most alluring voice. "Do you suppose there's really any hope for Clare as an artist?"

But Uncle Jack was completely bewitched by my mother's charm. In addition, he resented my indifference to his own work. Now was his chance. He did not miss it.

"If anybody could have made Clare into an artist, it was I," he boasted. "But I must admit that I've failed."

I smiled as I heard him answering her question, for I was recollecting an amusing struggle between them.

The incident started from a potted pink oleander. It happened just before the First World War, when we left London and moved to a pretentious house near Lowestoft, called Heather Cliff. At the bottom of the garden was a big greenhouse, and within this greenhouse, when we bought the place, stood a large oleander. There were very few oleanders in England. The plant, in fact, was so rare that scarcely anyone had heard of it.

"But in Italy, where I have lived so much, there were *real* oleanders," Uncle Jack loved to boast. "And when I say real oleanders I do not mean potted ones, Fiorita Mia. I mean great bushes of them, growing out of doors in the sunshine of Florence or Fiesole. Now if only you had been to Italy you'd see that this solitary oleander you're so absurdly proud of is a mere straggling, puny plant."

This made my mother furious. She resented it when our uncle started to boast about Italy.

"Let me tell you, Jack," she answered him, "it isn't the actual object that has beauty. It's whether the eye of the person who looks at it is really worthy. Now all those oleanders in Florence and Fiesole cannot possibly mean a quarter as much to someone like you as this one 'straggling, puny plant,' as you call it, does to me. To you oleanders are only pink flowers, but I am able to surround them with glamour and a dream."

My mother had read somewhere of a lover who, disappointed in his passion, had sought escape in death through breathing deeply of the fatal perfume of the oleander. The story placed a halo of glamour around our potted plant. We waited in trembling suspense for the first flower to appear, feeling that here, in this pink blossom, lay the power of exotic death.

But Uncle Jack was far more deeply involved in the blooming of our oleander. He was in love with his Fiorita Mia. My mother, in her usual manner, was anxious to put this love to the test. Besides, she was annoyed with his boasting about Italy. Now, here, was her chance.

"Jack," she said one day in the greenhouse when he was staying with us at Heather Cliff, "Jack, if you truly love me you can prove it by painting me a picture. You can paint me a picture of a lover drinking deep of the perfume of the oleander blossom, while the spirit of his beloved hovers in the air above and around him."

I was busy at the far end of the greenhouse with some young tomato plants, but I could feel the consternation in my uncle's voice.

"It is an almost impossible thing to do, Bien Aimée," he said, using his latest pet name for my mother.

"Oh, no," she answered him airily, "not at all. Here in front of your eyes is the oleander for you to do your study from, in case you've forgotten the shape of the oleanders you knew in Italy. And all the rest, of course, is in your imagination. Love, you know, fires the imagination. The picture should be quite easy."

I delighted in my uncle's discomfort because of my aesthetic grudges against him. Mischievously I waited for the morning when he would bring out his sketchbook and paints. I knew that the thing he lacked most was any form of visual imagination. I also knew that my mother was going to be very exacting.

As the pink blossoms of the potted oleander burst more fully into flower, I developed an interest in the tomato plants in the greenhouse. My uncle arrived each morning with his sketch book, and did not notice me crouching low at the far end. But the light was not right for him, or the blossoms were not yet far enough out, or something else must have been wrong; for pretty soon I heard him bang down the lid of his paint box and swear out loud. Each evening my mother questioned him about this picture, and each evening he procrastinated. It was great fun for me.

The picture was never finished. Knowing what was at stake, Uncle Jack did achieve some studies of the oleander, and on his return to London he actually drew a model in the pose of the phantom lover. But the small oil sketch of the picture seemed to my mother so lacking in imagination that forthwith she turned her attention from my uncle to a fat bank manager who had appeared on her horizon.

"The Leightons are so mediocre in their art," she said. "There's nothing to choose between them, whether it is Jack or Sarah."

And she smiled at the bank manager in her most beguiling manner.

"Just fancy trying to paint a passionate picture like this from such an utterly commonplace model, and against the background of Jack's dingy Bloomsbury flat," she went on. "Of course, it isn't the actual setting of the background that matters—though I must say that whatever the Leightons touch turns fusty. I believe they'd make Buckingham Palace look like a West Kensington boarding-house, and I know for a certainty that Jack took Tavistock Square, Bloomsbury, with him when he went to Sicily. They have the knack of impoverishing everything that comes their way. It's almost a form of genius. But heaven protect me from their muted tones, as they call them. If I were to see one bright color in Jack's flat I think I'd faint. Why, I even have to be careful what dress I have on when I visit him, for fear he'll have a heart attack. There's that pink silk coatee I love so much—the beautiful salmon pink one you're so fond of, that I wear with the black satin skirt and salmon pink ribbons in my hair; I can feel his eyes turning from it in pain, as though I wore something almost vulgar. And I suppose it isn't surprising, when you remember that all his curtains and his rugs look like a bowl of porridge. Now *you*, Silenus . . ."

She turned with tenderness toward the fat, red-faced bank manager with the pendulous double chin. And then a look of worry came over her, as she realized that she had let Roland's nickname for him slip out unawares.

Had he noticed it? And, if he had, would he know what it meant? She looked at him keenly, to discover. But a puzzled frown had come upon the fat, red face, as though he wished to understand what it was his beloved was calling him.

She rushed to the rescue. She knew it was not too late.

"That is my name for you," she cooed to him. "Have you forgotten who Silenus was? Well, you're a very, very busy man, and you haven't time to go reading up all the books on ancient days. So I'll tell you myself, which is much better. Silenus was one of the most important of the Greek gods. And the Greek gods, you know, were always supposed to be men who were more beautiful than anyone who had ever existed. Think for a moment of the beautiful Greek statues you've seen. Or perhaps you haven't seen any of them? One day I'll take you to the British Museum with me, and I'll show you the Elgin marbles, and then you'll realise it's a compliment that I call you Silenus. . . . They had always the most perfect male bodies . . ."

She had saved herself. "Silenus" would never know the ignominy of the nickname. He had not heard of the god of tippling. He burst into an enormous crimson grin, and his great bulging stomach seemed to tremble like an excited jelly.

"Darling," he said as he leaned forward to pat my mother's cheek. "Darling. Didn't I always say you were the most wonderful, wonderful, wonderful woman? Now my wife, you know, she hasn't any idea of the learning she lacks. If you were to ask her about a Greek god, she'd change the subject, and talk about the cook having just given notice, or something unimportant like that. Do you know, it seems to me that I've never been fully alive until I met you."

It didn't really matter much to my mother just now that Uncle Jack should have been found so inadequate in the painting of this passionate oleander picture.

"For the first time in a very long while," she said, as she waited one afternoon for the bank manager's arrival, "I'm being adored by a man with the protective instinct of the complete bourgeois. I can see now how uncomfortable it is to be involved with an intellectual. This is something to enjoy, for I can let myself go with 'Silenus' and don't need to argue, or use my brains. Above all, I don't have to exhaust my soul the whole time battling against the mental sterility of the Leightons. If Jack had any insight into me, he would know his days are over."

Uncle Jack knew only too well. He took it with bitterness, and retired to Swallowfield and the friendly company of Aunt Sarah, where the two of them would spend long hours at a stretch—my uncle reading aloud in Spanish and my aunt working at her endless embroidery in muted-colored silks upon neutral-tinted "Ruskin" homespun flannels—in resigned withdrawal from the world.

But Uncle Jack could not really disentangle himself from my mother. He needed to feed upon her vitality, and pretty soon he gave Aunt Sarah some reason for leaving Swallowfield, and appeared once more within my mother's aura. Aunt Sarah, who was wise, never questioned her brother, and, though she loved him deeply and dreaded his departure, she told him that of course she knew he must attend this art meeting, or that private view, or rehearse some puppet show he was organising. And then she filled his glass with Falerno, or Lachryma Christi, or, if she were out of stock of these Italian wines with their associational glow, with Australian Burgundy decanted into an antique Florentine wine bottle.

But before bidding him good-bye she gathered a bunch of the choicest roses in her garden. She grew these especially for him, and devoted a large part of her days to producing the most rare specimens for him. Each time he returned to London he took them back to his Bloomsbury flat, and laid them in the shallow black bowl my mother had given him. Whenever my mother visited him he presented her dramatically with the most perfect of them all. She took malicious delight in knowing that they had been grown by Aunt Sarah. I always hoped that never, by any cruel satire of circumstance, would my aunt discover the fate of some of her loveliest roses.

My mother rejoiced in torturing Uncle Jack. She may have done this as a means of getting her own back upon the Leighton family, for undoubtedly he was the most vulnerable. My father was so happily enslaved that he would have been miserable without her domination. But Uncle Jack still fought her, though he loved her so disturbingly, Love, to my mother, meant complete submission. Her adorers must think as she thought, and live as she demanded. It exasperated her to find that she could not change Uncle Jack's views on life.

"If I had been told that I would allow a man to love me who was a Liberal—even, perhaps, almost a Socialist—I would never have believed it," she said, after a wild quarrel with my uncle during the First World War. "Jack's opinions stamped him as being no gentleman. Look at the way he storms and rages at me for being what he calls a reactionary. Why I put up with it, I don't know. If he weren't your father's brother I would never allow him to cross our threshold again."

But she was fascinated by his intellectual independence. Never before had a man resisted her.

"He's utterly impossible," she sobbed. "What's more, he's wearing me out with this pacifism of his. Just think of it—I, a hard-working writer, have had to spend an entire morning arguing with him about the stories of German atrocities. It's the most absurd waste of my time. Brother-in-law or no brother-in-law, he'll have to go."

The worst times of all were when, during the war, he was staying with us at Lowestoft. There was then little escape for either of them. He and my mother strode up and down the morning room, like caged animals, while she tore Ramsay MacDonald to pieces and Uncle Jack defended him. Finally they both burst out weeping, and Uncle Jack ran from the room in a passionate rage, nearly knocking the housemaid down in his tear-blinded hurry, and locked himself in his bedroom until lunchtime. My mother recovered more quickly, and summoning Walmy, she continued dictating her overdue instalment. When my uncle reappeared, he was filled with remorse at his anger with "Bien Aimée," and for several days all would be calm.

There was one thing about Uncle Jack that entirely pleased my mother. He enjoyed reading to her.

"Not that I hold with all the books he gets through by himself," she would say. "He's somewhat smeared with the same highbrow intellectual anemia as Sarah. But then, that comes of his being a complete dilletante. While I'm slaving away all my life, at real work, he is able to live on his dead wife's money and spend his days in a brown velvet smoking jacket trimmed with frogs, and sip expensive pallid China tea while he cuts the pages of the latest novel from Mudie's Library with a silver paper knife."

But in the matter of French books, their tastes were alike. So, when he came to see us, Uncle Jack always brought with him a pile of plays and some pale yellow paper covered French novels. And then, from the nursery, we would hear his voice droning away in French over the hours of the evening, as he read to his Fiorita.

"I don't really think very highly of Jack's French accent," she would qualify. "It's entirely lacking in subtlety and style. But then, one can't have everything in this life. And it means a great deal to have someone read these French plays and novels that are too improper for Clare to be allowed to read to me."

Unfortunately for my mother, Uncle Jack wished to show his love for her in music. Here most decidedly their tastes differed.

Uncle Jack played the pianola. He did not know how to play the piano, but he had a way of making it seem a far more exacting work of art to play a pianola. When he went to Mudie's Library to change his books, he took with him a small black portmanteau that looked exactly like the kind of bag in which we had been told that doctors brought newborn babies. This was for his music rolls, which he also changed at Mudie's.

Each day he sat for hours at the grand piano in his Bloomsbury flat, playing these rolls. Each day, too, his drawing room ceiling shook as the pupils of the School of Dramatic Dancing in the flat above practised their steps. But Uncle Jack did not seem to notice this disturbance. He pedaled away at the piano, playing the "Moonlight Sonata" or the "Waldstein," apparently unaware that a rival piano filled the pauses of his own playing.

My mother, though, would giggle about it with the gusto of a schoolgirl.

When she honored him with a visit he put away the Beethoven music rolls and produced Chopin. He was very proud of her visits and conducted her with elaborate ceremony to the big sofa in the drawing room, from where she could watch him play.

He intended to be seen in action, as well as heard. We always supposed it was for this purpose that he had arranged a mirror on the wall, by the side of the piano. If he so chose, he could even watch himself perform when he was alone.

As he played Chopin nocturnes, he flung his head back with a gesture of passion. In the mirror a second Uncle Jack could be seen, making an identical gesture. Forward and back, mournfully shaking his long hair, or bending low over the music roll, he went through the movements of painful emotion, till my mother from her seat of honor on the sofa could restrain herself no longer.

"If you could only see yourself as you go through all these antics, Jack," she laughed, "you'd be every bit as much amused as I am. One of you would be enough to give me hysterics; but when it comes to *two* . . . !"

Uncle Jack never forgave her for these irreverences.

"Bien Aimée," he reproached her. "Have you *no* idea of the respect due to good music?"

"Good music—yes," she answered. "But you can't call what comes out of a pianola *music*. It's only one step removed from a barrel organ in the street—not but what I don't even prefer listening to a barrel organ, when it's playing Italian opera."

For some time after one of these outbursts Uncle Jack abstained from playing to my mother. But after a while he would forget his annoyance with her and produce the Chopin nocturnes.

However well he might behave, though, my mother never considered him a gentleman. She even felt she had to pick and choose where she was seen with him, and when invitations came for some especially snobbish affair at Lowestoft, such as a Ladies' Night at the Yacht Club, or a party on board a visiting battleship, she was always careful never to be accompanied by him.

"Why has he never learnt how to dress?" she would say to us in vexation. "That flowing Liberty necktie completely damns him. And his wide black hat is enough in itself to keep him out from any decent club. But what chiefly worries me is his hair. It is far too long and sweeping for a gentleman, and yet, if I have to be fair to him, I really don't see how he can manage to wear it any shorter, for he is beginning to get bald, and needs his hair long so that it can cover his bald patches. And, too, I have to admit that I'd rather his hair were absent and black than present and grey."

But then, just as she was beginning to get thoroughly upset about Uncle Jack's appearance, she would console herself by remembering that he had never grown a beard. My mother loathed beards. I used to wonder how she managed to reconcile this loathing with her reverent love for King Edward the Seventh. But perhaps there was a different rule for kings.

"There's no possibility of romance with a man who wears a beard," she always said. "Even a young Adonis would be changed into an Old Testament prophet if you were to stick a beard on him. And who, I ask you, could fall in love with an Old Testament prophet? The only admirer I've ever had with a beard was George Meredith, and this tempered my admiration for him to such an extent that, famous though he was, I let the friendship slide."

I never told my mother how, during one of those times when Uncle Jack had retired to Swallowfield in rage and disgrace, he and Aunt Sarah debated as to whether it might not be an interesting

experiment for him to grow a beard. Aunt Sarah was unaware of
the self-destructive revenge Uncle Jack planned. She merely thought
it might make her brother look even more distinguished and
romantic. He went without shaving for several days, and the beard
was well on the way when an especially tender letter arrived for
him from "Bien Aimée." Aunt Sarah was busy in the kitchen, over
the primitive oil cooking stove, making a preserve from the quinces
in her garden called "membrillo." Uncle Jack had procured the
recipe from a peasant woman on his recent visit to Spain, and
wanted to share the delight of this confection with his sister. But
him mind just now was occupied with other interests. He rushed
over to the kitchen sink and filled a pan with water. He sought a
place for the pan on the top of the oil stove; but there was no room.
He champed and raged, and my aunt turned to him in amazement.

"Why, Jack," she said. "What is the matter? Here, come and
taste this membrillo. Does it remind you of Spain?"

But all my uncle wanted was space upon the cooking stove to
heat some water for shaving.

He did not grow his beard.

10. *As the Dear Canon Said—*

Walmy arrived upon the scene several years before I was born.

"Miss Annie M. C. Walmisley, please," she always insisted when she was asked her name.

But we never found out what the "M. C." stood for. It was unusual in England to have more than one given name, and I think she must have felt that these extra initials added to her importance.

She needed this reinforcement, for she stood in a strange position in the Leighton household. Although she was employed by my mother, she was not of the servant class.

"Walmy is a lady," my mother quite willingly admitted. "But she is that awkward thing called a 'lady in improverished circumstances,' and you never know how to treat such people."

Her brother, "Captain Will," was a retired officer in the regular Army, which was, after all, exactly what my mother's own father had been. But in spite of this social equality, Walmy was never supposed to be present when my mother's friends appeared. My mother's adorers hated her, for they thought she spied on them. Whether she did or not, I don't know, but certainly she must have disapproved of them, for she was a devout churchwoman and would not have condoned my mother's views on romance.

She was a regular attendant at St. Mary Abbot's in South Kensington, where she rented her own pew and was even on friendly terms with "the dear Canon." This church was one of the most fashionable in London. To belong to it made you socially secure. But to be on the visiting list of the Canon stamped you as a lady. Walmy's conversation was punctuated with "as the dear Canon said to me only yesterday." Beyond all doubt, she was of the elect.

She was amazingly ugly.

"Sometimes I find myself wondering whether it is bad for me to spend so much of my life looking at such ugliness," my mother remarked. "But when all's said and done, I am glad of it, for I can leave Walmy alone with your father and know that nothing improper will take place. Men are so made that if they see a great deal of any woman who is even ordinarily good looking they'll be kissing her behind the door before many weeks have passed. But no man could possibly want to kiss Walmy."

My mother's admirers liked to make fun of Walmy, but my mother had an affection for her secretary which brought her staunchly to her defense. She would point out that Walmy's eyes were some of the most beautiful she had ever seen. They were a deep, rich brown, and were "put in with a smutty finger," as my mother described them.

"If your small pale blue eyes were only half as beautiful as Walmy's," I once heard her say to Mr. Bowles, "and if they had some of the moving depths of hers, I might even think it worth while to risk being caught in a fire with you, and come and see you in your office all those five flights up, as you are always begging me to do."

But the poor woman had characteristically English teeth. They

were conspicuous chiefly by their absence. Two great tusks stood
out prominently in the front of her mouth, and fascinated us. We
watched her at mealtime and wondered how she managed to chew
her food. Her greying hair was drawn back tight from her face, and
wound in a bun behind. Her extreme shortness was accentuated by
a slight hump upon her back, doubtless due to countless years of
bending over a work table. She wore severe striped shirt blouses,
with collars and neckties, but she insisted always upon pronouncing
these very masculine affairs "blouses," in a French manner, as
though they were the most seductive confections of ribbons and
lace. For she had stayed in Paris a great deal with my mother, and
was anxious that no one should forget it.

These visits to Paris took place about once a year.

"It seems to me, Marie, that you're beginning to be just a bit
stale in your work," Lord Northcliffe might one day be heard telling
my mother. "Your last instalment of *Sealed Lips* isn't as exciting
as most. This won't do, you know. I rely on your serials for keeping
up the circulation of the *Daily Mail*. You need a change. I'm going
to send you to Paris again, to the Hotel Meurice, for six weeks."

And so my mother went to Paris, taking Walmy with her.
Neither of them ever left the hotel. They worked through the days
in exactly the same way in which they worked in St. John's Wood.
The journey might almost have seemed unnecessary.

"But a change of atmosphere doesn't depend upon going out
into the streets sightseeing," my mother declared. "I may have to
stay in my room, dictating to Miss Walmisley all the day long in my
dressing gown instead of walking along the rue de Rivoli or the
Champs Elysées; but all the same, I am getting to know the spirit
of Paris. And the change is doing me good. My mind is working
better already."

Walmy never admitted to any disappointment at being kept
indoors. It was enough for her that she could boast of having stayed
at such a fashionable hotel. And so she followed my mother around

as they emerged from their rooms for the evening meal, looking like an endearing pug dog on a leash.

"I have a sneaking suspicion that Marie uses Miss Walmisley merely as a foil for her own beauty," the peeved wife of one of my mother's adorers was heard once to remark.

But in this she was wrong. My mother relied upon Walmy for everything, and could not possibly have managed without her.

After these visits to Paris, Walmy returned with all the Parisian affectations she could muster, and French phrases strayed into her speech. "Oh, la, la," she said, and "il me semble," and instead of kissing us good morning in the usual English way, she embraced us on both cheeks as though she were a Frenchwoman, and exuberantly said, "Bon jour." Roland told us he had even heard her swear softly to herself in French; but remembering St. Mary Abbot's, I can scarcely believe it. It was not long, however, before her Bayswater "self-contained," semi-basement flat and the world of "the dear Canon" in South Kensington reasserted themselves, and "oh, la, la" became the familiar "lo-ar," with which she prefaced most of her conversations. We were glad. She was our own Walmy again.

We loved her dearly. She was the only grownup of whom we were not afraid. She was a bridge between us and our parents, but she had none of their frightening power to hush us when we were being noisily happy. With Walmy we might play and laugh and sing with no feeling that punishment awaited us. Sometimes she was made to pay for this boisterous behavior in the nursery; she did not tell us so herself, but we would see her snivel and wipe the tears from her eyes, and for a few days we would have no visit from her, and we were very sad.

Although she was enslaved by Mother, she worshiped her and did everything in her power to copy her mannerisms. She even tried to develop my mother's fantastic handwriting, and decided that she could not see to read without holding up to her eye an enormous magnifying glass, exactly as my mother always did. In her slapdash, sloppy way she "ran" the Leightons. She was housekeeper as well as secretary, and she let the bills mount in an alarming manner.

"Lo-ar, Mrs. Leighton," she would say from time to time, "that grocer's bill seems every bit as high as it was last month. I can't think why it is, when I really do try to keep it down."

But my mother didn't worry. Bills weren't of much importance. They could always wait to be paid. Walmy was, in fact, entirely suited to our way of living, and, loving us so deeply, she never realized how completely different we were from the family of the "dear Canon."

She was our timepiece in life. Each morning the front door bell rang at five minutes to ten, and rain, fog, snow or thunder, influenza or bronchitis, nothing prevented her arrival. In the thirteen years that I knew her to be coming to the house, I don't think she missed one day of work. She always gripped an umbrella in her right hand, whatever the weather, and as she walked she jerked this arm with the umbrella backwards and forwards, like the piston of an engine. When she looked upwards to us at the nursery window she waved the umbrella vigorously in the air.

It would be interesting to know how many thousands upon thousands of words Walmy had written by hand during those years. There was a long time when my mother had no typewriter, and everything was put on paper with a pen. It must have been exhausting work, for Walmy had never learnt shorthand. Once my mother had started, she went ruthlessly on with her dictating over the hours, as she flung herself more and more into the destinies of her characters. And poor Walmy covered the sheets of manuscript paper with her handwriting which, though scribbled at a great pace, yet had to be legible enough for the printers to decipher.

But one day my mother succumbed to progress. She bought a typewriter.

"Lo-ar, Mrs. Leighton," sobbed Walmy as she looked at its complicated mechanism. "The good Lord gave us hands to write with. He didn't mean us to use contraptions like this. I'll never be able to learn it. I know I won't."

Her tears fell upon the terrifying machine. She did not belong to the age of mechanization.

But my mother was insistent.

"Nonsense, Miss Walmisley," she said. "You've got to learn. Why, if I go on sending in my manuscripts written by hand it'll look as though I'm not a success. All the best people these days are getting typewriters."

And so over many weeks Walmy struggled with the typewriter. She stayed to the midday dinner, in order that she might learn to type without interrupting my mother's work. Tears continued to fall, until it was a wonder that the machine did not get rusty.

"If Walmy can't change with the times," my mother told my father, "I'll have to force myself to be really hardhearted, and send her away."

Walmy was finding life very difficult.

Miss Annie M. C. Walmisley had a selfish sister who insisted upon being looked after by her. And so, when Walmy had finished working for my mother and walked more than two miles home to her Bayswater flat, she had to do all her housework and marketing before walking back the same two miles to our house for the evening's dictating.

She adored this sister Mary, and thought her the most beautiful and intellectual of women. Actually Mary looked like one of Cinderella's ugly sisters.

"It's perfectly obvious that Mary Walmisley drinks too much coffee," my mother would remark. "Look at her dry brown skin. It's like an old piece of leather. That's why nothing on earth will make me drink a cup of coffee—no, not even a demitasse after dinner. It's almost as though the coffee leaks through the stomach into the blood stream."

My family detested this selfish sister and saw as little of her as possible. But Walmy was so proud of her that on the occasion of one of our garden parties at Vallombrosa she begged to have her invited.

"It will give a cosmopolitan touch to the gathering," Walmy explained.

It had so happened that many years earlier Miss Mary Walmisley accompanied a family to China for a few weeks, as governess to their daughter. She never forgot this. It permeated her life and gave her a sense of superiority over her sister.

"What's Paris, I ask you?" she boasted to Walmy. "I tell you, Annie, it's all very well for you always to be bragging about staying in Paris at the Hotel Meurice, but when it comes to China, Paris seems like a suburb of London."

And so, in the middle of the garden party, as the guests were grouped around watching the arrivals, the imported butler announced in a loud voice that everyone could hear: "Miss Mary Walmisley, from China." Everybody turned to look, as the visitor from the Far East appeared, and our little Walmy trotted in proudly behind her, unannounced.

This was one of the peak moments in Walmy's life.

Walmy gave us such a glowing account of her sister's brain that one year, during the summer, when Mary was in Lowestoft for a holiday, our mother was persuaded to use her as a tutor for Roland. This worked for a short time, but pretty soon Roland began to find that he knew about as much as she could teach him. For several days Walmy went about weeping, while possible successors arrived at the house to be interviewed. And when my mother finally decided upon the bearded old man called Mr. Strickland, Walmy did everything she could to turn us against him.

The bespectacled old creature arrived each morning on the tricycle that he persisted in riding, his flowing beard and his square black hat and frock coat making him look exactly like a caricature of a professional magician. Unfortunately for poor Walmy, he and

Mary met one day, when she was fetching a book she had left behind by mistake. As luck would have it, instead of hating her rival this leather-skinned woman took a violent fancy to him. It was mutual, and it was based upon a common love for the Swiss Alps.

"What did I tell you?" laughed our mother, who was highly amused about the whole affair. "It's always the governess and tutor class that goes to Switzerland and loves mountains. This just shows you how right I am in condemning George for spending his holidays there. Nobody with an iota of romance in his blood could endure it. Nothing will ever take me one step inside that country."

We would see these two romantic creatures together sometimes along the Front, the old professor standing against his tricycle as he gesticulated into the sky, and "Miss Mary" looking from him to the sky and from the sky back, enraptured, to him. We supposed they were both seeing imaginary mountain peaks. But I think Walmy wasn't so sure. Anyhow, she went about that summer in a state of gloom, and my mother was heard to say to my father that if Miss Walmisley's nerves didn't get less jumpy she'd have to get rid of her. I don't know how far this romance would have gone if Mr. Strickland hadn't suddenly died of a stroke. The emotional excitement had proved more than his age could stand. Once more Walmy had her sister to herself.

But back in St. John's Wood Walmy continued to have her little struggles. The typewriter was not the only product of this mechanized age which bothered her. My mother thought it was due to her to have a telephone.

"All the best people are installing telephones. And I shall make you answer it," my mother told Walmy. "Not only will that save me trouble, but it will make me look more dignified."

As my mother had ordered her adorers never to disturb her during the working hours of the morning, she could be certain that when the bell rang before midday it would not be any of them.

For they dared not disobey her. No servant was allowed to touch the sacred instrument, and I was deputed to answer it when the family was out. Both Walmy and I were scared out of our wits at having to lift the receiver. We never rationalized this terror, but I imagine we feared an electric shock.

None of us were conditioned to electricity. My mother considered it dangerous, and refused to have anything to do with it.

"But it's all nonsense to confuse the telephone with electricity," she explained. "The telephone is something quite apart. It is when it comes to electric light that I put my foot down. It's all very well to point out that people in the neighborhood already use it, but I am deeply suspicious of it. I wouldn't so much mind having it in a new house—down at Lowestoft, you will remember, we are quite up-to-date in our lighting system—but I am afraid of a short circuit in this old St. John's Wood house. It might set the place on fire."

And so the study was lit by oil lamps right through the years of my childhood, because my mother didn't trust gas, either. There might be an unnoticed leakage, which could suffocate us. For some reason I never discovered, she made a distinction that certain rooms and not others were permitted gas light. The dining room and the day nursery had incandescent gas lamps, which gave a depressing pale cold light and made a mournful singing sound when the air got into the pipes; but we never went to bed by anything but candlelight, and the drawing room—on the rare occasions when it was used—was lit by candles.

But the exciting moment came when my mother decided to be thoroughly progressive. We installed a gas fire in the front drawing room. Not even Walmy was allowed to touch this. Only my mother might light it. It was lit once a week, on Saturday afternoons.

Saturday afternoon was my mother's At Home Day. This was a serious ritual. A line of carriages and, later on over the years, private cars, stood before the garden wall. We would have considered the family was "slipping" if the line had stopped before it turned the corner of Abbey Road and continued up Marlborough Road.

"The last carriage is as far as the house with the green gate. It has never reached past the doctor's garden before this," Evelyn and I told each other with pride, as we returned home from our walk on an especially successful At Home Day.

But though we enjoyed counting the carriages, we were frightened of these At Home Days because we had to be prepared, dressed in our best party clothes, in case some female visitor might "want to see the children." This was never encouraged by our mother, as she considered it bad for us; but sometimes it was unavoidable.

"If I refuse to let you come down," she told us, "the rumor will run around that you've got skin disease or a harelip or something."

When we were called to the drawing room, we were made to shake hands and be polite. We dreaded this, because we always felt we might say the wrong things, and be punished for it next day. Then, too, we had been told to keep our eyes from roving to the silver cake stand with the little round buttered buns and the cocoanut cakes and jumbles. We had bought all these things that same morning, on our walk with Nanny, and now we were greedy for them.

We liked the smell of kid gloves and sable muffs, ostrich feather boas, Parma violets and waxed moustaches, and listened for the particular sound of kid gloves being eased on at the moment of departure. These gloves seemed always too narrow across the palms, so that we were afraid of shaking hands with the ladies, in case we should split the precious kid. But too often the visitors wanted to pat us, which we hated. We were glad when each At Home Day was over. So too, was our mother.

"There's nothing really to be gained by them," she said. "You can't ever get to know anyone when you're not alone with them.

me of unexpected visitors for the remaining six days of the week."

The one real excitement for us on At Home Day was this new gas fire. Immediately after the midday dinner on Saturday, our mother braced herself for the adventure. Newspapers were torn in long strips and twisted into tapers with which to apply the light. For it was such a dangerous undertaking that you should be as far removed from it as possible. My mother wrapped a cloth around her head, lest her straw-colored hair get smoky, and cautiously turned the jet of the stove, having carefully seen that, whatever the weather outside, the front drawing room window should be opened a little at the top so that, should there be an unnoticed escape of gas, we would not be suffocated to death before we knew what had happened. Each time my mother applied the lighted newspaper there was a loud explosion, and the fire seemed to have backfired. We waited in suspense for the moment when the flame at last should burn blue instead of a flickering yellow; for that meant it was properly lit. But with each successive try the fumes smelt stronger, until the whole of the front drawing room seemed strangely unattractive as the setting for a fashionable At Home.

"Really, Robert," my mother said in exasperation, as she opened the windows wider to let out the fumes, "I don't see what is to be gained by having this gas affair. I have to let all the damp air in so that we shan't be suffocated. If it weren't that the best people are installing gas fires I'd send it back and go on with ordinary coal. Besides, I'm perfectly certain these fires dry the skin and give you wrinkles."

And so, each Saturday, Walmy had to place bowls of water in front of the gas fire and on top of any flat surface she could find in the drawing room, in order that the air might be kept moist. My mother was not going to let progress damage her complexion.

But down on the East Coast there was neither a telephone nor a gas fire. Life was far simpler.

It was during the summer half of the year, when Walmy lived in the house with us at Lowestoft, that we could really enjoy her. She slept in a room with a skylight, on the half landing, and within this room with its violent yellow distempered walls, she kept her Skye terrier Cona. Cona had been the runt of one of Tita's litters, and she never seemed to catch up with her brothers and sisters. But if she were a puny creature, she yet possessed the virtue of patience. She waited in this bedroom through the long mornings when my mother was dictating to Walmy, and never once, so far as we heard, did she misbehave herself. The bedroom, it is true, did smell most extraordinarily doggy—but then, that was an odor my family was accustomed to, and even liked. Unfortunately, our dogs seemed imbued with snobbishness, and couldn't stand Cona. They treated her like a presuming poor relation, and fierce dog fights occurred whenever Cona was taken for a walk.

"Run along to the kitchen and get me a bucket of cold water to dash over their heads," my father shouted to me as we hauled the fighting dogs over the garden gate. They hung there, on either side of the wooden gate, held together by the teeth of the one in the jaw of the other, until the shock of the cold water loosened the grip.

My mother then invariably scolded Walmy for letting Cona be seen by Kelpie or Roy, and Walmy would sob into a soaked handkerchief, and go and bind up Cona's wounds.

But these out-of-door fights weren't half as bad as the fights that took place in the house. Walmy opened her bedroom door at midday, to take Cona on to the Front for a few minutes, to "make herself comfortable" before dinner. Kelpie had followed my mother up the stairs, on the way to her bedroom. The two dogs met at Walmy's open door. The fight took place in Walmy's bedroom, where there was no way to separate them.

"Robert, come quickly!" shouted my mother. But he did not hear. In desperation she climbed the steep stairs to his front room—those stairs she hated climbing—and found him calmly looking out to sea through his telescope, while she had supposed him to be busy writing. She never trusted him up there so much alone after she discovered this; it is no wonder he began to dislike Cona. The fight was a terrible affair. Both dogs had to be sewn up, and there was a dark stain of blood all over the matting upon Walmy's bedroom floor.

But we took these fights in our stride, for our lives were spent among so many dogs of both sexes that there was nothing unusual in such complications. Although we were never told the reason for it, we were made to help segregate the sexes at certain times of the year. Of course, having read the *Manual of Medical Jurisprudence* from cover to cover, we knew the bitches were in heat; but we managed to assume a childlike innocence when our father said that on no account were we to take Selina for a walk with Donnie until we had been given permission.

From the incomparable vantage point of the nursery window we watched the love affairs of the Leighton kennels, and saw Nellie the cook rush out to disentangle the deerhound from the amorous clutches of a tiny mongrel that belonged, of all things, to the carpenter who came to mend a loose plank in the cabin at the bottom of the garden. The suitor was not even a gentleman's dog. We hoped that Nellie was too late, for it would be fun to see what sort of puppies could be half deerhound and half tiny yellow mongrel. Unfortunately the cook was just in time.

And so we did not sympathize with Walmy as much as we ought to have done, when these dog fights took their toll of poor little Cona. It was far too frequent an occurrence.

Sunday was the day we saw most of Walmy. My mother left her free then, because she knew her secretary believed in keeping the Sabbath. Every Sunday morning while we were in East Anglia, we sat with her on the pink upholstered window seat in the drawing room after breakfast until we had to get dressed for church in our starched white piqué clothes. She produced one of the books from the twelve volume set of *Wild and Garden Flowers*, and we were made to guess the names of the flowers. Outside the window the sun danced upon rows of white marguerites at the top of the terrace and sparkled on the North Sea. There were no brown sailed fishing boats upon this sea, for it was the Sabbath. There was nobody out upon the Front, because everyone was at home, dressing for church. Through the opened window came the salt smell of the sea, while from the dining room drifted the lingering odor of Sunday morning kippers.

My mother's Scotch adorer had arrived to greet her. At the other end of the house, in the front hall, he was singing "Auld Robin Grey" in a wheezy voice. He sat there in his Highland kilts, with a posy of honeysuckle and heather in one hand. When he had finished his song he would pin these flowers on "Mea's" bosom. Our mother pretended to listen to his singing, but half the time she was planning the next instalment of one of her serials.

While this was happening, our father was in the back garden, tending his rose bushes.

"If Alexander thinks he's the only one to bring her flowers, he's mistaken," he muttered as he cut some of his pink rosebuds. "These will put him in his place."

Out in the kitchen Nellie was preparing the Sunday dinner; there would be the inevitable roast rolled rib of beef, with Yorkshire pudding and roast potatoes and a vegetable, and perhaps a gooseberry pie with custard, among the many sweets.

Everything around us this Sunday morning breathed security and order. In a coaxing voice Walmy said to me: "Lo-ar, Clare, just you think again. You can't have forgotten it. Yes—yes—that's it. That's it. Ciner-aria." There was a rustle of pages as the next colored picture was reached. It was Evelyn's turn to guess the flower's name.

But the flower book was not supposed to occupy too long, for after we had guessed our allowance of flower names Walmy made us look at the pictures in the *Child's Bible*.

"Nobody can say you children have an overdose of religion," she sighed. "You're almost like a pair of little heathens during the winter months when I'm not with you on Sundays. Lo-ar, you know, sometimes it really worries me when I come to think about it —especially when I remember how you are exposed to Nurse's Baptist beliefs. If I'm not to be held responsible before the Lord God when I die, I'll have to do all I can now, in the summer."

And so, as the best way to prepare us for church, Walmy read this *Child's Bible* to us. The wheezy singing of Scotch love songs from the front hall blended into the frightening story of the flood.

Our mother left Walmy a free hand with us where religion was concerned.

"After all, Miss Walmisley can't do the children any harm," she decided. "Fortunately Walmy objects to any High Church antics that might put wrong ideas into their heads, and her religion has the solid lack of fervor of true good breeding. If a woman is a lady she can be trusted in all things."

We were taken to church by Walmy each Sunday morning while we were at Lowestoft. We hated the long hot walk in our starched Sunday clothes, and dreaded passing through the church-yard, among the graves. It scared us, for Walmy often talked about death. She had a literal belief in the Resurrection of the Body, and disapproved of heavy tombstones.

"Lo-ar," she said with a sigh, as she noticed some especially pompous graves, "if they think it's friendly to give that poor dead creature all that heavy weight to lift at the Judgment Day, it's not my idea of kindness. When *I* die I don't want anything on *my* chest. A small stylish headstone will be quite enough. I'll be able to rise out from my grave more quickly and easily that way."

By the time we reached the entrance to the church, Evelyn

and I were almost trembling with fear. We were a pair of frightened creatures, and whenever we were among a number of people, anxiously sought the possibility of an exit. We were not accustomed to crowds. We had never been allowed to play with other children.

"That there Miss Clare and Master Evelyn, all they wants to do is to 'ide be'ind a big bush so that they can't see nobody and nobody can't see them," our old nurse used to say.

And she was perfectly right. No one of the grownups knew what we suffered on summer Sunday mornings in St. Margaret's Church.

Before we started out from the house we compared notes:

"Do you feel 'thundery'?" we would ask each other.

"Thundery" was the word we used to denote the sense of anxiety that came over us. This expression must, I think, have originated from our terror of being caught in a thunderstorm on the long country walks with our nurse. It was accompanied by horrible feelings in our tummies, which made us wonder these Sundays if we wouldn't have to slip out of the church, somewhere to the back of the churchyard among the gravestones, during the sermon.

This terror of an internal upset was shared by our mother.

"It's all very well for people to tell me it's nonsense," she said. "But I know better. After all, my inside is my own, isn't it? And who should know how it behaves if I don't? I tell you for a fact, that if I don't watch every single thing I eat for a full forty-eight hours before I take a journey I'm in for trouble. Above all, I must keep off fruit or vegetables."

In spite of these precautions, though, our mother mistrusted her inside, and about an hour before she was due to start—whether it were a journey to London by train, or merely a visit somewhere in the neighborhood—she dosed herself liberally with Dr. J. Collis Brown's Chlorodyne, and carried a bottle of it in her purse, along with several lumps of sugar upon which to take some more in an emergency.

But there were certain foods she would never eat, though she might be staying safely at home. She feared mushrooms and shellfish.

"It's tempting death even to take one mouthful of them," she said. "They're bound to give you ptomaine poisoning. It isn't for nothing that mushrooms smell of the tomb. I may make an exception in the case of shrimps, because, after all, they're so small, but when it comes to things like lobsters and oysters and crabs, why, if you're fool enough to taste such sewage-eating things you deserve to die."

Walmy always insisted on sitting right up at the front of the church, in the first pew. This was especially terrifying for us, because there would be so much farther to go if suddenly we had to rush away with an upset tummy. Besides, we dreaded being seen by everybody. But Walmy felt that the Walmisley dignity demanded such a position.

"After all," she said, "it would be unseemly for us to sit anywhere else, when you come to remember that our pew at St. Mary Abbot's is right under the dear Canon's very nose."

Nobody else in our family went to church. Roland considered that he was too old to go with "the children," and our father and mother declared they hadn't time.

"But whether or not I choose to go makes no difference," our mother said. "On the whole I thoroughly approve of Walmy taking the children to church. For one thing, it's excellent discipline for them to have to sit still during the sermon. They've had very little of that kind of training compared with what I was subjected to in my own childhood. Papa never forgot he was a commanding officer and he would order me to sit still in a chair for an hour or two on end, without saying one single word, simply as a lesson in self-control. . . . I hope, Miss Walmisley, that you are particularly careful not to let the children fidget when the sermon is long?"

It is not surprising that Evelyn and I never enjoyed going to church. We did not feel close to God.

As the months at Lowestoft passed, and our mother turned out her flood of dictated words, or listened to the adoration of Judge Talbot or the Scotch love songs of Alexander, a pattern was being threaded into the family of which she was but dimly aware. It was chiefly Walmy who threaded this pattern. With her we lived the year's seasonal occasions, which to us, at our age, were of enormous importance.

Each April, soon after our arrival on the East Coast, we trespassed in the Corton Woods for primroses.

"Quietly, Clare. Quietly, I say," Walmy whispered as we crept past the gamekeeper's cottage. "And if you hear a sound just lie down flat on the ground, among the undergrowth, and don't move. Never mind if you do tear your coat in the brambles or on the barbed wire fencing. I'll see to it that Nanny doesn't punish you. Lo-ar, to think that a man could buy up all this beautiful woodland, and keep it so strictly to himself, just by making such a silly thing as mustard."

For the woods were owned by Mr. Colman, of mustard fame.

We returned home with baskets filled with bunches of primroses. And then, to our delight, our mother would wear our primroses in her hair and pin a clump of the flowers in the front of her dress. She did not mind that they had been stolen.

In September we obeyed another ritual, and were driven by Tarbox, in his governess trap, along the lanes near Blundeston and Hopton, to gather ripe blackberries. When this took place the Leighton family feasted upon blackberry and apple pie and stewed blackberries for many days.

On these occasions, like a character in a fairy tale, Walmy always had to be back in her place facing the typewriter at half-past six in the evening; neither coppice nor lane held the power to deflect her from duty.

"Just one more basketful," we would plead. "Please, please let us stay a little longer."

But Walmy's face would grow stern as she asked Tarbox for the exact time.

"None of that wheedling, you two," she always answered. "You know I'll turn into a pumpkin if I'm even half a minute late."

And sometimes she sounded so convincing that we almost believed her.

Occasionally, though, when special friends happened to be visiting us, or staying in the neighborhood, our mother gave Walmy an evening off. To celebrate this she took us by trolley car to the end of the line, past the town of Lowestoft, where the North Sea was eroding the land. We returned by way of one of the piers, and the fish market, and because she was still free, Walmy came to the nursery to eat with us, and there were shrimps for high tea.

Our lives in the nursery were such ordered existences that these treats were tremendously exciting. The excitement was intensified by a sense of danger, for we knew very well that had our mother discovered about these expeditions she would have forbidden them. She disapproved of our going in any public conveyance, expecting us to catch scarlet fever. We kept them secret even from Roland.

Walmy may have made the wheels of life run smoothly for our mother, but our father disapproved of her.

"Her ugliness is a perpetual eyesore," he moaned. "And besides, Chummie, she comes between us. Never do I get a chance of seeing you alone, except when I'm asleep at night. And if that woman could, she'd spy on me even then."

He felt convinced that Walmy was his enemy. And he may have been right, for she had no trust in men, and disapproved of them. There was little doubt that she continually watched my father from hidden corners of the house, to see if he were behaving himself with the servants.

But to us in the nursery Walmy meant escape from the old

nurse. She also meant exuberance and warm hugs, which we never got from our nurse. For this old Gloucestershire Baptist who controlled our days countenanced neither gaiety nor laughter. Already in her seventies, all she demanded of us was that we keep healthy, still and quiet. Our bowels must work regularly; our bodies must be kept warm; and twice a day we must take long walks, slowly, one of us on each side of her. Never must we run or play.

This nurse was a godsend to our mother. She made it possible for her to combine work with having a family. Because the old woman was so strict our mother realized that she could leave us entirely in her care. For she agreed with the nurse that healthy bowels and obedience were the chief things in childhood that mattered.

"Disobedience is a sign of weakness," Mother would tell us from time to time on her hurried visits to the nursery. "The strong character obeys. The weak one has to prove its strength by disobeying. I want to be proud of my children. They must be strong."

Old Nanny Vowles came to the family soon after I was born. She had taken the place of a nurse who had turned out to be a violent Salvationist.

"Not that I really mind what the religious views of my servants are," our mother explained. "But when things came to such a pass that Nurse Newby was covering the walls with texts about being washed in the blood of the Lamb, and spending most of her days doing a regular war dance around the nursery, and banging on a tambourine and shouting that she was 'saved,' it was about time to make a change. Now Nanny Vowles may be a Baptist, but she does keep her religious enthusiasms pretty much to herself."

Actually, though, Nanny obtruded her religion far more than our mother knew.

The Baptists in England were a rigid sect. Our nurse was a devout Baptist and she had a propriety of behavior that exasperated us.

Oddly enough, I remember that one of the main things I resented was her attitude of shame towards the human body.

"One of these days, Miss Clare, when you stands before the Judgment Seat, you'll be sorry as you 'adn't more sense of decency when you was young," she warned me. " 'ere you goes around the nursery in your birthday suit, and for all you knows the dear Lord may be 'aving to 'ide 'is eyes in shame. Now I 'ave much more respect for the Lord Jesus, and when I takes a bath I always sees to it as 'ow I places a big towel over the whole of the top of the bath tub, with nothing but my 'ead and shoulders a' showing, so as not to distress the dear Lord with the sight of my nakedness."

With a similar feeling of chivalry she did her entire dressing and undressing each day beneath a flannelette nightgown. We used to watch her from our beds in the night nursery, but never did we manage to see anything more intimate than her figure when she emerged, in her combinations, her grey flannel petticoat, her stays and a wonderful garment with two inset ovals in the front for her bosoms, that she called her "slip body."

In view of all this, I acted with obtuse boldness when I begged her once to pose for me as the naked Andromeda. This happened while I had my phase of painting mythological pictures.

Finding it impossible to imagine what a female looked like, I had tried to use my own immature figure as the model for this ambitious picture of Andromeda chained to the rock. One evening, as I stood before the mirror in the bathroom, pencil in my hand, trying in vain to take the pose of this naked adult female, Nanny discovered me.

"Oh, so it gets worse and worse," she thundered. "Not content with going around with nothing on, you 'as to 'ave the evil thoughts of making a picture of your nakedness. If you don't see the error of your ways I'll take all your pencils and paints and paper away from you and make you sew hems."

I was so hurt and desperate that nothing mattered to me but my picture.

"Oh, Nanny," I pleaded. "Please—please—won't *you* pose for me—just this once?"

Ignoring the compliment to her seventy year old body, the old nurse forgot her place and gave me a severe whipping. In addition, she went in a fury to my mother and threatened to leave this dirty-minded family. The only way my mother could appease her—for she dared not let her go—was by taking away my paints for an entire month.

Considering her views on the human body, I cannot help wondering if our nurse did not sometimes feel shocked at the way her mistress seemed to have no sense of sin or shame where her own body was concerned. For our mother never noticed it when her clothes failed to cover her, and often parts of her neck and shoulders showed which were never intended to be seen. Not only this, but she had some pictures of voluptuous naked ladies hanging on the walls of her bedroom. These must surely have upset the old woman, but being a well trained servant she never so much as breathed a word or hinted what she felt about the disreputable family.

Each Sunday evening Nanny dressed herself in her best clothes to go to the local Baptist Chapel. Lying in bed in the night nursery, watching, we scarcely recognized her when she was ready. To us she seemed to belong with her uniforms: starched white piqué in the summer, thick grey cloth in the winter, and always the black bonnet with nodding feathers, tied beneath her chin. Her boots creaked as she walked, and her breath was sweet with cinnamon and horehound—for she had a passion for a certain brand of herbal tablets, threepence a tin, that she bought for a nonexistent cough.

As she sailed out of the night nursery door, we were filled with longing to go with her. There was the excitement of the forbidden about the Chapel, as well as tales she told us of the baptisms performed there. But our mother ordered her never to take us into this chapel. Nonconformist chapels belonged to the lower classes, and we were not to be exposed to them.

There was no love lost between Walmy and the old nurse. For one thing, Walmy felt very strongly about religion, and had nothing but contempt for the Baptist Church. You could scarcely be a friend of "the dear Canon" without feeling this. Because she feared the Nonconformist atmosphere was influencing us, she snatched us away from the old Baptist whenever she could. The nurse, on the other hand, had that antagonism towards Walmy which is always felt, my mother said, towards somebody who is "betwixt and between." She never knew whether or not she had to obey her, or where she stood in relation to her. For though Walmy was most certainly a lady, yet she was, also, an employee of our mother—which put her in the servant category. The only thing to do, the old nurse must have decided, was to resent her. And this she most certainly did.

The subtle complications and shades of social difference in the world made life very difficult for us in the nursery.

11. *Education for the Leighton Children*

"The 'finishing school' I went to was a very prim place," my mother delighted in telling me whenever she thought I was demanding too much freedom. "It was so correct that the headmistress sewed flannel petticoats around the waists of the little naked cupids supporting the chandeliers in the school drawing room. The pupils, you see, had to be kept innocent and pure, for they were the daughters of British diplomats, and might one day become the wives of ambassadors. And they were never taught much because it was far more important to give them grace and subtlety than to fill their brains with facts out of textbooks. You can always leave those facts to the lower classes who will never have to govern."

My mother had very definite ideas about education for girls. While the family fortunes were in luck, her own schooling had consisted of short stays at this ultrafashionable establishment in the aristocratic town of Tunbridge Wells. But when the family funds ran low she was removed from it and remained for long periods of time at home, doing whatsoever she pleased, until the next legacy arrived from a deceased relative. Her parents had no interest in her education. Although they liked her to associate with these diplomats' daughters, they sent her to school chiefly in order to keep her out of mischief, in the same way that she had been dispatched to a convent in France, as a small child, to be out of reach of the window cleaner with whom she had fallen in love.

This idea of school as a place of safety for a straying young female persisted in her, so that when, at the age of thirteen, I fell in love with a lawyer friend whose portrait I had been allowed to paint, she threatened to send me away to a boarding school. As weeks passed and I fell more deeply in love, the paint on the canvas became thicker and yet thicker, till it must have been almost an inch in depth. Apparently my mother had noticed my lovesick condition, and was beginning to worry about me, for one day I happened to overhear a conversation between her and my father.

"Robert," she was saying, "if this affair goes on any longer there's nothing to be done but send Clare off to Miss Dothie's as a boarder. This man's intentions are not honest. He's merely playing with her. Besides, he's far too old. And he drinks whiskeys and sodas at teatime, which I strongly disapprove of. I'll give them one week more and then if things haven't changed, I'll send her away."

She was probably remembering her window cleaner.

I don't know how she supposed the situation could have altered in one week. If I had not happened to overhear this talk I would certainly have been yet deeper in love, and the paint on the portrait would have stood out even half an inch thicker. As it was, I told the lawyer what I had heard, and suggested an elopement. But he never came to the house again. I was not sent back to school. And some little time later I recovered from my infatuation.

Actually I would have enjoyed returning to school, for it had nearly broken my heart to be taken away when I was twelve. But my mother informed me that already I had received more schooling than she had, and far more than was necessary.

"School," she said, "takes all the character and charm from a woman. Suppose Juliet had been sent to high school or college, Shakespeare wouldn't even have found her interesting enough to write a play about, and most certainly Romeo could not have loved her with such passion. Besides, if you do not need schooling in order to be able to write books, much less do you need it in order to become an artist. . . . And don't forget, my child, that I had my first novel published when I was only sixteen—*The Lady of Balmerino;* and a three volume novel, at that."

But when I remember the extent of my schooling, I scarcely think my mother could have had even less education than I. The old nurse started me off with the usual "A cat sat on a mat," out of a paper-bound speller, and gave me copybooks to teach me how to write. Then a woolly old lady called Miss Birks appeared on the scene. She was completely ignorant and I cannot imagine how or why she called herself a governess.

"But she was quite good enough for you," my mother told me later on in my life. "It would have been a downright waste to have given you anyone better when you were so young."

I twisted Miss Amelia Birks round my little finger. I never learned the homework she gave me, but I always managed to know one of the subjects better than the others, and when she asked me, in her gentle voice: "And what's your next lesson, dear?" I would leave the one I knew best to that moment when I thought my mother was coming into the dining room.

This schooling took place in the dining room in St. John's Wood, and often we had to wait until the breakfast table had been cleared before we could start. The smell of bacon and toast hung in the air and seemed to rest upon my school books. Every day at about eleven o'clock my mother entered the room to fetch her unvarying refreshment of a glass of Burgundy and two Osborne biscuits—seeming to forget the cold bacon on toast that had been saved from the breakfast table for this occasion.

"Good morning, Miss Birks," she always said in a detached tone of voice. "And is Clare getting on well with her lessons?"

If I were lucky, I was at that moment repeating, without fault or pause, the one lesson I had learnt. Sometimes I miscalculated the moment of my mother's arrival, and was caught; and then Miss Birks, anxious to keep her job, managed to help me out.

These lessons were varied with music lessons in the icy cold back drawing room, and dancing lessons with Evelyn in the same arctic temperature. Miss Birks put on a pair of black satin quilted slippers and padded round like a baby elephant. Her breath always smelt of onions, even in the early morning. She wasn't supposed to play the piano for these dancing lessons, lest it should disturb our mother at her work in the study. And so she steered first one and then the other of us around with her, breathing onions upon our faces, while she wheezed:

> One, two, three-four-five,
> Catching fishes all alive.
> Why did you let them go?
> Because they bit my fingers so.

In this way we managed to learn the steps of the polka. But it was not so easy to learn the set dances that were still the fashion those days, such as the lancers, the quadrille, or Sir Roger de Coverley, because we had to imagine the many partners who weren't there. One day Miss Birks hinted to our mother that she knew several little boys and girls who could come and learn these dances with us. But our mother forbade her to bring to the house these possible spreaders of measles and scarlet fever, and we went on learning the dances alone. We circled round nonexistent people. We held hands with phantoms. We were whirled by imaginary partners. And Miss Birks jigged up and down, with her cheeks growing pinker and pinker, twisting and twirling in her black satin quilted slippers, the feathers in her bonnet tossing, as she hummed the tune for the dance.

All this was warming to the constitution, especially on a damp, cold, winter's day; but it was strangely ironic. For we were never allowed to go to any parties or dances, and so there was little purpose in our learning these elaborate figures. But that, unfortunately, did not strike me just then. I merely knew it was more exciting than sitting in the dining room repeating my lessons.

Miss Birks also taught me music.

When it came to these music lessons, the problem of not disturbing my mother was more complicated. The playing had to be muted, so that it could not be heard beyond the closed doors of the back drawing room. I was accustomed to the way my mother banged the keys when she played, and the timid little tinkle Miss Birks and I produced from the piano seemed all wrong. My mother hated to hear me practising.

"It is a common sound these days," she declared. "It is nearly as common as the sight of washing on a line, for the world has come to such a pass that the lower classes are forgetting their places, and every girl child of every greengrocer or plumber is being taught the piano in order that she may be changed overnight into a lady."

My mother felt especially bitter, because, at Lowestoft, our carpenter had a daughter who was a musical genius. This little Marjorie Palmer was being given piano lessons by the best possible teacher, and the cook and the old nurse, who were friendly with Mrs. Palmer, made the mistake of reporting the child's progress.

"Oh, so they think they're going to make her as well-bred as anyone else, do they?" my mother said later. "It won't be long before they find the error of their ways. For as soon as all these common people take to teaching their children the piano they'll discover that the ladies and gentlemen of the world have ceased to teach *their* children. And then it will be a sign of underbreeding to be able to play."

There was not much enthusiasm over my music lessons.

Auntie Pollie, who specialized in the banjo, ventured to suggest one day that perhaps it might be interesting if I were to be taught the zither. It was a more uncommon instrument, she said. She even gave me a small one for a Christmas present; but I never knew how to play it. My mother had other ideas. She thought the harp might be even better.

"But," she said, "it will be wiser to wait and see how Clare's arms develop. The one advantage of the harp is that it shows off the beauty of a woman's arms as nothing else does. Men love to see a woman playing the harp. It gives her allure."

Meanwhile I continued learning the piano.

But the sounds of my playing could not possibly have penetrated the closed drawing room door to the world of the study. My fingers were always so numb with the cold that I wouldn't have had the strength to do more than brush the keys like a butterfly's wing. For there was never any heating in the back drawing room. When she came to us first Miss Birks bravely ignored this, but soon she decided to wear her outdoor coat, and sometimes even her gloves, as she sat at the piano by my side. This damp of a London winter cannot be described. It has to be experienced, to be fully understood. A film of near-freezing moisture seemed to hang over everything. We always had some windows of the house open the whole year long, whatever the temperature might be. The only time all the windows were closed was during one of the London pea soup fogs. My mother said that foggy air gave one pleurisy.

Although Walmy always found her way to Vallombrosa in the thickest of these fogs, Miss Birks was less courageous, and sometimes she failed to appear. But even when she had managed to reach the house in the fog there would be no music lesson, for the only means of illumination in the back drawing room was a few candles, by the light of which it was difficult to see the keys. I knew this for a fact because my mother sometimes took it into her head to play the piano at midnight, by the light of one remote candle, and she struck many wrong notes. Or so it seemed to me, listening enraptured, in a half-asleep stupor, in the night nursery above.

My mother's playing was extraordinary. In my childhood I thought it was the most wonderful thing this side of the music of the spheres—which I had read about, and would stay awake night after night trying to hear. She banged the keys till the piano shook, and Tita would sit by the drawing room door and give out a continuous howl. I never knew if the dog was approving or disapproving, but we were so accustomed to this howl that something would have been lacking in my mother's playing if it had not existed. It was like a strange violent duet. There was no variation of tone in my mother's playing, and never a soft note. Looking back upon it now, I do not see how she managed to make such a volume of noise. But then, she was a mighty woman, as we knew when we were spanked. There was the strength of the Amazon in her massive arms, as they crashed down upon the keyboard.

In those days I had not heard anybody else play the piano except Miss Birks, with her occasional strummed "one, two, three, four, fives" for the dancing lesson, when she knew my mother had run upstairs for a moment to her bedroom, beyond the sound from the back drawing room, and once a year Walmy's sister Mary, who was supposed to be a musical genius. Every winter we went to a tea party at the Walmisleys' flat in Bayswater, and, as the grand climax of the evening, Miss Mary sat and played us the Rachmaninoff "Prelude."

"It's supposed to represent a man buried alive in a coffin by mistake," Roland whispered to me each year. "And these are the sounds of his trying to make himself heard."

I trembled with fear as I listened. Miss Mary's playing, though undistinguished and timid, terrified me so much that I did not enjoy it.

My mother's repertory was limited. She generally played somewhat vamped accompaniments to popular sentimental songs, such as "The Honeysuckle and the Bee." I used to look through her music on top of the piano, when I was supposed to be wading through Czerny exercises, with a feeling that within those garish colored sheets lay glamour and romance.

"I very much want you to learn to play 'The Apache Dance,'" my mother said to me one day as she handed me a sheet of music with a passionate picture on its cover of a woman in the embrace of a masked man. "It reminds me of Paris, and helps me with my work. You may leave the drawing room door open when you're playing it, so that I can hear from the study. And, by the way, I'd like you to learn the 'Merry Widow Waltz' as soon as you are able to play anything so advanced. I shall feel justified then in having allowed you the extravagance of music lessons."

She condemned anything classical. Uncle Jack tried his hardest to reform her, but the only result was a remark that the fustiness of the Leighton family even ran into its taste in music. *The Merry Widow* was her standard, and *The Merry Widow* it should remain.

And so, when Uncle Jack tried in vain to persuade her into going to a concert with him, she gave one of her little flutey gurgles.

"Classical music is like tepid diluted boiled water," she said. "Your pet darling Beethoven is nothing but a stuffy old man with a beard."

"But he had no beard, Fiorita Mia," Uncle Jack pleaded. "Bien Aimée, I assure you he had no beard."

She was firm in her convictions, and even when Uncle Jack took the trouble to bring along a photograph of his "pet darling Beethoven," she remained adamant in her opinion.

"There may not be a beard visible on his physical face," she said. "But there's a beard evident upon the face of his soul. They're all the same, whether it is your Beethoven or your Brahms, your Mozart or your Bach. The only one of the whole crowd who would ever have been capable of loving a woman was Chopin; and even he could have learnt something of the art of love by going to *The Merry Widow*. If you don't believe me, I'll put the dull Beethoven record on the gramophone and then you'll see I'm right."

Some misguided friend had once given us one of the "Leonora Overtures," and my mother always used this to emphasise her opinion. She considered it the epitome of dullness. In it there was neither beauty nor rhythm. Above all, there was no passion. Music should lilt with passion. It should throb with romance.

The nearest she ever achieved in tolerating classical music— apart from some Chopin, which only held its power over her because it was woven into her sentimental feelings at that moment for Uncle Jack, and because, after all, Chopin had been in love illicitly with George Sand—was almost to enjoy Mendelssohn's "Spring Song." This was because Mr. Bowles's eyes had been seen to grow moist while he heard me stumbling through it in the distant drawing room.

"I want you to play the 'Spring Song' again this afternoon," my mother commanded me sometimes when she felt Mr. Bowles was a little detached. "I find it has a most softening effect upon George."

And I would put aside my five finger exercises.

But just then I despised Mendelssohn. I was finishing an orgy of Grieg and discovering Brahms, and so it must have been in a perfunctory manner that I ran through the command performance, if I could tell from the conversation I heard a little later, as I was passing the study door.

"Funny," my mother was saying to Mr. Bowles. "Funny how one can produce such an utterly unimaginative daughter. Clare has neither looks nor charm. The looks don't matter, for some of the world's sirens have been the most hideous of women. But charm is a necessity. What do you suppose happened to make her so dull? To think that an offspring of mine could play the 'Spring Song' with such complete lack of feeling and passion! I simply cannot understand it. Why, that music should be played with the kind of swimmy feeling one has when one looks at an envelope written by somebody one is in love with. That, as you know, my dear George, is, to me, one of the most unfailing tests of whether one is in love with a man. If I am in love with a man, I cannot even see clearly the address he has written on the envelope. The writing is enchanted and blurred, and if it weren't that the postman doesn't feel the same about it, the letter would never reach its destination. Now you, George, you have before now had this power over me. I have known days when, as I came down to breakfast and saw a letter in that exquisitely beautiful handwriting of yours, everything even beyond the letter—the eggs and bacon and the toast in the toast rack— swam before my eyes in a swirl of passion. But now I can look at your handwriting on an envelope and say to Robert in quite a calm tone of voice that George has a most distinguished handwriting, hasn't he?"

That afternoon George had started to hint that he needed a holiday. My mother was determined to make him suffer.

But it was the first part of her talk with Mr. Bowles that puzzled me. She had accused me of lack of feeling and passion. She did not know that at that very moment this dull young daughter of twelve was herself indulging in a violent love affair. Never yet having met anyone of the opposite sex, I had flung the whole force of my emotions into love for the woman who now taught me music.

A year or two before this, my mother had supposed me to be beyond the scope of Miss Birks, and had sent me to a local dame school. It was called The Elms, and it was typically a "dame school." The standard of scholarship was grotesquely low, and because it was a private concern there was no authority to dictate how it should be run. One of the mistresses actually got a degree while I was at the school, and there was rejoicing over this. On every possible occasion she had to appear, weighed down by her cap and gown, in order that the parents of the girls might appreciate the high quality of her teaching. But it was only the seniors who were privileged to come anywhere near her.

This school was kept by a woman who would have fitted into the world of the Brontës. She was tall, and straight as though she had swallowed a poker, and her name was Miss Fanny Dothie. She was a caricature of a schoolmistress. My mother never ceased to make fun of her to me. She looked like an upright goose, and sailed into a room as though she were running on invisible wires. So silently did she appear in a classroom that no one of us knew she was coming until she loomed above us.

"The Elms won't do Clare any harm for just a little while," I heard my mother say to my father. "All the teachers have got the mark of the beast on them, of course; but a short stay there may not damage her. And anyhow, she's not the sort to get emotional about anything or anybody as I did over in that convent in France."

But my mother had forgotten that I was her daughter.

The music teacher whom I adored went by the unromantic name of Miss Elsie Rooke. I would have liked her to be called something less commonplace, remembering how my mother had once said that nobody with the name of Elsie could possibly be worth knowing. I would have liked her, also, to look more beautiful, but my love soon managed to weave a veil of enchantment around everything connected with her.

Never, I then supposed, had human being in this world felt such love. My worship of her took the form of kissing the seat of the chair she sat on, and the floor upon which she stood. If my mother had known of this love, I might have gone up in her estimation, and have been considered less of a Leighton than she feared; but I kept it secret. It was too holy to be discussed.

I grew suddenly envious of my mother's beauty. I remembered

how the old nurse had told me that I was "neither good looking nor bad looking, but just passable," and felt I must do something about it, if I were to try to be worthy of my beloved. So I took to stealing my mother's famous Crème Simon. The face cream she rubbed so assiduously into her skin might, I imagined, give me something of her beauty and her power. Each night, after my bath, I slipped into her bedroom. No character in my mother's melodramas lived more dangerously. But I rejoiced in my recklessness. Had I not heard what my mother's heroines risked for their love?

I had to find my way about in the dark. I had, also, to be careful not to knock anything over, and thus make a noise.

My mother's dressing table was an amazing assortment of things. It was covered with empty Crème Simon jars, old pieces of ribbon, jewel cases filled with rings, hair curlers and odd bits of red wax that had been used to seal the envelopes of her manuscripts. One or two postage stamps and some old love letters leaned against the other empty jars, while dead flowers from the hair adornments of many weeks lay sadly against the pincushion into which were stuck numberless hatpins. Among the empty jars, I had to find that particular pot of Crème Simon my mother was using. My fingers strayed upon my mother's hair curlers, and suddenly I wondered whether part of her power over her admirers lay in the beauty of her yellow curls. I thought of my own long hair, straight as a ruler, with the wisps that hung around my neck and ears. If I could curl and frizz these, I might not be so displeasing in the eyes of Miss Rooke. From out of the collection of twisted, used hair curlers, I stole four—two for each side of my face. Among my straight braids, those days, appeared ridiculous frizzed curls.

But my mother noticed nothing of all this.

Unfortunately Miss Elsie Rooke disapproved of *The Merry Widow*. She would not let me learn it, but said that I had the makings of a Brahms player. Until now I had obeyed my mother; but love was stronger than daughterly obedience. With the insight of this passion, it seemed to me that suddenly I understood music, and all that my mother had told me about it was wrong. I began to play Bach, Beethoven, and Brahms. I wanted to go to concerts. And my mother, yearning from her study for the romantic sounds of the "Spring Song," grew vexed at my stubbornness and threatened to take me away from The Elms, where I was growing even colder than before.

"I suppose it's the Leighton blood running through your veins," she sighed. "You have no conception of passion or romance or anything colorful in life. You're nothing but a fusty puritan. That's what comes of tying oneself with such a family, I suppose. Now Roland has no Leighton in him. He, at least, has color."

Unknown to her, at that moment Roland was entranced with Gregorian chant, which she would have considered worse even than Beethoven. But as he continued to spend his pocket money on buying her scarlet silk stockings she had no suspicion of his heresies.

"I may not be able to wear these scarlet stockings in the common light of day," she said, as she looked fondly at them on the study table where they lay among quill pens and empty Stickphast pots, "but that doesn't really matter. They give a meaning and a glory to life, even though I should never once put them on. It's enough to be able to look at them. Thank goodness I have produced one child who has understanding. And I don't forget how fortunate I am, for where, I ask, would you find anyone of Roland's age spending all his spare time from his school work in setting Verlaine's poems to music, or doing drawings of Spanish ladies with black mantillas and crimson carnations in their hair? Most young males think of nothing but cricket and football."

As was customary those days in England, there was a vast difference in my family between the education due to a boy and that due to a girl. While I was being sent for a short time to Miss Dothie's, Roland was attending a public school on his way to Oxford and a diplomatic career, and Evelyn was being coached for the Navy at one of the preparatory schools which specialized in producing naval cadets.

"It's useless for you to think you need any serious schooling," my mother would remind me. "I disapprove of education for women. Never forget that a blue stocking is a woman who has failed in her sex, and that the few females who find their way to a university are inevitably far from being the well-bred women of England. A career woman never belongs to the aristocracy. A woman is meant for marriage, and once she is married she has lost all chance to pursue her career."

And without a glance at Father who was idly drawing a little fishing boat, Mother would turn round to Walmy and go on dictating the instalment of one of her serial stories which was to feed and clothe the three children.

She must herself have had an amazing upbringing. Her Trelawny mother and her Irish father had little interest in her. Left to her own devices, she had devoted her time to writing. When she was only just able to form her letters she saved her pocket money for many weeks, and with this accumulated wealth bought a large supply of paper, pens and ink. Little Pattie, as her parents called her, was always a quiet child, and so nobody wondered what kept her satisfactorily occupied in her bedroom all the day long. But a few months later they discovered, for someone from a London publishing house came to visit her. It seems she was copying an entire novel by Mrs. Henry Wood, word for word, and sending it to the publisher as her own. The trick was found out, but the publisher was so puzzled by the childish handwriting that he took the trouble to come and see what sort of person had undertaken such an absurd labor.

Thwarted in this, Pattie had other ideas. Already the incipient melodrama writer lay within her. She looked through a local street directory and picked out some attractive names.

"This is to warn you," she wrote to one man who lived in a

nearby road. "Things are not as they seem to be in your household. Your wife plans to deceive you. It would be advisable for you to watch her more closely. We have information that points to her running away next Wednesday night with Mr. Jonathan Wetherby, who lives in Acacia Road."

She wrote to an unknown woman and told her not to trust her husband so implicitly, for he had been seen in a saloon with a chorus girl while he was supposed still to be at his office.

She spent her pocket money now on postage stamps, and the anonymous letters must have reached their destinations.

By the time she was through with these escapades, my mother was seriously writing poems. On her return from the French convent, she fell in love with Wilson Barrett, a well-known actor of those days, and he became the inspiration for her poems.

She also grew stage-struck. This caused many family tussles. Finally her parents decided that the only thing to cure her would be a short time on the stage, in order that she might see how glamourless it was. And so, when she was about fifteen, Wilson Barrett took her on tour. She was chaperoned and accompanied by her self-sacrificing Aunt Pollie.

"And oh, how dreary it all was," she often told me. "Nothing on earth can equal the dismal squalor of theatrical lodgings in a place like Nottingham, on a rainy afternoon in November. I found no romance anywhere—only hard work and the tiredness of everybody, and the dusty appearance of the boards in the daytime, in an empty theatre."

So, as soon as she could, she returned home, completely cured. And while her Aunt Pollie Trelawny breathed a sigh of relief at being back again in her own comfortable setting, my mother informed the family that she had made up her mind to write books, and that she would leave the stage to people who were so insensitive that they didn't know what sordidness meant.

But Wilson Barrett remained her hero. He became even more

idealized in her imagination, as she understood the background against which he worked. She felt now that he needed her. He needed a dream world into which to escape from a theatrical lodginghouse in the Midlands. To this end, she became friendly with his daughter Kitty, so that she might be aware of all his movements.

He went to America on lengthy tours, and for a year or two my mother's young life was a six months of ecstasy alternated with a six months of waiting. For he told her to be patient while he was away, and, leaving with her a copy of Walt Whitman, he asked her to stay quiet and study until he returned. Over the dreary months of his absence she would weave her dreams of him into: "When Lilacs Last in the Dooryard Bloomed," and write her own poems to her hero. She remembered some of these poems, and often when she was anxious to show us how backward we were in a sense of poetry, would start off with the first verse of one of them:

> Pass on awhile, that other lands may hear thee,
>   That other hands may weave the laurel crown.
> Let perfect art to other hearts endear thee,
>   And Transatlantic tongues thy greatness own.

He was her introduction to America, and he wrote back to the romantic young girl, waiting patiently in a walled doll's house in St. John's Wood, dramatic accounts of the Rockies, New York City or Niagara Falls. This was my mother's only knowledge of the New World, though already she had had her struggles and uncertainties about the North and the South.

"I'm glad, really, that I shall never be forced to make a decision," she said, "for I find myself distinctly worried. Part of me is for the North and yet another part is definitely for the South. But now, after long years of conflict, I have settled down to the conclusion that the Northern States appeal to my heart, and the brighter, gayer South appeals to my temperament."

"Mightn't it be interesting to come to America with me next

time I go there?" I asked her once, many years later, when I had just returned from a visit. But she would not come. She had strange ideas about American food.

"I have never known an English person who ate American hotel food for any length of time who didn't break up in general health," she answered me. "Your American godmother used to say that the air in the United States was so exciting that one couldn't eat restfully in it. I think it will be best for me to stay over here in England."

And so my mother's views of America remained the world of Emerson, Walt Whitman and *Uncle Tom's Cabin*. In our childhood we could not understand Emerson or Whitman, but a profusely illustrated copy of *Uncle Tom's Cabin* was one of the delights of the nursery. We gazed in rapture at the pictures of Topsy, and shivered at the sight of Eliza escaping over the ice floes. The only Negroes we had ever seen were the "minstrels" upon the beach of Lowestoft; but even these were really white people who had blackened their faces for the occasion. We would have been excited had we known we were to meet our first colored people in the front drawing room at Vallombrosa.

For some reason or other, my father was idolized by a certain Negro in West Africa. He was Cornelius S. May, the editor of the Sierra Leone *Weekly News*. Every week of our lives this paper arrived, in its pale yellow-green cover, and every week it was tossed unopened into the wastepaper basket in the study. One day a letter arrived for my father. It contained the news that Mr. and Mrs. Cornelius S. May were coming to London, accompanied by their eldest daughter Isa. Isa, it appeared, was being sent to a "finishing school" in Highgate. They wished, during their short stay in London, to pay their respects to Mr. and Mrs. Robert Leighton.

"Do you realise they'll be as black as pitch?" said my mother. "These will be no half-castes or such. These will be really as black as your hat."

My father did realise it. He had only recently finished writing a thrilling boys' story about Africa, called *In the Land of Ju-Ju,* and there was little he didn't know about every tribe of natives. But he was clearly worried by my mother's attitude.

"Chummie," he pleaded, "how can I help it? We'll have to see them and be nice to them. There's no way out."

I was listening to this conversation in great excitement. To my joy I heard my mother's decision.

"Well," she said, "there's one thing to be said about it. It'll be an excellent chance of initiating the children into the existence of the colored race. I'll make them come downstairs and shake hands with the whole family."

The day arrived. There was a ring at the front door bell and we rushed to the nursery window to see our first Negroes. There they were: father and mother and daughter. We could hardly believe our eyes.

But my mother had mixed a hint of malice into this decision. She had told our nurse to dress us in white, from top to toe. As we marched into the drawing room we must have looked terribly like a trio of angels to poor little black Isa. We hesitated as we drew near to them. We had had no idea that colored people could be so black. And then, with the most gracious manners we could muster, we shook hands with them.

Later, when I was at my dame school, I made great use of this little encounter with the Cornelius S. Mays. It didn't happen to every schoolgirl in St. John's Wood to have had tea with three West African Negroes. I think it probable that, being my mother's daughter, a sense of drama may have stirred me to slight exaggeration, for I cannot help recollecting that pretty soon I was known as the girl who had stayed with a whole tribe of African cannibals.

But I think my ego must have needed this drama, for I had little chance of gaining popularity at school. My mother did not approve of the social level of The Elms.

"I would never have sent you there if I had been able to find *a* better school as near home," she explained. "As it is, I do not wish you to make friends with any of the girls. Nurse will stay with you in the cloakroom until the bell rings. I'm decidedly worried about the background of some of the pupils. Miss Dothie assured me she had no tradesmen's children, but I've just found out that the poulterer in Circus Road has sent his daughter there."

I was always wanting to show off my mother at The Elms. I wanted especially to show her to my adored Miss Rooke. My mother was not like the mothers of the other girls. They seemed so drab and inconspicuous. She was something completely different, in her wonderful big hats and her queenly walk. One day the opportunity came.

Our nurse was ill and couldn't bring me home. As it happened, my mother had hired a carriage that afternoon to pay a call on Lady Northcliffe. She decided to fetch me from The Elms as she drove back. Now my adored music teacher would see her.

But a terrible thing happened. My mother towered above Miss Rooke, in all her splendor, and made her look so frail and insignificant that I grew confused and ashamed.

"How extraordinary it is that the moment a woman becomes a teacher all the glamour forsakes her," my mother said to me, in the carriage on the way home. "Why, you would think that music might have enough magic to counteract the smear of the teaching profession, but even your little Miss Rooke has the mark of the beast upon her. I was disappointed, for I had gathered from you that she had personality. But she has none. She ends where she ends, and has no aura surrounding her. She's every bit as commonplace as the rest of them there at The Elms."

I decided after that to keep to myself the world in which I was living.

And so I never talked to my mother about the exciting people who came into my school world from the outside. Neither did I tell her about the poets and writers I discovered. It might have been supposed that, coming from a literary household, I should already have been aware of them, but my mother did not feed upon a diet of Shakespeare or Dryden, Shelley or Keats. While I lived in an enchanted world of Shakespeare's tragedies and Wordsworth's "Prelude," and the poems of Southey and Cowper, she moved about the house quoting Swinburne and Byron and the lyrics of Henley.

But in spite of our different worlds, life was happy. Down in the study my mother and father worked. Up in the nursery in the evening Evelyn and I worked. In his own bedroom Roland worked. We were hedged by security, and it seemed impossible that this pattern to our lives could change. My music lessons with Miss Rooke made Tuesday and Thursday for me into moments of delight. As Wednesday and Friday evenings came around, the barrel organ in the street outside our house could be heard playing tunes from Italian operas while we did our lessons. Monday, Wednesday and Friday, on our return from afternoon school, Mr. Bowles's top hat and overcoat greeted us in the front hall. Saturday was a holiday, and we went with our nurse to the florist in Abercorn Place to buy the weekly flowers I was allowed to arrange: sweet-scented yellow mimosa in the wintertime, tulips and daffodils in the spring, sweet peas and roses in early summer, before we left London for the East Coast. When, many years later, I visited the Mediterranean and found myself living among great bushes of this mimosa, my mind turned to the study in St. John's Wood, and blue sea and silver olive trees and the songs of Provençal peasants held little power as these fluffy branches carried me back to a lamplit room, with a London fog outside, and my mother dictating her love stories to Walmy at the enormous table. By her side sat my father, writing one of his boys' books. Around the study lay sleeping dogs.

12. *A New Center of the Universe*

"Stop making that noise," a male voice called to me as I sat at the piano in the back drawing room and began to practise my five finger exercises. "I refuse to be interrupted when I'm busy thinking."

Startled at finding I was not alone, I closed the piano. I looked in the direction from which the command came and saw a man on the sheepskin rug in the distant front drawing room. He lay flat on his stomach, his head buried in his hands. It was the same figure that I had often seen on the rug before the fire when I went into the study to fetch a book.

It was Lord Northcliffe.

"There's absolutely nothing to be surprised about in someone choosing to lie on his stomach," our mother reproached us when we seemed bewildered. "The sooner you children learn to accept any eccentricity as though it were a commonplace, the better equipped you will be for life. A well-brought-up person should never under any circumstances show amazement. Why, if you saw your father or me sitting at the study table working, without a stitch of clothing on, you ought to be able to behave as though it were the normal way to sit and work. I even think it might be worth while to try it one day, just to see how controlled you are. . . . And, by the way, I am perfectly certain Northcliffe is scientifically correct in supposing he can think best when he's flat on his stomach. The blood doesn't have to make the effort of running uphill to the brain."

Whether it was a scientific truth or not, Lord Northcliffe did imagine he could do his best thinking lying down. He had a great sense of the value of time, and never believed in wasting a single minute of his life. While he was waiting for my mother to come into the room to discuss her work, he might just as well sprawl on the floor and do some planning for the future.

Evelyn and I never spoke to this Napoleon of the Press, for we had been ordered not to. He was a busy man, and he didn't like being bothered by children.

"As a matter of fact, it isn't only because he's so busy," our mother explained to us, after we had been hurried out of his way. "Actually he's sensitive about children. He's never had any of his own, you see, and it's been a dreadful blow to him. But there you have another unfailing example of the Law of Compensation I'm always telling you about. Destiny makes him into a millionaire, but withholds from him the one thing he most wants, which is a son and heir."

And so, whenever we saw this prostrate figure before the fire, we tried to move quietly away before he would discover that we had even entered the room.

But although we did not really know him, we thought of him in fear and awe, realizing that he held the keys to our existence. It was from the man on the hearthrug that we received our bread and butter, our beefsteaks and our flannel undergarments.

I had a special reason for being afraid of him, which I kept secret from everyone else. It was through his family that I had received some of my deepest suffering.

Our mother never allowed us to go to any children's parties.

"If you don't catch infectious diseases you catch bad manners," she said, as she refused the various invitations.

But there was one party a year that she would not turn down. It was given by Northcliffe's brother, Lord Rothermere, who had a large family of children.

"I've got to let you go because of my work," she sighed each January, as she came up to the nursery to talk to Nanny about our new party clothes. "If I were to refuse, Northcliffe would be bound to know, for he always goes to these parties—though why he should torture himself by looking at all those children I never can understand. And he might take it as a personal insult. He's such an impetuous, touchy creature that he would be quite capable of telling the office not to give me any more stories to write. . . . And after all, even though you *may* get measles and whooping cough and all the diseases of the young, yet I can be pretty sure you won't catch any very serious bad manners that I can't rectify. The children you meet there shouldn't do you much harm."

My elder brother, Roland, was always clothed by our mother with extravagance and care.

"He is the only one of my children who is beautiful enough to be worth dressing," she would say, as she took time off from her work to buy him the velvet suits and silk blouses of the Little Lord Fauntleroy period. My younger brother, Evelyn, inherited the splendors which Roland had outgrown. But my wardrobe was supervised by the nurse, whose aesthetic taste was not of the best.

"It seems to me, m'say, the only thing that matters is for everything to be serviceable," she would say, as she fitted me out in the unexciting navy blue sailor suits I detested. "Once a little girl begins to get ideas into 'er 'ead about wanting frills and satins, it opens the door wide to the world, the flesh and the devil. And it's always the plain, fat children like Miss Clare what gets carried away by finery."

One winter Lord Rothermere's party happened to take place on a wet day. The Leighton family was terrified of rain, and both our mother and the nurse hinted that we might not go to the party unless the weather cleared. All morning long they looked at the sky, but the rain fell unceasingly.

"What do you think about it, Robert?" we heard our mother repeatedly ask of our father. But he went on writing. We did not hear him give an answer.

"If the children are wrapped up well, perhaps it won't give them pneumonia," our mother finally decided. "I've been having a few difficulties lately with Northcliffe, and frankly I don't want to annoy him just now."

And so we went to the party. But beneath my party dress I wore black woollen stockings and high black boots.

"That there Miss Clare always was delicate in the stomach and susceptible to chill," Nanny said. "And for a delicate inside in the rain there is nothing like flannel drawers, flannel petticoats and thick woollen stockings. And on a soaking wet day like this, even though we carries 'er right down to the carriage, she's as like as not to turn her ankles, what are so delicate. The only safe thing to do is to make 'er wear 'er boots to the party."

I sat on my chair at this party, among boys and girls in white silk socks and satin slippers, and pulled my accordion pleated dress as far down over my knees as I could, while I kept my black legs under the chair.

"Surely you're the little Leighton girl," said a voice I recognized.

There stood Lord Northcliffe, looking straight down at me. I felt certain he was staring at my black woollen stockings and my high boots.

Ever after that, I dreaded seeing him. He reminded me of my suffering.

But though our mother always appeared anxious not to displease him, she never seemed to be really afraid of him. In talking with our father she laughingly referred to him as "the Chief." More often he was "Alfred," and she did not scruple to make fun of him.

But suddenly Lord Northcliffe and our mother quarreled. No longer would she be writing her stories for his newspapers. The *Daily Mail* and the orange-colored weekly paper called *Answers,* which she and Northcliffe had inaugurated together, would carry no more serials signed "Marie Connor Leighton."

She was not worried. She had unfailing belief in Destiny. And Destiny just now seemed to be busy.

"What's the use of making oneself look old and wrinkled by worrying about things beyond one's control?" she asked. "In that way one would defeat one's own ends. Destiny has something up its sleeve for me, and it's no good my fighting it. How do I know that this break with Northcliffe isn't intended so that I can have time to produce the things that are worth while? Now, perhaps, I can write my play."

This play had been in the back of her mind ever since the visit to Cheiro, the celebrated palmist. For not only had he told her of the gruesome nature of her early death, but he had informed her that before this death she was to write a successful play.

"Apparently I'm to go out in a fanfare of riches and fame," our mother laughed. "If I wanted to delay my untimely death, I suppose I'd put off writing the play. But you can't trick Fate. And after all, I admit that it will certainly be most pleasant to make a fortune— even if I *do* have the example of Northcliffe's continuous unhappiness before me."

The mirage of this play was one of the excitements of our childhood. As we lay in bed, before falling asleep, we acted the most glamourous first night, and surrounded ourselves with indescribable splendors. We were convinced that this world of make-believe would one day become reality.

"Yes," decided our mother, "perhaps my quarrel will turn out to be a godsend. I can see in it the hand of Destiny. Now I shall have time of my own."

Destiny was very hard at work with the Leighton family. It took our seventy year old nurse to hospital, with cancer. Within a few weeks she was dead.

"If there's one thing on this earth that terrifies me it is cancer," said our mother. "I'm very much afraid, Robert, that we'll have to move from Vallombrosa. How do we know the old woman hasn't left some traces of the disease in the house behind her?"

As if this were not enough, something suddenly went wrong with the drains of Vallombrosa, so that there was a fear we might catch typhoid fever. Everything fitted in like the pieces of a jigsaw puzzle. Fate decreed that we must leave St. John's Wood and go to Lowestoft.

"You can't go and bury yourself like that, away from the center of everything," Mr. Bowles kept on telling our mother as the plans for the removal developed. "You of all people belong to London."

She looked at him in consternation.

"Since when have I been dependent upon my surroundings?" she asked. "Where I am becomes the center of everything. If I chose to live in Timbuctoo I assure you I could make London and Paris and Vienna seem as suburban as Balham or Tooting or the outskirts of Birmingham. You see if all of you don't soon begin to feel drawn to Lowestoft by some magnetic power of intellectual stimulation."

But certain standards of living were expected of the Leighton family, wherever it might settle.

"We'll have to find a different house, Robert," our mother told our father. "It's all very well to live in a semidetached place like The Red Croft when we are known to have a house in London as well, but it's altogether too lower-middle-class for us as our sole establishment. We must find something with more dignity. I'll get Silenus to help. He knows all about houses and mortgages. What's the good of his being a bank manager in the City if we don't make use of it?"

Before we knew what was happening, our mother's faithful Silenus had found us our house.

It was the kind of mansion one might think up in a nightmare. It's name was Heather Cliff, and it stood alone on a bluff overlooking the North Sea, not more than a mile or two from the lower-middle-class semidetached Red Croft. We thought it wonderful, but when Uncle Jack first set eyes on it he visibly squirmed.

"It's obvious you have no aesthetic awareness, Bien Aimée, or you could never possibly have brought yourself to live in such a place," he said in a superior voice, conscious of being the artist of the family. "There's no purity of form or design anywhere about it. And it's the most absurd, grotesque conglomeration of architectural styles you ever saw."

"Oh, nonsense, Jack," answered my mother. "Your taste is so impoverished and anemic that you can't understand the need for romance in a building. Now passion and romance could be lived richly here in Heather Cliff—far better than in one of those austerely correct houses you would want me to have. Think of the many towers and passages in which one could hide one's lover—not to speak of the beauty of the moon shining down through the dome in the hall. This place is made for love, I tell you, and illicit love at that."

But nothing would make Uncle Jack change his mind.

And it was not surprising that he should have felt as he did about Heather Cliff, for one part of the structure was Tudor, with oak beams patterning the white outside walls, another was like a copy of a French chateau, with round towers and turrets, while yet another part had a number of square balconies and bay windows. But the central attraction was an enormous dome, like a miniature copy of the Duomo in Florence. This mixture of strange features outside was even more amazing from within. The dome was an especially impressive affair. Walmy, when she first saw it, put her finger to her lips.

"Hush," she said to us. "You feel you've got to behave yourself here. Lo-ar, if it isn't just like some sort of a heathen church."

I didn't quite follow her, but I, too, felt awed. The stained glass in the dome cast magical colors upon Walmy as she stood there, till her face was splashed with blue and a band of crimson ran down the front of her "blouse." I moved to her side, and across my dress streaked a bar of brilliant green.

Into the pretentious mansion moved the Leighton family, bundles and servants, dogs and children and all. The annual migration was as nothing to this. The furniture from two houses sprawled over the rooms of Heather Cliff, with neither order nor concern for style. White enameled tables and chairs from the summer residence of The Red Croft hobnobbed with old oak settles and the ancestral grandfather clock. Easels and gramophone, study table and dog kennels, everything was transplanted from Vallombrosa to the clear light of East Anglia. The dome in the hall cast its magical blues and crimsons and greens upon unpacked crates of books and manuscripts, model yachts and my mother's winter dresses. The whole place looked like the backstage of the Metropolitan Opera House.

But the family did not mind this confusion. My mother and father had settled upon the room in which they would work, and the study in Heather Cliff became a near duplicate of the study in Vallombrosa. The important thing was that the pattern of life should continue unchanged.

Walmy, though, had other ideas. The splendor of this mansion had gone to her head.

"Lo-ar," she said with pride in her voice, "this is not a house. It is a 'place.' We shall have to live up to it. You will see that the 'County' will now call upon us. When we were merely summer visitors, it was your mother's charm and fame that made her accepted by local society. It wasn't where we lived. Now we shall 'belong.' You see if I'm not right."

To what extent she was right, I am uncertain. I have a suspicion that it was a good deal curiosity that brought people to see us. But whatever the motive, there is no doubt that we had entered upon a new phase of life, for vicars and their wives and their curates called and came to tea, and the local nobility and gentry left their visiting cards upon the silver salver in the front hall.

My mother, though, did not mean to be trapped into the life of Lowestoft.

"If they think I shall interest myself in all their little comings and goings, they're quite wrong," she said. And she would take the train to London with a mysterious little smile, as though she were disappearing to a world of which these rustic locals could know nothing.

For she was busy just now, recovering from the break with Lord Northcliffe. She was writing stories for a rival firm, and writing with the same terrific output. Though they were appearing these days in different papers, the same blond heroines emerged from the clutches of the same dark villains, and the family meals had still to wait until my mother should have found a means of escape for the imprisoned hero. Piles of maroon bound volumes already stood in odd corners of Heather Cliff, as the completed serials appeared in book form—*Convict 99, Put Yourself in Her Place, Fires of Love, Was She Worth It?*; they had grown in number over the years, till they could be counted in scores.

"I wonder what Mother is going to do when she has used up all the names ending with 'ine,' " Roland used to laugh. "Aline, Bettine, Ellaline, Justine; Mother says she'd have no luck if she didn't give her heroine a name with this termination. But she's bound to come to the end of them one of these days. And then she'll have to invent names for herself, like Lanoline or Vaseline."

But our mother was serious about this little superstition.

"It's all very well for you to be amused," she reproached my brother. "Actually I *did* call one of my heroines something without this ending. And what do you suppose happened? Why, that was the very story I was writing when I quarreled with Northcliffe, which only goes to prove that there is something in the superstition. Never again will I be so stupid as to tempt Providence in such a matter."

Although my mother had established herself in this new setting and was working just as if no change in her surroundings had taken place, I was not able to do so.

I was unhappy. I had been taken away from The Elms. My school days were ended. What was even worse, I had been snatched from my adored Miss Rooke. I felt that I knew the fullest extent of sorrow. I spent my time writing sonnets of grief and lovesick letters to my music teacher. When the postman came each morning I shared my mother's anticipation of what he would bring.

For though she might no longer be in London among her adorers, she kept in close touch with them. Letters arrived with handwriting that "danced" before her eyes. Understanding now how she was feeling, I watched her those mornings at breakfast, as she waited for the meal to be over in order that she might open the envelopes. There was an unwritten law in the Leighton family that nobody should be so ill mannered as to open his mail at the breakfast table. I saw her glance with impatience at my father. Would he never finish eating? Why should he want to choose this moment, now, to discuss the plot of his next book.

"I wonder, Chummie, if it wouldn't be more exciting if I were to make the Indians kidnap the boy," he asked over his bacon and eggs. "What do you advise me to do?"

But my mother's answer was casual. Her mind was on the pile of envelopes by the side of her empty plate. In the middle of that pile was an enchanted letter. I watched her turn the pile over and over, hurrying past the business letters and bills. I knew that as soon as the breakfast was finished she would carry all her letters with her

to the study and there, while appearing to glance at the business communications and the bills, she would subtract the one precious
envelope and, tucking it down the front of her morning jacket, take
it with her to the privacy of the lavatory.

She did not intend to be isolated from her admirers.

If I had not been so unhappy just now on my own account I
would have enjoyed this new life. Here, upon our premises, we
owned an ornamental pond, a tennis court, a croquet lawn, stables,
a greenhouse and terraces with stone urns to hold flowers. A drive
curved from the front gate round by the house and past the stables
and the greenhouse to the back part of the place, and then out to
the gate on the Corton Road. We possessed, in fact, entrances upon
two roads.

"Silenus" had done well by us.

But although my mother was always making her little trips to
London, to see publishers, dressmakers and admirers, she was not
able to escape the visits of the local gentry. She pretended to be
bored by them, but actually I think she would have felt piqued if
they had not called upon her.

"After all," she sighed as she said good-bye to a curate's wife
who had wasted most of her afternoon, "one should be willing
to pay for one's sense of glamour and romance. These poor creatures
have so little opportunity to see what it is they have missed in life
that one has no right to deprive them of this chance. And it is
enormous fun to see how quickly one can shock them. I had an
especially amusing time this afternoon with this visitor. I told her
the wildest stories about St. John's Wood and the actresses that
Edward the Seventh used to visit there. And of course she couldn't
really say anything, for he *was* our king. The trouble is, of course,
that I have probably whetted her appetite so much that I shall be
pestered with her from now on. As Mamma always said, so truly,
if a woman doesn't *do* naughty things herself she delights in hearing how other women have done them. If I'm not more careful

I shall find myself used as a source of enlightenment and entertainment by all these little curates' wives. And then I'll get no work done. Yes, I really must be more careful."

To this end, she managed to find out when they would be away from home before she returned their calls. Then she could merely leave cards and know that she had behaved as was demanded of her.

Pretty soon, though, the splendors of Heather Cliff began to go to her head as they had gone to Walmy's. My mother decided to enter into the life of the country and enjoy it.

"This doesn't mean that I shall accept invitations to open church bazaars or flower shows," she declared. "Neither does it mean that I shall be available to any little Tom, Dick or Harry who might choose to come along and waste my time. If you read your French literature you will see that the chatelaine of the chateau in France rarely went beyond the gates of her estate. She surrounded herself with a mist of inaccessibility, which gave her additional magic and glamour in the eyes of the people. There is no reason whatsoever why the same kind of atmosphere should not be possible here at Lowestoft as in Touraine."

And so my mother, dressed in her flamboyant clothes, and looking like an illustration to *La Vie Parisienne*, took her daily exercise in the grounds of Heather Cliff. But the walks were more varied than those she had taken up and down the center path of the back garden at The Red Croft. She went all the way round the front lawn with its terraced slopes and the stone urns, past the ornamental pond at the back, and the stables and the orchard. Rarely did she turn aside to look at the plants in the greenhouse, except when the pink oleander was coming into bloom. She would pass our father as he hoed some flower beds, and sometimes, when she was in trouble with her plot, would stop and shout to him for advice.

"I can't seem to get the right setting for this new serial, Robert," we would hear her complain to him. "How would it be if I were to lay the story in Russia this time, and let my heroine get banished to Siberia? Robert, listen to me. Do you think that would keep my readers' attention, or is it too far away?"

But Father was busy with his hoeing, and his reply was apt to be perfunctory. This vexed our mother, who thought he was spending far too much time in the Heather Cliff garden.

"You know perfectly well, Robert, that there's no need for you to do all the work here yourself. It's much too big a place, and we can afford a real gardener."

"And let him dig up my treasured plants," moaned our father. "I've had that happen twice within the last month, before I sent the wretch away, and I tell you I'd rather slave out here myself than let any more so called professional gardeners ruin the place."

"Which means," answered my mother, "that you might just as well give up the idea that you are a writer who is helping to earn the family income. It's bad economics, you know. It would pay much better to employ a gardener."

But our father shook his head. Only a week or so earlier he had found a whole row of seedlings heaped, uprooted, on the rubbish pile.

The place really was far too much work for him. The grounds of Heather Cliff waged a winning battle, till the grass of the slopes grew tall and the hedges sprawled wildly beyond their limits. It began to look quite pleasantly familiar, like the garden at Vallombrosa. Only the croquet lawn and the tennis court were kept under control, for the Leighton family now varied its walking exercise with mild games. As a concession to life in the country, our mother took to playing tennis.

"So long as no one sees me playing, I must admit that it is good for the figure," she said, as she strolled across the court to return a slow ball sent over to the net to her by our father. "But I refuse to play with Jack or George or any of my other friends. It is not conducive to magic and romance."

There was one diversion that took our mother beyond the gates of Heather Cliff. During the summer months concerts were held in the municipal park called The Sparrows Nest. Into the marquee sailed our mother, to listen to her favorite baritone. As she entered, all eyes were turned her way, to gaze upon the rows of frills on her figured silk dress with its short sleeves and perilously low neck, and the enormous hat with its burden of blossoms and its floating ribbons.

"Doesn't Mother look wonderful," Evelyn and I would say to each other, as we watched her step into the carriage that was ordered three afternoons a week, to convey her to her singer. And we hoped everybody in Lowestoft would be there at the concert to see her.

But our mother's adorers were not happy. They were jealous of her interest in this baritone.

"You think you go up in my estimation by sneering so cheaply about him," she said to Uncle Jack one day as she came home with him from The Sparrows Nest. "Actually, you are damaging yourself in my eyes, for it only goes to show that you don't understand real feeling. And then you wonder why it is I find it so difficult to be emotional about you. . . . This passionate, dark baritone holds magic for me. The dreams I weave around him help me with my work. I only have to sit there in my seat and listen to him and I know exactly what to make my hero say to my heroine, and—"

"But Fiorita," interrupted my uncle, "don't you see that he is just a cheap sentimentalist? What sort of a song is Tosti's 'Goodbye,' I ask you? Now if only I had a voice I'd sing you songs that would make you leave all this nonsensical dross behind you. I'd sing you arias from Mozart, or songs by Schubert or Hugo Wolf."

The mere mention of these classical composers seemed to do something to my mother. She turned to Uncle Jack with withering contempt.

"I'm sick of you, Jack. You damage my power to work. You'd better leave."

This time Uncle Jack's pride was deeply wounded. He packed his bags and left.

But though our mother was upset at his reacting to her in this way, it was not long before she found comfort in a comparative newcomer.

He was a French Baron.

My father was editing the memoirs of the Princess Caroline Murat. This involved getting to know various members of the Napoleon Bonaparte family. The particular one who was helping him came to Lowestoft, to be near at hand.

"The Baron so exactly looks the part, that it's almost ludicrous," said our mother. "Why, one could see his double any day at the gaming tables at Monte Carlo, or sauntering along the Promenade des Anglais at Nice, or taking the waters at Aix les Bains, or Baden Baden.

Evelyn and I had lately been reading French history, and it filled us with awe actually to see in the flesh a relative of the great Napoleon.

But behind his back we called him Belshazzar.

It was our old nurse who had started the nickname. This perfumed gentleman with the little black waxed moustache and the suits that curved in at the waist had appeared on the scene just before her death. She had disapproved of him. In her staunch Baptist faith she had decided that he was unholy.

"That Frenchy don't bode no good," she had sighed. "Regular evil I calls 'im, with the wicked look in 'is eyes and all the stinky perfumes on 'im the whole time—yes, even at ten o'clock in the morning. And with that ridiculous long foreign name as no one in their senses could pronounce. Beelzebub is what I think 'e should be called. It sounds very nearly the same as 'is own."

"Not Beelzebub, Nurse," our mother had commanded. "You

know what that name means in the Bible. It would never do for
him to hear the children call him that, and they might easily let it
slip out by mistake."

Our mother had learnt her lesson over her own carelessness
with "Silenus."

"Well then, m'm, if it isn't to be Beelzebub, it 'ad better be
Belshazzar, which is the next nearest in sound," Nanny had
answered. "But I tells you what, m'm. If that there evil man comes
around 'ere much more, there'll be changes in this 'ousehold. It's
all these stinks I'm thinking of. In my young days no lady would
'ave been seen with scent on 'er in the daylight. She 'ad the decency
to wait till the evening, when respectable people were out of the
way. But to 'ave a man smelling like this—well, as I says, either
'e goes or I do."

"But we have to have him around, Nanny, because of Mr.
Leighton's work," my mother had tried to console her. It would
be disastrous for the old woman to leave.

The nurse had hobbled off, still grumbling. But not before my
mother promised that the study door should be shut tight whenever Belshazzar was there, so that the scent of his shaving soap
and toilet waters should not offend her nostrils in the prosaic
hours before the midday meal.

If the old nurse had been still alive during the months at
Lowestoft when Belshazzar haunted us, I don't know what might
have happened. Her crusading spirit was inflamed, and on
those rare occasions when her religious scruples were disturbed she
had been known to forget her "place."

But even as it was, Belshazzar plagued us.

He stayed at the best Lowestoft hotel, in company with one or
two effete English noblemen. They visited us and drank whiskeys
and sodas at times of the day that my mother considered decidedly
degenerate.

"I don't think anybody could exactly call me a Puritan," she said, as she shook her head over their behavior. "But I must admit that I disapprove of drinking whiskey in the daytime. It is something that belongs to artificial light. To drink it before midday, though, is utterly impossible. And here they go, at eleven-thirty in the morning, with their Scotch and soda. . . . But then, nothing would ever make me touch a drop, except medicinally, when I have the beginnings of a chill in my inside. It is unromantic for a woman to drink and, besides, it gives you a double chin and a bloated complexion. I feel the same about smoking. It's all very well for a man to smoke, but not for a woman. It is only the really tame, dull, insignificant women like curates' wives who do it, to try unsuccessfully to prove they are progressive and modern. A really wise woman knows that her power lies in what she refrains from doing rather than in what she does."

And so she produced the whiskey and soda, the cigarettes and the cigars, for Belshazzar and his friends; but she did not join them in their drinking.

Neither, really, did she enjoy their company, though she delighted in talking French with Belshazzar. Some integrity within her despised people who did not work. Besides, Belshazzar was too completely interested in his gentlemen friends to be susceptible to her charms.

This piqued her considerably. It had never happened to her before, and she could not understand it.

"Am I losing my looks, Robert?" she asked my father, as she gazed at herself in the bedroom mirror. "This Belshazzar of yours doesn't seem to have any interest in me whatsoever—except to talk French with. Upon my word, it worries me. You'd think I was beginning to get crowsfeet around my eyes, or wrinkles on my forehead, or a few white hairs on my head."

But my father patted her cheek and told her not to be silly.

"There are some people in this world, Chummie, who are so made that they prefer the company of their own sex," he told her.

"And when this happens Venus herself could walk among them unobserved."

My mother felt better after this; but still she was bewildered.

If Uncle Jack had only known, it was a propitious moment for him to return. This time, however, he had been deeply wounded in his pride, and his self-elected absence continued.

My mother was quite deeply annoyed at the way Belshazzar ignored her, and perhaps it was as a revenge upon the entire race of men that she flung herself now into friendship with a woman.

This woman was a Russian whom she had met in London. She happened to be extremely rich. It was rumored that she was probably a millionaire, but this did not influence my mother, who had no interest in the worldly possessions of other people. She took a suite at the best hotel in Lowestoft, near to Belshazzar and the effete noblemen, and spent a great deal of her time with us, talking in French with our mother.

"But how *can* you be so much interested in a woman?" Roland asked our mother one day, after she had sat throughout an entire afternoon with this Russian friend. "If she were a man I could understand it, but you aren't the sort of person to waste your time upon some one of your own sex."

"Don't you see that she has a very special quality to her?" she answered him. "She's a cosmopolitan aristocrat. If she were only an English noblewoman she might be as dull as ditchwater—they generally are, if the truth were told—but a Russian aristocrat is bound to be vital and exciting. What, I ask you, have Mr. Bowles or your Uncle Jack to give me that I cannot get far better from this woman? She has an understanding of life and romance that I have discovered in very few men."

Fascinated with her new friend, my mother slipped more and more into the world of Russia. She began to decide that there must, after all, be something Russian in her own ancestry.

"Sonya is so extraordinarily like my Trelawny mamma," she said. "And I am recollecting that that time we visited Russia I was often mistaken for one of their own people. Do you know what I am beginning to think? I am beginning to believe that some ancestor of ours in Cornwall, centuries ago, must have got emotionally involved with a visiting Slav who had sought tin from the family mines. They did come to Cornwall for tin, you know. They came from places like Ragusa. It's an historical fact that you can't get away from. And, now I come to think of it, that would explain everything. Yes, I am convinced that is what happened. I am certain of it."

Actually, my mother did behave somewhat like a Slav. In many ways she resembled Lyubov in Chekhov's *The Cherry Orchard*. Her romantic emotionalism and impetuous generosity were combined with a complete lack of concern over material things.

"All that matters, my child," she would say to me from time to time, "all that *really* matters is to cherish the world of your mind and your soul. You know how much I love luxury, but I assure you that I would never allow possessions to dominate me. You should be able to abandon your worldly goods at a moment's notice, and remain every bit as rich as you were before—and perhaps even richer, I would say."

As my mother spent these hours with her friend, it brought back to her mind her holiday in Russia.

This had happened some few years earlier. Both my father and my mother were boastfully proud about it.

"We went there long before anyone supposed it possible to go to Russia," my mother always reminded us. "And it was no tourist agency affair, like the underbred holidays George takes to Switzerland. Neither was it one of the organized trips to the over-frequented countries of the Mediterranean, such as your Uncle Jack indulges in. If you are going to travel anywhere the only thing possible is to go to the aristocratic parts of Europe, such as Holland and Denmark, Scandinavia, Germany and the heart of Russia, as your father and I did."

"Oh, Chummie, what I would give to go to some of those places again," sighed our father, who had happened to overhear what our mother was saying.

But she ignored him.

"Most of the rest of Europe has been made commonly popular," she went on, "and filled with the sort of English you'd run a mile from over here in England. But in those Northern countries you may feel pretty sure you won't meet any of these schoolteachery kinds of people. Even in Paris you have to be careful where you go, for fear of coming up against them suddenly. That's why, when I am staying there, I hardly ever go beyond the doors of the Hotel Meurice. I know I am safe inside there. But if I were to stray into Montmartre, and visit places like the Folies Bergères, I'd be certain to see some English clergyman in plain clothes, or some tittering English schoolmasters, salaciously watching the naked women as they paraded before them, and imagining they were seeing the real Paris. On the whole, of course, it's safer for your soul to stay at home."

My father felt a little sad those days at Heather Cliff at the mention of Russia. As it might be expected from his writing of adventure stories, he yearned for foreign lands. It was hard on him that my mother should feel so strongly against the benefits of travel. I remember the light that came upon his face one day as she admitted that she would never be quite the same again after her one week's memory of Moscow and the "queer, sinister people in it." Was she, perhaps, changing her mind? But he was too wise to say anything to her about it, and, while she settled down to her own world of story writing as though nothing could ever take her away from it, he took comfort in poring over maps for hours at a time, a soft look in his eyes.

Sometimes he could be seen smiling tenderly at his Gladstone bag, upon which was pasted the label of a Moscow hotel. This was one of his most treasured possessions, and on the infrequent occasions when he used it he took care always to carry it with the label side outwards. This label was the symbol of adventure. He cherished it as though it were a relic in a church.

"You may stroke it carefully, Clare," he said to me sometimes. "It has magic in it. I want you to remember where it came from, and to think of all the wonderful things it is associated with."

And he would tell me stories of this memorable journey.

But a very cruel thing happened to him. It was the fault of the good sticking quality of English paste. Once it had occurred there was no possibility of mending matters. It was irrevocable.

A few years after the visit to Russia, my father had to judge at a two-day dog show in Croydon.

"I'm sorry it should be in Croydon," sighed my mother. "It is one of those completely common suburbs of London which one would never even admit to having visited. It is most unfortunate that you should have to go there—and even more so that you should have to stay overnight."

My father packed his Gladstone bag with the Moscow label and, at Victoria Station, gave it into the care of a porter. But when he arrived at Croydon, and got the bag out from the luggage van, he found that the porter had pasted a Croydon label on top of the Moscow one. He stormed and raged all over the station, cursing all porters of all railways for all time. He tried to remove the Croydon label; but the paste had stuck it so fast that there was no way in which it could be taken off. He went to the station master and demanded that the label be removed. It was no good. The Moscow hotel was hidden from sight forever.

But though this tangible sign of the visit to Moscow had been destroyed, the sudden friendship with this Russian aristocrat was bringing back to my parents all the glamour of their one great journey. These three people who knew and loved Russia lived within a magic circle, which it was impossible for outsiders to enter.

"What did I tell you, George?" said our mother one day when Mr. Bowles was staying with us. "You supposed I'd be bored down here, away from London. Not a bit of it. All the best people live in the country these days, and those who can't wish they did."

Physically my mother and father lived at Heather Cliff, and my mother took her daily exercise along the winding drives, past the tennis court and the orchard, the greenhouse and the ornamental pond, and back again to the house; but spiritually they were in a world of their own, beyond reach of the local inhabitants. It was a world of Paris and Russia, my mother's romantic melodramas and my father's Wild West. When the local rector and his wife, the curates and even the naval officers who were stationed at Lowestoft, came to tea, they saw no more than a shadow of the Leighton family.

13. *War Years*

It was the first summer at Heather Cliff. While our mother and father lived within their own world of the imagination, Evelyn and I found excitement in the life of Lowestoft. For suddenly we were free. No longer held down by the old nurse, we perspired over bicycle rides with the curates and got drenched to the skin in boating expeditions on the Norfolk Broads with naval lieutenants. More wonderful still, we were seeing a great deal of our brother Roland.

Now that we had emerged from the nursery, this remote god whom we worshiped seemed to be aware of our existence, and came for walks with us, and laughed and talked. Joyfully we worked together. While Roland was writing poetry, I painted pictures of Heaven or the Day of Judgment, and Evelyn drew warships and diagrams of the flags of all the nations. Together we made plans for our future. After triumphs at Oxford, Roland would be a poet and a diplomat. Evelyn would end up as an admiral. I would become a great painter.

The summer days were golden with promise.

Our lives were so rich that we did not seem to realize what was happening in the world. Everything appeared secure.

The weeks of that summer of 1914 passed.

Roland did not go to Oxford. Instead, he became a second lieutenant, and disappeared to a camp. The god, whom Evelyn and I had so recently laughed with and played with, forsook us. We were desolate and inconsolable.

But our mother rebuked us.

"This," she said, "will be your test. It is all very well to be able to cope with life when everything is going smoothly. The important thing is to discover whether you are strong enough to cope with it when it turns against you. Now look at me. I shall go on as usual, whatever happens, for as long as I can. Do not let me have to be ashamed of you."

And she turned to Walmy, who was sitting before the typewriter in the study at Heather Cliff, with a look of defiance upon her face.

"Where was I, Miss Walmisley?" she asked. "This instalment is already overdue. Let the children mope if they choose to. It won't do them any good. They'll have to learn sooner or later that there is such a thing as self-discipline."

The war gathered force, yet the pattern of our life remained the same. When we passed the study door we heard the customary tap of the typewriter and the sound of our mother's voice, as she dictated to Walmy. Each day she took her exercise along the winding drives, past the silent tennis court and the orchard, and back to the house.

It was Evelyn and I who came first against the tragedy of war.

"Whatever are those little fishing boats?" Evelyn asked me one morning, as we were looking out of the dining room window after breakfast. "I don't recognize them, and I thought I knew all about every boat that passed along the North Sea. They're so tiny. They're even smaller than some of the shrimpers. And how they're tossing. It's almost as though they'd get sunk."

We rushed upstairs to the attic, to look through our father's telescope.

The little boats were filled to overflowing with women and children, and even babies in arms. They flew the Belgian flag. Suddenly we recollected some of the war news our father had been reading aloud at breakfast. These must be Belgian refugees.

"They're heading for the harbor and the fish market," said Evelyn. "Let's go and meet them."

The Belgian refugees staggered from the storm-tossed little boats to the quay, seasick and scared. There was a look in their eyes we had never seen before. It was something outside of the security of our childhood.

When we returned home, we heard our mother's voice still dictating to Walmy. But we did not enter the study. Instead, we crept upstairs to our separate bedrooms. We were confused. Life was no longer simple. Our mother's world was stamped with unreality.

The war grew closer to us.

"Funny," said our mother one morning, as she read through a letter she had opened. "They suddenly say they don't want the next serial from me. And I was perfectly sure of it, too. This is most upsetting and vexing. They add that their decision has nothing to do with the quality of the work I have been doing, but that they have to cut down the space given to my melodramas to make room for the casualty lists. This is awkward. I must think things out and make plans."

It was decidedly awkward. Our father did not earn enough with his boys' stories to keep the family at our present standard. Besides, we had always lived above our income. We had nothing to fall back upon.

"I suppose some people would say we ought to have saved over the years," smiled our mother. "But that's all very well for the great mass of the population, with its ideas of caution. I was never brought up to have such notions. My family considered it a sign of lack of breeding to save. I'm not *really* worried. Something always has happened and something always will happen. And at any rate, we can live for quite a long while on our overdraft."

It was fortunate for us that there was still that British institution called the overdraft. For some time we continued to draw checks upon a nonexistent bank account.

Outwardly the Leighton family went on as usual. We ran up the same enormous bills, and kept the same number of servants. The servants' wages, it is true, began to slip into arrears, but our mother felt confident that she could handle this.

"So long as I treat them as human beings, they won't mind waiting for their money," she said.

She spent a little longer than usual in the kitchen each morning after breakfast, talking with the cook.

"When you come to think of what those men are having to put up with in the trenches," I overheard her saying one day, "and when you pause for a moment to imagine the cold and mud and danger, you will realize how fortunate anyone is who has a roof over his—or *her*—head, and food enough to keep from starving."

"Yes'm," answered the cook. But there was a lack of enthusiasm in her voice. Big money was being paid in the munitions factory a few miles away.

Rumors began to surround us, over the first months of the war. Tales of possible German invasion sent the local population slinking inland each night to sleep. My mother was contemptuous of this cowardice.

"Poor souls," she called them, as she heard of their flight. "I scarcely think they're worth saving, if they've got so little ordinary sense of courage and adventure. It would almost serve them right if the Germans were actually to land and destroy them all. What really upsets me, though, is hearing that one or two colonels' wives have been seen on the 'heroes train' for Norwich. They are supposed to be ladies, and ladies should show no fear. I don't know what the world is coming to these days."

But in spite of our mother's courageous spirit, we did realize that we were exposed to special danger.

"Heather Cliff stands alone against the skyline, Chummie," our father tried to impress upon her. "It's on a cliff overlooking the North Sea, and it's probably about the nearest dwelling to Germany. And the war has only just started. There's no telling what may happen to us before long. . . . At any rate, I do think we'd be wise to bury some of our more precious belongings in the garden."

"You can do it if you want to, Robert," answered our mother. "But as far as I'm concerned I don't see much point in it. You see, *things* don't matter—especially in wartime. War elevates one to the basic values in life, till the only important consideration is the mind and the spirit. However, if it will make you feel happier, go ahead and bury anything you want to."

Our father had greater interest in possessions. He cherished some of our belongings. But it was not so much the intrinsic value of the thing that concerned him as his associations with it. And thus it was that he was most worried about the grandfather clock.

"To think that it may be exposed to a German bomb," he sighed as he stood in front of it, where it ticked away in the hall, beneath the dome of many-colored glass. "And after the glory of its past, too. The hiding place of Bonnie Prince Charlie deserves a worthier end."

"Well, you can't very well bury the grandfather clock, Robert," said our mother as she passed through the hall on her way to the study. "It would be even more humiliating for your poor Bonnie Prince Charlie if it ended up as food for the worms. I'd rather be dramatically destroyed by a bomb any day than undergo slow disintegration by earthworms."

Reluctantly my father decided that the grandfather clock would have to stay where it was and take its chance. But there were other things that would not be damaged by earthworms. One morning he was seen to search the kitchen quarters for all the available empty biscuit tins.

We were going to bury the family china.

Neither the Leightons nor the Trelawnys had ever been rich in this world's goods. The Trelawnys, though, had a substantial collection of old Dresden and Sèvres china. When Grandmamma Trelawny died she left this precious china to her sister, our Aunt Pollie, along with an enormous bronze statue of Phryne and quite a lot of valuable jewelry.

"I bear Pollie no grudge about all the jewelry," my mother had said, "for, as you know, I don't hold with wearing jewels. Neither do I want the china. But I do think Mamma might have given *me* the Phryne. She has left me nothing except a perfectly hideous heavy diamond ring that is suited to a dowager. But she knew perfectly well what the bronze statue meant to me. I've told her many a time how the voluptuous curves of that nude female figure satisfied my soul. Phryne was 'made' to stand in the corner of the hall at Vallombrosa, where it could be seen as you entered the house. As it is, Pollie is ashamed of it, and hides it away in the downstairs lavatory, where it is in semidarkness."

But one day, without giving us any warning of her extraordinary behaviour, Auntie Pollie vanished. It turned out that she had gone to Canada, to spend the rest of her life with my mother's half brother and his family, in Toronto. The first intimation we had of her sudden disappearance was the arrival at Vallombrosa of half a dozen big packing cases filled with the china. The jewelry, apparently, went with Auntie Pollie to Canada. Phryne vanished as completely as our aunt.

The fragile, delicate-colored Dresden shepherds and shepherd-esses were covered with numberless rivets. This had been one of Auntie Pollie's particular caprices.

"Of course I have broken my china on purpose," she boasted. "In this way I can prove that it is genuine. The rivets show that. Nobody would have bothered to get mere copies of Dresden figures so abundantly and expensively mended."

And now, during the early days of the war, we wrapped these much riveted little figures in tissue, and packed them in the empty biscuit tins. Evelyn and I went to the garden with our father, to dig holes where we might hide our treasure.

"One of these days, when the war is over, we'll have a great time digging it up again," laughed our father.

We had difficulty in deciding where to place these holes.

"Better have them some distance from each other," Father advised. "In that way, if a German shell or a bomb should drop among them it wouldn't be so apt to destroy all the tins at one time."

Already, during an unexpected German bombardment, our tennis court had been ripped by a shell.

But I cannot remember exactly where we hid our treasure. It is still there. Heather Cliff is no longer ours. Today, I believe, it is an Anglican convent, unless, of course, it has been destroyed during the Second World War.

But although I have forgotten where we buried the china, I do recollect the excitement we felt as we replanted disturbed daffodil bulbs and irises on top of the biscuit tins beneath the earth. Our garden housed hidden treasure. Never again would it be a mere garden. Magic had been added to it.

So excited were we two children over this romantic adventure that we could not understand how our mother could stay indoors working, instead of joining us. But she was busy just now with her play.

Finding herself suddenly with no serials to write, once more she perceived the hand of Destiny. This was the heaven-sent moment to write her play.

"The war won't go on forever," she said, "and even as it is, the world needs to escape into something other than fighting. I can't help thinking that palmist meant me to get my play written now, while there is an unavoidable pause in my potboilers."

And so she kept Walmy in front of the typewriter all the day long, as she plotted her play.

But there were unplanned interruptions. The evening work was sometimes badly disturbed.

We were troubled by air raids.

Most of the zeppelins intended for raiding London arrived over England near our part of the East Coast. Some of them hovered in the sky above us and, hovering, dropped their bombs.

We had a very large cellar at Heather Cliff. Over the months before the war we had used it to store the many pieces of furniture we did not need. But now it was to be put to another purpose. Because it occupied only the back part of the house, so that on one side it was banked with earth, it was an exceptionally safe retreat in an air raid, or even a bombardment. The townspeople knew this, and women with tiny babies walked the three miles out to our house, so that they might shelter from possible bombs. At the first news of an approaching zeppelin the electric lights of the town were extinguished. Somehow or other these people got to know about this even before it happened, and often when we were working in the carefully curtained house, we heard high-pitched voices shouting to us to let them in.

"Dear me," said our mother, as the frightened voices called to us. "This means another night of disturbance. And just as I was in a thoroughly good working mood, too. Of course, you might say that there is no reason why I shouldn't go on with my dictating, as though nothing were happening. But apart from the fact that a bomb might quite easily fall on the house and kill me, there's far too much noise about for me to be able to concentrate."

Our mother joined the crowd in the cellar.

On these nights of air raid alarms, the atmosphere of the cellar soon became disagreeably close, for there was little possibility of fresh air percolating into it. But it was not only because of the airlessness that our mother suffered.

"War most surely does make one put up with things one would have thought impossible," she whispered to me one evening, as we sat huddled in the darkness. "If there's anything I consider important, it is the sanctity of the home. And now our home has suddenly been invaded by the outside world—and not the kind of outside world I would have chosen to come closely against. If I had been told, at Vallombrosa, that unknown mothers and children were going to sleep one of these days in the upholstered armchairs that used to stand in the front drawing room, I would never have believed it. Somehow, it reminds me of the stories of the French Revolution. I suppose I'm living history."

But not only did children sleep in the upholstered furniture. Babies even wetted the chairs that had been sat in by velvet-gowned guests on At Home Days in St. John's Wood, while mothers opened their dresses and fed their infants on a sofa that had stood in the hall at Vallombrosa.

Sometimes, when a bomb fell a little way off, one of the women shrieked and wakened all the babies. It was then that my mother suffered most. For if there was anything in the world she disliked, it was the crying of a baby.

"It's such an impoverishing sound," she said to us later. "It's bad enough to have had to put up with your own, when they were at the screaming age, without being forced to listen to all these strange ones. Their mothers ought to be able to control them better. But then, these women have got the psychology of the refugee. It's a funny thing, you know, but all refugees look and act alike.

Whether it's those Belgians you told me about, or the dismal, dreary creatures that one sees pictures of in the newspapers these days, they puzzle me. I find myself wondering where they come from, for one never notices them in the ordinary course of life. It's only when something like a war comes along that they appear suddenly in the limelight . . . But I do wish they had more self-control. You see if I'm not right in saying that if a bomb were to fall especially near us these women who gather here in our cellar on air raid nights will probably faint and moan and want brandy."

However much my mother might talk like this, though, she opened her doors to anyone who wanted to come.

"There's a sense of drama even to their dreariness," she decided. "And whatever you may choose to think, this is an epic age. As I said before, we are experiencing history."

Heather Cliff was not an easy house to live in during a war. Because it stood alone on this bluff, overlooking the North Sea, it was a conspicuous landmark. As such, it had to be blacked out with special care. It was difficult enough to darken the countless windows we had been so proud of, but to obscure the dome seemed an impossibility. Try as we might, we could not prevent rays from shining skyward and seaward. Soldiers patrolling the coast knocked at our door at all times of the night, ordering us to turn out our lights. People even reported they had seen them burning in the early hours of the morning.

We began to wonder why it was that we were looked at in such a strange way when we walked through the town. It was the cook who enlightened us.

"They says as 'ow you must be spies, and they'd better be watchin' you," she told our mother. "Of course, I tells them as they is all wrong, and that it's only because they don't understand your queer ways. But they won't believe me, and they is always asking me about you. Why did you 'appen to come to live 'ere so short a time before the outbreak of the war, they says, choosing to forget all those years at The Red Croft. You don't earn your livelihood in Lowestoft, so there seems no 'onest and good reason for your deciding to come 'ere—and especially to this 'ouse with the dome. It's the dome, m'm, what gets them feeling bad and worried. Why, they says to me, that 'ouse as you works in, it's the very place for a German spy. If it 'ad been built special, it couldn't be better, what with all those windows and the dome that is being used to signal from. And then, of course, I tells them as you is all of you queer, being writers as you might say. If I don't take care, m'm, I'll be 'aving them suspect me too."

My mother's appearance scarcely helped to dispel these suspicions. In her Paris clothes and her elaborate hats, she did not belong to the provinces, and the local people might be forgiven if they mistook her for a typical conspirator.

But my father's deafness added fuel to the rumors. One evening he did not hear the sentry's challenge as he came back from mailing some letters, and was almost shot. He stormed at the soldier, which only made matters worse. The neighborhood was getting increasingly suspicious of us.

Meanwhile, we crept about after sunset with difficulty. If the dome had been isolated from the rest of the house we could have managed the blackout more easily; but it was in the center of the hall, and each time we opened the door of any room the light would have streamed out and been visible from the sky. For a long time we felt bewildered as to what to do. But suddenly my father had an idea.

"Let's get more of that black stuff we pin over the windows," he said, "and make hangings across all the doors. Then we can come in and out of the rooms when the lights are on without even a gleam escaping to the dome."

But already it took so long each night to pin the draperies across the windows with thumbtacks, that we decided to leave the door hangings in position during the daytime.

"I know what it reminds me of," laughed our mother, as she stood in the middle of the hall with the draperies in place. "All these black hangings, and with the dome above, make the house look exactly like a Continental church during a funeral. I find myself searching in vain for the catafalque."

But our mother could not see how amusing she herself looked as she suddenly pushed aside a black drapery after breakfast and emerged hatless, low-necked and bare-armed, in one of her pink, frilly morning jackets.

"If you aren't careful, Chummie," chuckled our father, "you'll find there's a priest lurking somewhere round a corner, ready to tell you that you are not decently attired for being inside a church."

The servants in their uniforms seemed equally out of place, and the "Merry Widow Waltz," played on our gramophone, sounded deeply sacrilegious. As Walmy had once said, here in this house you felt you must speak in a hushed voice.

Considering that it never entered our heads to cover the dome with a coat of black paint, the most sensible thing would have been to go to bed early and get up next day correspondingly betimes. But this seemed an impossibility with my mother.

"I have nothing but contempt for people who retire early," she said. "And why should I change my habits, just because there is a war on? That would be a form of defeat. I've never gone to bed before two or three o'clock in the morning, and I've never wanted more than five, or at most, six, hours of sleep. There's an old rule about sleep I believe in: 'six hours for a man, seven for a woman, and eight for a fool.' You might think I ought to class myself as a woman, but when it comes to the things of the brain, I class myself as a man."

My father, though, suffered from this austerity, for he seemed to need far more sleep.

"Your mother just doesn't seem to understand," he confided to me one day. "I'm terribly behindhand in my sleep. I've been adding up the hours of which she has deprived me, over the years, and they have reached an unbelievable figure. I'd never be able to make them up, even if I lived to be a hundred and were to stay asleep all the time."

Around midnight my father would try to escape to the bedroom, but my mother was wide awake and intercepted him.

"I would like you to read to me, Robert," she told him, "while I paste together these fashion pictures from the *Daily Mail*. I never have time to do it during the daytime, when Walmy is here."

Midnight passed into one o'clock. Two o'clock struck. And still she acted as though the day were young.

"What your mother never realizes, of course," my father went on in confidence to me, "is that she makes up for these late nights by dropping half asleep during the daytime, while she is being read to. Many a time I've seen her close her eyes and nod her head. But it would never do to let her know I have noticed this, and you must promise me you won't say a word to her about it."

It must have been because of her nocturnal activity that she did not seem to see how tired the war was making us children. As the months went by, the fear of invasion increased. More and more of the local inhabitants went inland each night to sleep.

"They do say that if the Germans land it will be on the particular strip of coast near Heather Cliff, where there is a break in the sandbanks," our mother told us with composure. "You know I don't believe in getting panicky, but I am beginning to think it might be wise for us to be prepared. Conceivably we may have to flee—and in the middle of the night, too."

And so when we went to bed we were made to place food, warm clothing, some money and any little treasures we wished to save, on the chair by the bedside.

We did not tell our mother of the fear we felt, or let her know how our sleep was broken by nightmares.

But this sleep was short. She decided that the safe thing to do was to keep watch through the hours of darkness for the electric light to be turned off. This would be the signal that something was wrong. When she herself went to bed between four and five in the morning—having had a short sleep earlier, while our father kept watch—she wakened me and my brother in order that we might keep a lookout until daylight came.

"It's safer to waken both of you," she decided, "lest one or the other should fall asleep. Not that I expect you to do so. You are too well brought up for that. Now it wouldn't be safe for me to make the servants take their share in keeping watch. They'd have no sense of responsibility, and the next thing to happen would be the Germans upon us, with no warning given, and the servants sound asleep in their beds."

However exhausted we were, our mother considered this good training for us. She did not let us go to bed any earlier the night before.

"One must be properly disciplined for an emergency," she told us. "My papa always impressed that upon me—and he was a soldier, and should have known. That is the way never to let life get the better of you."

But there were things other than fear of a German invasion that might be supposed to worry us. Our bills had been mounting. Knowing the Leighton habits, the tradespeople had been lenient, but there was a point past which even our family debts could not go.

One day the parlormaid came to my mother in confusion.

"If you please, m'm, Mr. Thompson is at the front door, and wanting to see you," she said apologetically.

"And *who* is Mr. Thompson?" asked my mother.

"It's Mr. Thompson the butcher, m'm," explained the parlormaid, getting red in the face.

"Tell him I'm busy," loftily answered my mother. "Oh, and

you might mention to him that I shall be writing to him in a day or two."

It was many months since the butcher had received a penny.

"To think of his daring to come to the house—and to the front door, too," she said. "It's enough to make me change butchers. People like that don't seem to realize that it's an honor for them to be owed money by us. But there you are. That's war. It upsets civilization. It gives a chance to the common people of the world, and makes them forget their place. They aren't capable of understanding the glory and glamour of war. They only see in it an opportunity to raise themselves in the social scale. It's always the upper classes that suffer most in time of war. You see if I am not right."

She was deeply outraged.

"In the glorious days of the Boer War it was different," she went on. "People knew their places more then. They had a queen they worshiped, and I don't care what the rest of the world says, a country is only at its best when it has a king or queen at its head that it can revere. The whole trouble about this war of ours now is that it has happened a few years too late. If Edward the Seventh had still been alive and on the throne you would have felt a pulse and a throb all through England; and Thompson the butcher would never have dared to come and ask me for payment of his bill. Wars are no longer the stimulating things they once were. Now in the Boer War we almost worshiped Lord Roberts and Lord Kitchener. That was an aristocratic war."

As far back as I could remember in my earliest childhood, I had been told of the greatness of Lord Roberts. My mother insisted that his photograph should stand in the place of honor on the nursery mantelpiece, as an example to us. We had only a vague idea, though, who he was. We knew he didn't belong to the family, but we never understood why he was important enough to be placed in the center of things. As we grew older our mother told us stories of the glory of the Boer War, and quoted poems by Rudyard Kipling; and the man with the row of medals and the elaborate military uniform, whose faded photograph stood next to Nanny's membership card for the Social Society of her Baptist Church, was woven into legends of a place called Ladysmith.

On the mantelpiece in my mother's bedroom, next to the photograph of Lily Elsie as the Merry Widow, stood a picture of Lord Kitchener. He had as many medals as Lord Roberts. In addition, he had a more imposing moustache. He, too, was one of her idols.

"When you grow up," she said to me, "you'll know—or you should, if there isn't too much of the Leighton side in you—that the only man worth giving yourself to is the man who has kept aloof from women. There is no satisfaction in seeing yourself as one of many, but if you are the great passion in the life of a man who has managed to live independent of sex, then you may know the gods have been good to you. I always feel that about Lord Kitchener. He never found the woman who was worthy of him or of his love. He could have been one of the world's greatest lovers. He would have been like Nelson with his Lady Hamilton. I tell you, if you want real passion you must go to the man of action. It is there you will find tenderness and love. You've only to look at people like your Uncle Jack to see how right I am. Intellectuals aren't any good. They're always thinking of themselves, and analyzing what they are feeling. They never lose themselves in the woman they love."

But Lord Kitchener had just been drowned. The World War did not produce heroes for my mother.

Meanwhile, there was the visit from the butcher.

And it was not only the butcher. Somehow or other, the grocer and the fishmonger, the coal merchant and the fruiterer must have heard of the butcher's visit, for we received communications from all of them, in letter and in person. The ring was tightening around us. The casualty lists in the papers grew longer each day, and still there was no need for my mother's melodramas.

Suddenly everything came to a head. The bank had foreclosed. We dismissed all the servants. Cook, parlormaid, housemaid, kitchen maid and my own maid Martha, they left us in a bunch, their wages still in arrears.

"You are victims of the war," my mother told them. "Never before have I had any of my servants leave me except to get married. But there are forces which are stronger than we are."

Walmy decided to stay with us for a while longer, although her salary was owing.

"Lo-ar, Mrs. Leighton," she said. "As if I'm the sort to be worrying about money. It'd be more than I could face, to think of you having to move from Heather Cliff without me to help you. When I remember the move from Vallombrosa, and the muddles we had, I know perfectly well how much you'll be needing me. Don't you think any more about it. I'm staying."

We were leaving our pretentious mansion. My mother's adorer "Silenus" was ill, and had retired from the City. No longer did we have a friend to help us.

Day after day we read through the advertisements of cottages in the newspapers.

"It's really rather exciting, if you come to think about it," smiled our mother. "There's absolutely nothing in the world to stop us from going to live anywhere in this entire island. What's that you have found? An inexpensive furnished cottage in the Lake District? The climate there would make me lethargic and romantic, and that isn't good in wartime. And not the Midlands, either. They are unstimulating and dull. I think our choice had better be narrowed down to the South of England. It will save time if you bear that in mind."

One day we found an advertisement of what seemed the ideal cottage. It was at the foot of the South Downs, in Sussex.

"I'm not half as much interested in how many rooms it has as in where it is," said my mother. "This sounds perfect. It is only about ten miles from Brighton, and Brighton is even more fashionable than London. I think we'd better telegraph straight away and take it. How much did you say they are asking for it?"

Without even seeing a photograph of the place, we rented this tiny cottage in Sussex.

My mother was not unhappy at this turn of events. It mattered very little to her what our setting might be, for she carried her own world around with her always, and that world was the center of things.

"After all," she said, as we first set eyes on our new home, "the war won't last for ever. And coming here only goes to prove that if you're all right in yourself it doesn't matter whether you live in a palace or a hovel. I consider that this cottage in Sussex is exactly the right place in which to spend the war years. Anyone who lives in grander quarters elsewhere is acting unpatriotically."

And so the family moved in. Considering the smallness of the place, it was fortunate that we had sold most of our possessions and that almost all of the dogs had died by now of old age. But even as it was, there was congestion. Trunks cluttered the miniature rooms, and my mother's bundles lay around all over the cottage. They had arrived unsorted from Heather Cliff. The contents of some of them went back to the early days in St. John's Wood. This time they even strayed into the kitchen. For there was no longer a cook to keep us and the bundles in our place.

"Really, you know, there's something to be said for being free," decided our mother. "If Nellie were still cooking for us we'd have to keep out of the kitchen. As it is, I find it the most inspiring room in the entire cottage, and I shall turn it into my study. You may work wherever you choose, Robert, but I mean to stay here, in the kitchen. Besides, this is the only good-sized table in the place. All those in the sitting room are so ladylike and tiny. I can spread my papers out here, and not have to pile them up every time we need to lay the table for a meal."

My mother's work covered everything in the kitchen except the cooking range.

It turned out to be a most sensible arrangement. We could combine work and cooking with the least amount of inconvenience. While my mother dictated her play to me—for now that Walmy had left I had taken her place as typist—we could watch the pots on the stove and even peel the potatoes for the next meal.

Neither my mother nor I knew how to cook. We children had never been allowed inside the kitchen. But now we did not even own a cookbook.

"That doesn't matter," said my mother. "If you have brains and imagination for one thing you have brains and imagination for another. We'll manage somehow. In fact, I shouldn't be surprised if we didn't turn out to be most ingenious cooks. After all, it's in our family. Think back to my mamma and Pollie. Have you ever tasted more perfect food anywhere? And they despised cookbooks. I don't suppose any of the world's great chefs follow printed recipes, any more than the great dressmakers use paper patterns. I am certain we can invent wonderful dishes."

One of the first things we made was a suet pudding.

"We must begin by deciding what the ingredients are," my mother told me solemnly. "Undeniably there must be suet, else it would not be called a suet pudding. Then, too, there must be flour . . . I suggest you chop the suet while I think over what else to do . . . Yes, I know. Surely we need something liquid, to bind the mixture together. How would it be if we were to use some milk? That would anyhow make it nourishing."

We stirred the contents of the milk jug into the mixture, tied the result into one of my father's handkerchiefs and dumped it into boiling water. No suet pudding had ever tasted so good before.

My mother's time sense, however, was unreliable. Never was

she ready for any meal at the proper hour, and I have known us to sit down to the midday dinner around four in the afternoon, just as the rector's wife was walking up the garden path to pay us a call. There was a scramble to remove the dishes of food to the kitchen before we should open the front door.

"Not that I'm ashamed to be seen eating at this time of the afternoon," my mother said as she sailed out of the sitting room with the steak and kidney pie. "It is, in fact, fashionable to eat late rather than early. You've only got to think for a moment of the sort of people who indulge in high tea, instead of late dinner, to realize this. No, the only thing that makes me take these things away is that there is something unpicturesque about a half-finished meal. It is even somewhat sordid."

By this time the rector's wife had waited at the front door, and might have supposed the Leightons were out had she not seen dim figures moving around within the house and heard Mother's voice. When she entered the room, there was only the tablecoth left, upon which stood a cruet containing salt and pepper, and a few knives and forks. But I knew that the house must smell strongly of steak and kidney pie, and I was not surprised when I saw the nostrils of the rector's wife unwittingly dilate, as though trying to discover what was being cooked at such a queer hour of the afternoon. She was far too polite on this occasion to make any comments.

But as time went on, the rector's wife grew fond of us, with our unorthodox ways, and named us "the dear disreputables."

"What can you know about cooking, when your mind is on your writing all the time?" she laughed at my mother. And, supposing us to be half starved from lack of any sense of domesticity, she would bring pies and cakes and vegetables and leave them on the front doorstep.

"I really can't think why she should imagine I don't know how to run an establishment," said my mother. "I've given far bigger dinner parties than she'll ever be called upon to have. Just because

I'm what she calls a 'Bohemian,' is no reason why I can't cook. When you come to think of it, some of the world's greatest creative people have been the best cooks. If I chose to I could feel really insulted."

Remembering this, I never told my mother that occasionally, when I met the rector's wife in the village, she would haul me into the Rectory for what she called "a good square meal at the right time." I knew my mother would be angry. But I was often quite glad of this food, as she grew increasingly careless about mealtime.

"What about supper, Chummie?" my father would ask, as the clock showed it to be half-past eight. "If you're busy I'll go along and get it ready."

"Oh," answered my mother, "it's far too early for supper. Why, in the old days at Vallombrosa Walmy never stopped work until nine o'clock. Besides, it must have been nearly seven o'clock before we finished tea. Let me go on for a little while longer."

Actually my mother was not working. She was in the mood to talk. The hands of the clock moved round in a complete circle and then nearly into a second circle, before either Father or I could find a pause in her conversation during which we might suggest that as it was now past ten o'clock, supper would be a good idea. Over the years her structure of living had been held in place by the punctual sounding of the dinner gong, or the arrival and departure of Walmy. Now that these supports no longer existed, the days sprawled.

They were strange days, in their busy shapelessness. They were filled from morning to night with cooking and scrubbing and washing. Though my mother was publishing a few short stories, in addition to plotting her play, there was little money for anything except actual food and rent. But we did not seem to care.

"A lady can remain a lady whatever housework she may have to do," my mother continually reminded me. "And this applies to a gentleman, too," she added, turning to look pointedly at my father, whom she never considered as quite a gentleman. "Why, when I remember how my mamma and papa used to wash dishes and cook and scrub while the family finances were low, I assure you that they made it into the right thing to do. They even made it seem underbred *not* to do it. But there is no need to let the whole world know what you are doing. Mamma was very wise about this. When she went out anywhere she looked exactly as though she employed at the very least a dozen servants. Nobody would have supposed she had just finished scrubbing the sink."

My mother took her full share of the housework. The typewriter was moved from room to room according to what she was doing. When she made their bed it was hauled upstairs to the little bedroom with the dormer window, and although she probably did no dictating, yet she felt happier when she could see the machine.

"It reminds me that I really *am* a writer," she said. "Otherwise I might find myself getting caught up into the entanglements of domesticity and, before I knew it, I would be concerning myself with the dust on the mantelpiece or thinking up cakes to make for tea."

As it was, she used the cooking as a background for working. Interested in the story she was dictating, she stood at the kitchen table kneading the dough for an apple pie.

"I find myself almost sorry I never had this chance those years at Vallombrosa," she said, as the kneading went on over an hour or two. "It's an interesting thing, but my mind works much better when I'm doing something with my hands. I wonder if I have made an important discovery, or whether anyone else had known this?"

The apple pie was ready for the midday meal around the middle of the afternoon. It was unexpectedly good. No one could possibly have said that the pastry had been made in too much of a hurry.

But behind all these domesticities hung the background of war. Brought up by a military father, my mother had no horror of war. She was a romanticist, and saw in it color and drama. The world was peopled with heroes. She belonged to the sanctified community of women throughout the ages, whose sons had fought the enemy in foreign lands. And it was well for her that she felt this, for, though we had left behind us on the East Coast the immediate danger of zeppelin raids, and the fear of invasion, the war was still close to us. As I went to the farm to fetch the afternoon milk I heard the guns from France, ceaselessly pounding. The farmer's wife said it was the well that carried the sound. When I walked along the ridge of the Downs the boom of the guns echoed among the hills. Casualty lists filled the daily papers, and more and more of Roland's friends were being killed.

But my mother held her head high, and quoted Byron and Rupert Brooke.

> "Blow out, you bugles, over the rich Dead!
> There's none of these so lonely and poor of old,
> But, dying, has made us rarer gifts than gold."

Roland was out in France, among the guns. He was a Knight of the Round Table, a shining knight in armor, a dreamer, an inheritor of all the glories of the world.

If she were afraid for him, she kept this to herself. Outwardly she assumed a certainty that he would not be killed.

"He'll come through it all right," she said with lightness in her voice. "Nothing has ever gone wrong for him. He has a charmed life. The gods couldn't possibly let him die, even though they must love him so. There's so much for him to do in this world. Besides, didn't Cheiro tell us that he would end up as an important military figure and die in battle at the age of sixty? And he's only just twenty now. No, there's absolutely nothing to worry about."

And so she took her walks gaily along the little Sussex lanes. Our cottage garden was too small for this daily exercise.

"But you must go some little way in front of me," she told me.

"I've got to be absolutely sure there are no bulls about in the fields. Take good care to look over the hedges."

Even in the midst of war and bombs and shells, she still felt certain that it would be through some member of "the second order of creation" that she was to meet her death.

She walked through the village street, wearing her ermine stole and her sable-trimmed velvet coat, as though she were treading upon the pile carpet of a palace. She sailed into the village post office, carrying her ermine muff. But the Parma violets upon that muff had had, these days, to be imaginary. Who was to say that the imagination could not produce Parma violets as magical as any that could be bought at a florist's? And what did it matter that the sable-trimmed velvet coat was growing shabby and worn with time? She looked around her in the village post office, at hobbling Miss Gander who sold the postage stamps, and at rosy-cheeked Mrs. Heathorn who kept the bakery at the far side. She smiled at them and at the doctor's wife who had just entered the shop in severe tweeds; and it was the smile of indulgent graciousness.

As I write this, I find myself back in a pension at Cannes, on the Riviera. This pension was kept by a Russian princess. The man in the green baize apron, who carried my luggage to my room, was her son, with whom she had escaped when he was a few days old. All around me, at the dinner table, sat Russian nobility in exile, dressed in shabby splendor that had belonged to the pre-revolution era. Their minds lived in the past, too. They addressed each other with a graciousness and a courtesy that was very moving. In the next room, upon an easel, stood a large painting of the Tsar and the Tsarina, heavily draped in black. Looking then at these people, I had found myself placing my mother among them. These were the people who had outlived their age. They were people who no longer belonged . . . They sat there and bowed in exactly the same way in which my mother bowed to the doctor's wife.

There was something all of them carried which life could not strip from them. Inside their hearts they nursed the same desolation. Their worlds had been destroyed. But upon their outward persons they would wear the ermines and velvets of their former glory. No one should ever see what had happened to them.

And so, as my mother walked down the street of this little Sussex village in her shabby sable-trimmed velvet coat she, too, carried an emptiness within her. But, holding her head high, she did not mean to show her suffering. The world must never know.

For Roland had been killed.

He had been killed in France half an hour before he was to start home on Christmas leave.

My mother's love for him had amounted almost to idolatry. He was the child of her atonement. Married when she was only seventeen, she had let her first baby die from a nurse's neglect. In Roland she determined to make amends. Besides, had he not loved things like scarlet silk stockings, red carnations and poetry? And was he not beautiful, like a knight in shining armor?

My mother went about in a state of exaltation, proud at the remembrance of him.

But suddenly she was ill.

"This is strange," she said, after being many weeks in a dangerous condition. "I can't think what has happened to me. They say it's my heart, but I have never been ill in my life—except when my babies came. These stupid doctors seem to be worrying about me, keeping me flat in bed all this long time, as though they expected me to die if I were to stir. Little do they know how strong I am. I'll fool them yet. You see if I don't . . . Where did you put those last poems of Roland's? I'd like to look at them again."

As she lay reading some of these poems that had been returned to us with Roland's belongings from France, she discovered one that had a weak line in it.

"How could he have written it," she sobbed. "It must have been the Army life that affected him. He would never have put such a line down on paper in the old days before the war. He was always so aware of his standards. I simply cannot get over it. He would have been so ashamed of it himself. I know he would."

She wept over the line that did not scan. She was beginning to recover.

"People are so queer in the way they take their grief," she said. "They seem to expect you to go all to pieces. Now I know enough about Roland to be perfectly certain he'd much rather have me go on living my life than just lie down and moan. It will be a far greater tribute to what he and I have always considered worth while. As soon as the wretched doctors will allow me to do so—and perhaps even before that, if they get to be a nuisance—I mean to begin work once more, and finish my play."

A few days later she started dictating the third act of the play. Not even the entreaties of my father could stop her.

I was able now to spend more time at the typewriter, for, during my mother's illness, we had discovered someone to work for us.

She was an extraordinary woman with long gold earrings and intricately plaited shiny black hair. She looked as though she should be telling our fortunes, and it seemed strange to see her innocently washing dishes or making a bed.

"There's no doubt about it, Mrs. Chatfield *must* be a gypsy," my mother decided. "Whenever she comes into the room with my tray I seem to see a background of caravans and circus tents, and baskets of lace and clothes pins, and white clay pipes. I even feel I have to be careful not to annoy her, lest she should cast an evil spell upon me. And I don't mean this only in fun, for we have, as I may remind you, cause to be scared of gypsies."

It seemed that the day before the young nurse accidentally smothered my mother's first baby, a gypsy had come to the house in St. John's Wood, with laces and ribbons to sell. The servant who answered the door had sent her away with anger, and the gypsy had spat upon the doorstep and said, as she left: "Very well. There'll be a death in this house within twenty-four hours."

If Mrs. Chatfield had only known, she could have twisted us round her little finger.

But there was one important thing she did do. During those drear days in the Sussex cottage it was she who kept our spirits high, and diverted us with her gaiety. It was impossible to stay gloomy with her about the house. In the frilled calico skirts that swirled around her ankles, and her gaudy-colored bodices, she was like some one from the chorus in the second act of *Il Trovatore*. Gypsy music seemed to surround her, even while she emptied the slops, and when she answered a ring at the front door she stood there in the entrance, her arms akimbo, as though she were about to break into a wild Romany dance.

"Sometimes it amuses me to imagine what these ultrarespectable local people must think when they come to call on us," laughed our mother. "They would expect to see a severely uniformed servant open the door to them, instead of this figure who looks as though she were waiting for her cue to whirl herself behind the footlights."

But the neighborhood was beginning to get to know us, and little would have surprised them. It was a good thing for the respectability of the Leighton family, though, that Evelyn returned from Osborne for his holidays, wearing the uniform of a cadet in His Majesty's Navy.

The guns still echoed from the well at Mrs. Bye's farm, when I fetched the milk. They thundered night and day, in March 1918, and every young man we knew had been killed. I had grown afraid to walk alone over the Downs, against the sound of these guns; the air seemed blurred with ghosts.

November brought the Armistice. I could get the milk now without fear. The well was silent. War was over. The men were coming home.

But to us no one returned. My mother walked along the Sussex lanes like a creature in fancy dress that had strayed from some carnival, and lost its way.

Life had been unable to defeat her. She did not even feel bitterness about Roland's death. The powerful alchemy of a sense of drama had infused a cosmic quality into her desolation.

"Why won't people see that it isn't what life does to them that matters, but how they cope with what life does?" she said. "Women have had their sons killed in battle from time immemorial, and they have not whined. And why should I be inferior to them in my spirit?"

She began to go to Brighton. In that seaside resort which retained its Regency atmosphere, she seemed more completely at home. There she entertained her London friends and admirers. Mr. Bowles, who was the only one of "Mother's Old Men" still living, again pinned Parma violets upon her ermine muff. Even Uncle Jack had grown gentle and understanding.

She was enjoying Brighton.

"It's one of the few places in England which has had the power to retain its true values," she said. "It has been able to withstand the rising tide of that drab thing called democracy. No sooner do you emerge from the railway station than you feel you are in a world to which you belong. If Brighton begins to succumb to this new-fangled glorification of the middle class, I shall begin to worry about life."

And she smiled her most engaging smile to the new friend opposite her, a Grenadier Guardsman just back from the trenches, who could have stepped straight out of a novel by Ouida.

Sitting there in this Brighton hotel, clothed in her mourning for Roland, she was enjoying herself with this young captain. She was touching the fringes of war. Life had lost none of its drama. Her personal grief had been merged in the common pool of human suffering. The violets on her ermine muff were still sweet.

14. *The Last Edwardian*

A new sense of protection had come into our feeling for our mother. Though she did not know it, we were aware of the desolation within her. I had seen her sometimes, when she thought she was alone, standing bleakly in the pose of the Tragic Muse, her head held high like a challenge.

We were doing everything we could to occupy her mind.

And so we were glad when a new adorer appeared.

It was my father who had introduced him. They had worked together in an Army camp.

"I look upon him as a perfect godsend," my father confided to me. "What your mother needs just now is to get interested in someone who never knew Roland. It will switch her mind into fresh channels."

But this adorer caused considerable consternation among my mother's friends. Uncle Jack was openly jealous.

"If you had chosen a man who was my superior—or even my equal—I could have put up with it better," he fumed. "But this is a downright insult. Why, the fellow is completely devoid of intellect. He has never read a real book. He knows absolutely nothing about music. In fact, he isn't even educated."

Mr. Bowles took a more definite stand. He refused to visit us.

The newcomer was a handsome Welshman, with the dark, bullet-shaped head and the blue eyes of the Celt. He had neither intellect nor education. So far Uncle Jack was right. My mother, though, rejoiced in this.

"I am so tired of all these people who think they have minds," she sighed. "At last I have found a man who knows how to love. For true love comes from the heart, and not the brain. As I've always said, the brain is the enemy of passion."

The Welshman was a man of action. He had lived recklessly. This fascinated my mother for, despite her outward appearance of abandon, her own behavior remained exemplary. But she found it exciting to live adventure through someone else.

Her Celt was the son of a parson in Wales.

"And isn't that exactly like life?" our mother said. "You will see that it is from the rigid, inhibiting rectories of Great Britain that our swashbucklers emerge. And have you ever noticed how the severe military families throw up our wildest eccentrics? It's almost as though drastic pruning is as necessary for the human being as it is for the plant."

Llewellyn Hughes had run away from school when he was very young, and gone to sea. Now, on his weekly holiday from the Army camp, he sat by the hour before our cottage fire, telling us stories of his seafaring years. What did it matter that we had scarcely any money? We fed upon tales of the last of the blackbirding days, when his sailing ship went to Africa to seize Negroes for slaves.

"You have simply no idea, Pattie, how gorgeously beautiful the bodies of those colored girls were," he told my mother.

And as he described them she would turn to him, with a worried look in her eyes, wondering how many women had interested him before he fell in love with her.

These days were lived to the rhythm of sea chanteys he had learnt while he climbed the riggings of a sailing ship.

> Sally Brown was a bright mulatto,
>   Way-ay roll and go,
> She drinks rum and chews tobacco . . .

As the cottage fire sank to embers, the sea chanteys merged into fabulous accounts of his experiences in the lowest seamen's dives of San Francisco and Shanghai, the East End docks of London and the seaports of Australia.

"Quiet, Lew," urged my mother. "All this is very well for me to hear. I'm a married woman. But I won't have you teaching Clare too much of the wickedness of men. She's far too young to realize that there is one code of behavior for seamen and quite another for the men she will come up against. You know my views about the bringing up of young girls. I hold with shielding them from everything I possibly can. That's the only way to keep them alluring and romantic."

But the Celt looked across at my mother with a soft twinkle in his eye, and went on singing his unexpurgated chanteys.

Llewellyn had a wife. She was a Frenchwoman he had married on one of his voyages abroad. We had not yet met her. I think we were somewhat afraid of doing so. For were not Frenchwomen proverbially jealous? And how could we be sure she would understand that all men always fell in love with our mother? We seemed to be living the plot of one of our mother's own melodramas. Anything might happen. I rather think she herself was apprehensive, for she kept on questioning the Celt about his wife.

"But you haven't told me yet what Celeste looks like?" she asked him. "Is she dark and tragic, or small and chic? And can't you show me a photograph of her? Then I'd know what to expect and how to treat her."

But Llewellyn seemed to have no interest in discussing her. His mind just now was on our mother.

The French wife, meanwhile, had written a letter to my mother, in which she thanked her with polite impersonality for the kindness we had shown her husband. But this did not reassure us. On the contrary, my mother, who professed to know the wiles of women, read into the lines all sorts of hidden meaning.

"I'm afraid there's going to be difficulty with Celeste until I manage to win her over," she confided to me one day. "But I'm not seriously worried. I shall know how to treat her."

Celeste arrived. A plump, squat little middle-aged woman stood on the doorstep, looking like an uglier version of our Aunt Pollie. She had, it is true, the same high breasts that, Grandpapa had once said, possessed such allure for men. Perhaps it was these that had won the Celt's heart. They seemed, though, strangely out of fashion, for women at this time were making themselves appear as flat chested as possible.

"I'm sorry she's so ugly," my mother said. "Ugly women are always the ones to boast about the great and wonderful love their husbands bear them. Now if she were a beauty she would feel fundamentally sure of herself, and could afford to be humble and generous. Yes, it's a pity she's so hideous."

But Celeste was not going to be the trouble we feared. From the first moment she looked at my mother she became her willing slave.

The Celt, though, could not live on love alone. His wife was aware of this. Now that the Army camp was closed, she found work for him in London. They went off and left us.

My mother looked about her in the Sussex cottage. While her Welshman had been there he had chased away the ghosts. But they surrounded her now, and she was afraid.

She did not admit to this fear. Perhaps she was scarcely aware of it herself, so determined was she to hide it. But suddenly she decided to leave and go to London.

"It's absolutely essential for my work that I should live within reach of possible editors," she told my father. "The remote country-side was all right during the war, but it would be cultural suicide to stay here any longer. Somehow, I'd rather like to go to St. John's Wood. What do you think, Robert?"

And so we went back to St. John's Wood. The years we had spent in the Sussex cottage were sealed away, as a thing of the past.

"How wonderful it will be to walk down Elm Tree Road again, and hear the birds singing, and smell the lilac in bloom," she said, as we settled into the furnished house we had found.

But St. John's Wood did its utmost to betray her. Progress had stepped in, and standardization, and the thrushes sang no more in the blossoming pear trees. For great blocks of flats had been erected, hiding the sky. Vallombrosa had been demolished, and where our thirty-six lilac bushes once blossomed stood a row of shops.

My mother, though, was not going to allow herself to be upset by all this.

"If you have the right kind of vision, you can see the spirit of a place even through bricks and mortar," she declared. "I refuse to be depressed by the changes here since we left. St. John's Wood will always be St. John's Wood, even though it were leveled to the ground. Progress is powerless to destroy it. Believe it or not, I can see our row of linden trees and the high garden walls just as clearly as if I were to touch them with my hand. Anything that was so full of magic as the life of St. John's Wood could never really disappear. It is indestructible within the memory."

The Celt and his French wife came to live with us. As we moved from furnished house to furnished house, they moved with us. Lew went to work each morning and Celeste cooked our meals with the skill of a Frenchwoman. My father wrote his boys' stories, and my mother went on with her play.

It was significant that my mother had asked her Celt to call her "Pattie." This had been the name of her childhood, and not even my father was supposed to use it. There seemed to be something in common between this Welshman and her own Irish father. Both had an aggressive contempt for intellectuals, and both were men of action. It was as though my mother were being drawn more and more into the shelter of her past. As she sat beside this latest adorer, listening to his tales of hunting and shooting in Wales, on the family acres, her face took on the expression of an enraptured child.

"You know the cry of the little hen pheasant when she is disturbed on her nest, Pattie?" asked the Celt. And he would imitate it so exactly that the living room seemed as though it had been transformed into the wind-blown wilds of Wales, and I held my breath and waited for the rustle of a gun dog among the bracken, or the whirr of wings as a bird was flushed.

"You see if you can't imitate it," said the Celt. My mother tried to, but failed.

And then, as I laid the table, I would be startled by the sudden call of a quail, and know that the man sitting by the fireside was still out among the heather and the bracken, and that it would not be easy to draw these two Celtic creatures in from the moors, to the evening meal.

Neither my father nor Celeste felt any resentment against my mother and the Welshman for their preoccupation with each other. They lived in the background, serving with devotion these two human beings they loved so deeply. The only time there was any sense of friction was when Uncle Jack appeared.

For Uncle Jack was still feeling bitter.

"That only goes to show what a little man he is," said my

mother. "He is ungenerous and possessive. But he defeats his own ends. It gets him nowhere."

"Don't you realize you are letting yourself slip out of life?" he asked one day, when he failed to interest her in a new French play he had brought for her to read.

But my mother gave a little laugh.

"Slipping out of life?" she questioned him.

"But you never even go to a theatre these days, or talk with me about ideas," complained Uncle Jack.

My mother was not hearing what he said. Someone had opened the front door. It was time for the Welshman to return home.

And then, as Uncle Jack went on grunting in vexation, up from the hall of this house in St. John's Wood came the call of a quail. The walls of the living room seemed to vanish from sight, and Uncle Jack sat in an armchair among heather and bracken, as his Bien Aimée let out her answering call.

He knew now that she had left him.

But he failed to realize there was so much else she was leaving these days, that he took it as a personal insult. From time to time he made a valiant effort to bring her round to what he called reason. But always, just at the moment when he felt he was succeeding, the Welshman returned home, and up from the front hall came this call of a quail. My mother's face ceased to be the face of his Fiorita Mia, as she answered from the bracken.

"The funny thing is," laughed my mother one day, "that I don't *really* belong among the moors and the heather—except in so far as they are the background for aristocratic house parties in Scotland, with trains running North for the 'Twelfth.' I'd hate to be living out there in the wilds myself."

This Celt held the power to lift her out of her own world into his own. His clergymen brothers visited us, and gentle, shabby little Welsh sisters came to London for the first time in their lives and cooked and sewed for us. My mother wrote lengthy letters in her wild handwriting to their aged cleric father, and the entire family saw in her a power for good. Their wandering boy had come home at last. A paean of praise to this strange woman who had worked such a miracle went up to heaven from a remote rectory in Wales, and little parcels, tied together with old pieces of knotted string, brought us sweet-scented violets, and the first wild daffodils of the year. We dined, in the autumn, upon Welsh partridges and pheasants.

There was only one thing that somewhat troubled my mother. The Celt had little interest in her clothes.

"And this is really rather serious," she said. "It takes away my chief impetus in earning money. Money to me means beautiful clothes. But why should I want them just now? Lew doesn't even notice it when I dress up for him. All he does when I put on some fashionable garment I've looked after with such care for many years, is to laugh a little and give his pet call of a quail. And that makes my stylish clothes look actually vulgar. For who could be among heather and bracken in velvets and furs?"

She did not even have Mr. Bowles to dress for. Although we were now living within easy reach of him, he continued to stay away. But this did not do him any good in my mother's estimation, for if there were anything she despised it was someone who sulked.

"If George only knew how completely stupid he looks," she said, "he'd give it up. I feel the same contempt for him that I used to feel for your Auntie Pollie when she indulged in her fits of the sulks. They lasted three days, and during that period she locked herself in her bedroom and came out for food only at nighttime, when the family was in bed. We all laughed at her behind her back. She looked thoroughly undignified."

But Evelyn and I were sorry for Mr. Bowles. Surreptitiously we saw him and tried to console him. We were deeply attached to him. In this changed world, where everything of our childhood had vanished, we clung to him as to a link with the past, and our allegiance never faltered.

We did not feel so well disposed towards Uncle Jack. We knew he could fight his own battles. But he would not seem to realize that vituperative belligerence was the wrong weapon these days. Our mother turned from him to the Celt, who was gentle and understanding.

But she also made a great friend of Celeste.

The two women held many of the same ideas. They spent hours together at a stretch, talking, over the remains of a meal, till they would notice that the table was still uncleared, and decide that it wasn't worth while removing the cloth, because already it was about time to set things for the next meal.

Celeste shared my mother's views on purity and perfect womanhood.

"It's zis way," she said, in her broken English accent, looking double her real size in the wide-striped woolen jacket that followed the curves of her voluptuous bosom. "It's zis way, I say. If I 'adn't been pure as a lily when Lew met me, 'e say 'e would nevair 'ave loved me. Mon dieu, 'ow 'e loved me! I was a little pocket Venus, 'e say. And Lew's love, it will last for evair. If evair I was to feel that 'is love for me 'ad died I would leave 'im. I would leave 'im and nevair come back. But 'e is not like zat. I could nevair 'ave loved a man like zat."

My mother gave her a curious little smile. Later in the day, when she was alone with me, she put into words what, earlier, she had put into that smile.

"What did I tell you?" she said. "It's always these women who are as unattractive as sin who talk like this. It's so ridiculous that it doesn't even make me angry. The only time I get enraged with Celeste is when she dares to tell *me* about Paris. As if she could know anything about Paris. She may have lived there for years, but she has never been there in spirit. It isn't where you've been in your body that counts. It's where your mind and spirit have taken you. She's got all the pettiness of a French provincial. And believe it or not, I can speak French better than she can. There are several words she's never heard of, and her accent is decidedly common. Whatever Lew saw in her I can't imagine. I've always meant to ask him. I really must do so."

The only time I got angry with Celeste was when she agreed with my mother about the bringing up of a young female. Together they determined that I should remain as innocent as a wild rose bud. Lew's French wife carried on where Judge Talbot had left off.

"It's zis way, Pattie," she would say. "It's wiser always to be on ze over-careful side, where young girls are concerned. Nevair should zey be given a latchkey until zey are safely married. Now even *you* are not as watchful as you should be. Perhaps you don't know zat Clare is going about wiz someone? And I don't like ze look of 'im, I can tell you. Foreign looking, 'e is, I would say. No good evair comes of a foreigner. If 'e were a nice, clean, upright Britisher, like Lew or Robert, you could feel 'appier about it. Zese foreigners are evil where women are concerned. What I could tell you!"

I was made to confess that I had found a new friend, who was a Serbian poet.

"Serbian!" said my mother, in a shocked tone of voice. "But that's even worse than I feared. They're the sort of people who are always having massacres. They aren't civilized. And they have the strangest ideas about women, too. They're half Eastern. And how do you know that he is even clean—I mean, of course, he might perhaps have unmentionable insects on him. I hope you don't get too close to him?"

The two women shook their heads in deep concern.

"We'd better not tell Robert or Lew about it," decided my mother. "We don't want blood about the place, and there's no telling what they might not decide to do, to defend their women-folk. The best thing is to lock Clare in her bedroom for a few days."

And so my meals were handed to me through the bedroom door, for the better part of a week, lest the Serbian poet should kidnap and seduce me.

Although I resented Celeste's interference in the matter of my virtue, I had to admit that her cooking was superb. When the family finances fell exceptionally low she was invaluable in producing an attractive meal out of practically nothing.

And the family finances most certainly did fall low, though my mother refused to admit it.

"You are an impoverisher," she scolded me, as I voiced my worry. "It's the Leighton in you that gets so upset. It makes me angry when you talk about our being poor. We're not poor. We're temporarily impecunious. Just wait until my play is produced, and you'll see what I mean. Then we'll have more money than we know what to do with. The difference between being impecunious and being poor is all a matter of class."

My mother was searching for the emerald ring we were disposing of, to pay the rent that was due.

"That's the one difficulty the war has made," she went on. "Before the war one could run up bills and nobody thought any less of one. In fact, one was esteemed. But nowadays it always has to be ready money. In those days one scarcely saw actual ready money. Once or twice a year one made out a check, and hoped there was some money in the bank to meet it, and then thought no more about it. But today we have to bother our heads with silly little shillings and sixpences. It's all so humiliating. And it's such a waste of time, too."

The overdraft at the bank was a thing of the past. My mother felt that the structure of England was cracking.

But more important things than family finances were occupying our minds. Suddenly the Welshman was transferred to the country. A change was imminent.

"Do you know, Robert," our mother said to our father, while

Lew and Celeste were packing their belongings, "I have been wondering for quite a long time whether it really is healthy to live in a city. When we were at Vallombrosa we were kept strong by the good air at Lowestoft, during the summer. But both you and Clare are looking pale these days. How would it be to move to the country? We needn't go very far away from London. Somewhere like Bishop's Stortford—where, by the way, Lew and Celeste happen to be going—would be ideal. It's only twenty-nine miles from Liverpool Street Station. And Liverpool Street is my favorite railway station. Do you remember how all the porters knew us there, those days we went to The Red Croft? I'd feel much safer living on the Great Eastern Railway line than somewhere in the West. Yes, I really do thing it's a good idea."

"But Chummie," pleaded my father, who hated change, "you used always to say that the air of St. John's Wood wasn't city air."

"Oh," answered my mother, "that was before they went and spoiled the place by building all these enormous blocks of flats that use up far more air than they're entitled to."

Within a week or two we had packed and joined the Welshman and his wife in a furnished house in the little market town of Bishop's Stortford.

And there we lived for several years. Each morning Lew went to work, and each evening, as he returned, the front door was opened to the call of a quail.

It was a somewhat uneventful existence. My mother made no friends in the neighborhood.

"And why should I?" she asked. "There seems to be nobody here with any sense of beauty, romance or class. If you can't find someone really worth knowing it is always better to live with yourself. You can at least be sure, then, of not coming up against spiritual impoverishment. Upon my word, I can't understand people who always seem to have to go gadding."

As she finished her sentence, she looked pointedly at Celeste.

Lew's French wife was finding this little Hertfordshire town boring. She was growing restless.

"But Pattie," she said. "I feel my mind is shrinking to ze size of a pea. If we go on like zis, living completely alone, we won't know what's 'appening all around us. I should 'ave zought zat you, as a writer, would need to expand. You don't even go to ze cinema."

No sooner had she said this than she realized she had made a mistake. The less said about the cinema the better.

For friendship had sprung up between Celeste and my father. It's roots were in the cinema.

"Your mother doesn't seem to see that I can enjoy the moving pictures because that is the only time I am not bothered by my deafness," Father explained to me.

But my mother very definitely disapproved.

"You'll only catch some infectious disease there, among all those common people," she said. "For only common people frequent such places. I wouldn't object to your going to a real theatre. That's completely different. That can enrich your spirit. But a cinema is a sign of the times, and not an encouraging sign at that."

The tea hour was supposed to be five o'clock. Rarely, though, did we sit down until five-thirty, at the earliest. The picture began at six.

"How about a little visit to ze cinema zis evening, Robert?" suggested Celeste after the midday meal. "Zere's a good Western showing at ze Royalty."

Father and Celeste would bustle around in the kitchen early that afternoon, preparing the tea. They did not intend to miss the opening.

I think it was this hurry with the tea that vexed my mother as much as anything. She did not approve of punctuality at meals.

"It's a waste of time," she said, "for whenever you may chance to sit down to the table, you always get up from it at the same moment."

But perhaps the worst aspect of these visits to the cinema was the way Celeste, next day, spent several hours telling us the entire story of what she had seen.

"It zis way, Pattie," her voice trickled on. "After ze 'ero 'ad found out that 'e was being followed 'e—"

"Oh, Celeste, don't you see I'm not interested?" my mother interrupted. "I believe in living life at firsthand. Don't you agree, Lew?"

And the Celt, who never went to the movies, smiled back at her.

There was, however, one weekly excitement in our lives. It was of a frightening nature. Bishop's Stortford had a thriving livestock market, which took place each Thursday.

"If I had known about it I am not at all sure I would have come here—not even to be near you, Lew," our mother said. "It looks exactly as though Destiny has been at work. And, of course, if that's the case I couldn't very well have avoided coming, try as I might. I must say, I can see the workings of Fate as clearly as I can see you sitting there opposite me. I have been brought to this particular town of Bishop's Stortford in order that my bull may escape one Thursday from its pen in the cattle market, or from the vehicle that conveys it to the market, and attack me and gore me to death."

Life may have seemed drab, but it did not lack drama.

And so, though my mother took her exercise each day with unfailing regularity—walking up and down the tree-shaded roads of the residential district where we lived—nothing would drag her from the house on Thursdays.

"And I even think it might be wise to bar the front door that day," she said. "You can never tell. The bull *might* try to break in. Where Destiny's concerned, anything could happen."

Every Thursday morning I was dispatched to the cattle market, in order that we might ascertain the extent of the danger that week.

"How many were there today?" my mother would ask, on my

return. "And what are they like? Do they look particularly fierce?"

So convincing was her terror, that I had almost as much fear of the bulls as she had.

And yet this terror of hers was qualified. Had not the palmist said that she would write a successful play? Until this should have happened, surely she was secure from death. For the same reason, while our family finances were so low, she was buoyed up by the certainty of future riches.

"All this period of lack of funds is nothing but preparation for the money we shall have one of these days soon," she said. "Haven't I always told you, my child, that the Law of Compensation is the one thing in this world which never fails? Now, if life hadn't given me some nasty hits I wouldn't be worthy of the great success I *know* I shall get. And then, by the way, I shall buy myself a new coat."

She was, I noticed, beginning to want clothes. The power of the Celt had started to dim.

But something else was happening to her. The first shock of Roland's death was wearing off. No longer did she need to escape into anything which could keep her mind from the past. She dared now to think of Roland. She was slipping back into the world of memory. And it was here that the Welshman could not follow her.

"I remember spring in St. John's Wood, with the pink hawthorns against the wrought-iron gates of MacWhirter's house, and our lilac bushes at Vallombrosa, and the sweet sadness of those May evenings, when the blackbird sang and the lilac hung down over the front steps with the weight of its blossoms, and Roland, as a little boy, stringing the tiny separate lilac flowers on a piece of thread for necklaces for me. He would twine these necklaces in my hair, and one day—"

My mother stopped. Suddenly she had seen the lonely look upon the Celt's face. He could not walk with her along the paths of the past. He had not known Roland.

"Do you think Roland would have liked Lew?" she asked me

one day. "Sometimes I find myself wondering. They belong to such utterly different worlds. I don't even know what they could have found to talk about."

As she asked me this, I knew that the Celt's days were numbered.

A few weeks before Roland was killed he had become a Catholic. We had known nothing of this until the chaplain paid us a visit. But my mother now was thinking about it a great deal.

"It's the queerest thing, his going and doing that," she said. "And somehow, it has the odd effect of taking me right back to my own childhood, and those days at the convent in France, when I was such a good little Catholic."

"Now then, Pattie, none of that nonsense," said Lew, in a sure voice. "You know perfectly well you're not suited to turn Catholic. Leave that to hysterical people. You've too much commonsense. Besides, Roland couldn't have known what he was doing—out there in all that danger."

My mother turned on her Celt with rage. She saw in him a betrayal of Roland.

"You," she said in anger. "And what right have you to talk about Roland? You never saw him."

It was fortunate that outside events were changing the pattern of our lives. The Welshman's work was about to take him to another part of the country. Already Lew and Celeste had started packing their trunks.

But this time we did not move with them.

Celeste was badly worried.

"It's zis way, Pattie," she said. "If you stay on 'ere in Bishop's Stortford it won't do you any good. You've been 'ere far too long already. Now in Croydon, where Lew and I are going, you could be nearer to London. You could get to Piccadilly Circus in a very short time. And you could 'ave all ze lower part of ze 'ouse to yourself."

"Croydon!" sneered my mother. "My dear Celeste, how *can*

you suppose for one moment that I would live in such a common-place neighborhood. It's aristocratic to live right out in the country, as we do here, but no one with any conception of style would ever dream of settling in Croydon."

Although they did not mention it, both these women knew that there was more at stake than a mere neighborhood.

"And when it comes to priests, Pattie," Celeste went on with complete lack of tact, "zere's nothing I don't know about zem. It's zis way, I say: zey're after your money ze whole time. I've lived among zem so long in France zat I know all about zem. What I could tell you if you would let me—but you won't, I know. Now Lew is a purer man zan all zese priests put together. Mon Dieu, what I could tell you."

My mother did not deign to answer. She looked at Celeste with a cold stare.

But Celeste smiled thinly at my mother and at her husband, and the smile seemed as if it were straining to bind them closer together.

For she knew that she was afraid to live alone with Lew.

After they had left us it looked as though my father were going to have his "Chummie" to himself again. He reinstated the teatime readings that had ceased over the years of the Welshman's dynasty. He could cherish her now to his heart's content.

But he was not entirely happy. He was, in fact, worried.

My mother was determined that he should become a Catholic.

"The way you go on about it, you'd think I was asking you to plunge into an ice cold pond on a winter morning," she laughed at him. "Where's the difficulty? I don't see it. Here you've always done everything for me I've asked you—ever since those days we were first married, and lived on nothing at all up in that lonely Highland glen. Do you remember those days, by the way? And how we borrowed fifty pounds from Alfred Harmsworth, to last us for a month or two? And how happy we were, writing *Convict 99* together? And how we bought cheap classics, and read them to each other in the evenings, by candlelight?"

She was back in her mind to the far past, when, lonely in her own home, she had spent her days writing poetry. My father was editor then of the children's magazine to which she had sent these poems, and so deeply impressed was he with the poems that, against the rules of the firm, he had asked the little contributor to visit him in his office. He fell in love with the seventeen-year-old girl, but lost his job. She eloped with him, to the lonely glen in Scotland. From the very beginning they had been bound together by work.

"After all," went on my mother, "Roland became a Catholic without my even asking him to do so. He didn't seem to find any difficulty."

But my father's conversion was not going to be easy. The Leightons were staunch Unitarians.

He tossed and turned throughout the night. He could not sleep.

"There's nothing on earth I wouldn't do for you, Chummie," he moaned. "But, try as I may, I simply cannot seem to embrace the conception of the Trinity."

My mother was not going to fail.

She had discovered a very attractive priest at Bishop's Stortford. This priest was invited to tea with increasing frequency. She would get him to help her in saving my father's soul.

Over the months my father grew attached to the priest. My mother even thought she had achieved her purpose. But still my father held back.

"You mustn't ask me to do it, Chummie," he said. "There are certain things belonging to a person that nobody has a right to question. And religious belief is one of these things."

My mother had a sudden inspiration.

"Very well, Robert," she answered him. "I understand. And I won't say one single word about it. I'm sorry, though—genuinely sorry. For, you see, we shall be separated in the next world. Roland and I will be in one place, and you will be in another. Oh, no, I'm not suggesting that you won't go to Heaven, too. I have no doubt but that you will, even though you do happen to be a Unitarian. But there's one place in Heaven for the Catholics and another place for the non-Catholics. And we shall be a long way from each other, and shan't ever be able to meet."

My father was converted. He surrendered his Unitarian beliefs, and was baptized into the Catholic Church. He could not face this separation. It would be no Heaven to him if he were not near his "Chummie."

He became devoutly religious. My mother grew more and more deeply attached to the priest. Both of them looked forward with excitement to his frequent visits. When he was coming to tea my mother decked herself in her gayest clothes.

"The poor Father," she said, as she wound a bright-colored ribbon in her hair. "His life must be dreadfully dull always. Most people who are religious seem to dress in such drab clothes. If they aren't in deep black, as though they were attending a funeral, they go about in garments that don't hang right, and that have neither poetry nor beauty. Father Anderson hardly ever has the chance of seeing a *real* woman. There can be nothing of the glory of renunciation for him in denying any interest in the sort of women I see about me in church. It would be a form of penance to have to make love to them."

And she gave an extra brush to her yellow hair before fixing into the ribbon bow the posy of flowers my father had just gathered for her from the garden.

Life appeared to run smoothly. It did not seem to matter to my mother that she was not working much. The untidy bundles still cluttered the house, filled with sprawling outlines for stories she planned one day to write. Designs for dresses, torn from the *Daily Mail*, still worked their way to the top of the particular bundle in circulation at that moment; but they no longer gave my mother the same delight.

"And it's nothing wrong with me that I don't feel the same rush of joy when I look at them," she said. "It's the dresses themselves. The glory has gone from women's clothes these days. Everything seems to aim at hiding the seductiveness of the female figure. And the strange thing is that just as everyone is supposed today to show as much arm and leg as possible, so there is no magic in what they exhibit. As I've always told you, my child, romance lies in what is hidden, Why, if I weren't right in believing this the world would be a cesspool of lower-class sex these days, when you come to think of the yards of flesh that are exposed. But oh dear me, not at all. A man no longer stays awake all night feverishly imagining the curve of the leg above a certain ankle he had caught sight of, as an unknown woman lifted her skirts to enter a hansom cab. When he can see the leg on the street, he no longer wants it. Believe me, it will pay you to hide as much of yourself as possible."

In spite of this, my mother continued to show a great deal more of her neck and shoulders than even fashion demanded. All her dresses carried a hint of the days of the Restoration. They could easily have been worn by the ladies in a Congreve play.

So devoted was she to the priest, though, that she did not resent it when he rebuked her for her way of dressing.

"As a matter of fact," she told me one day, "I can understand. And I can realize too, for the first time, how strong and fine he is in keeping so true to his vows."

He had remonstrated with her for coming to the Communion rail in too decolleté a dress.

"You remember that green velvet one, don't you?" she said. "It really was perhaps a bit low in the front—but there, you see, I knew I looked attractive in it, and I wanted to please the Father. Well, after he had told me about it, I suddenly realized how unfair I was being to him, so next time I went to Holy Communion and knelt at the altar rail I was careful to see how I looked, and I filled in all the space in the front of the dress with a mass of white roses. And when I saw the look of gratitude on the Father's face I was well rewarded."

My mother and father loved this priest like two little lost children. My father obeyed him in everything, but my mother obeyed him only when she wanted to. If he should exact something of her that she did not approve of, she would leave him for a moment and go upstairs to the bedroom. Soon she would reappear in some specially alluring dress.

"What you are asking me to do is all right for other people, Father," she told him in the warm, soft voice she kept for such purposes. "But of course you can't possibly mean it to apply to me."

And turning from him, she played the "Merry Widow Waltz" upon the gramophone.

"Do you know," she said suddenly, as the record came to an end, "I believe Roland would have loved you. Yes, I really do believe so."

My mother and her priest sat before the fire. She was dressed in a pink tunic over her black velvet skirt, a salmon pink ribbon binding her yellow hair. In her hand she held a lace-edged handkerchief. It was exotically perfumed, and it had been kept in a cardboard Roger and Gallet soapbox, along with a pair of dove grey suede gloves, for "worthy occasions."

As she held the scented handkerchief before her, I knew that she must consider this a "worthy occasion." She was asking the Father if it were *really* a sin to allow men to fall in love with her.

"I will do my best to try to stop them from doing so, Father, if you want me to," she told him.

The firelight danced upon her beauty. She had the gracious dignity of a great lady of the French Court. She held her salon here, with one provincial priest, against the background of a shabby sitting room in a little furnished house in Bishop's Stortford. But it contained all the splendor of all time.

"Father," she called to him softly. "Father." And the lace-edged handkerchief was waved towards the austere priest. It was waved towards him till the perfume should reach his nostrils; for it was a most special, seductive perfume. "Father," she called to him, still more softly.

I watched her as she sat there, and knew the privilege it was to be a man—even though that man might chance to be a celibate priest.

I knew, too, that she was invincible.